WOMEN AND INTERNET

CREATING NEW CULTURES IN CYBERSPACE

Women and Internet
Creating New Cultures in Cyberspace

D N Prasad

MD Publications Pvt Ltd
New Delhi
www.mdppl.com

Published by :

MD Publications Pvt Ltd
"MD House", 11, Darya Ganj,
New Delhi - 110 002
Phone : +91-11- 45355555
E-mail : contact@mdppl.com
Website: www.mdppl.com

ISBN : 978-81-7533-343-7

Published and Printed by Mr. Pranav Gupta on behalf of **MD Publications Pvt Ltd** at Repro India Limited.

Preface

There is a widespread, but false, belief that time and technology necessarily improves people's lives. Society does not improve automatically. The situation for women in computing has both improved and worsened many times in computing's short history. Less quantifiable is the effect of computers on girls and women who are not computer professionals. With the rise of the Internet, the influence of computers has broadened. The purpose of this newsletter is to explore how the Internet and other computing advances subvert or reinforce gender roles.

Women are the emigrant minorities of cyberspace. Every study from 1985 through to 2003 of the World Wide Web demonstrates that it is a male construction: it was begun by men and exploits technologies many women have not been trained to use or are not comfortable using. A strongly masculinistic ethos produces and structures many regions and norms in Net life; much of cyberspace culture is still controlled and dominated by men, and reflects and encourages sexual and sheerly competitive aggression, hostility towards, and debasement of women, and disparages what's thought to be female points of view of social life.

Studies of cyberspace social interactions reveal that repeatedly and increasingly women are moving into and active on distribution lists, web rings and other cyberspace forums which are women-only, controlled by one or more women list owners and moderators, or are vigilantly moderated so as to enable women to voice points of view seen as distinctly feminine, to talk about issues specific to women, and to feel comfortable or safe. In distribution list and games or computer- mediated communications, women have recognizably more conciliating, tactful and relational behaviors than men. If a cyberspace area is not moderated so as to prevent aggressive and adversarial postings directed at women, such postings will occur, and, in response, most women fall silent, or move away from the area.

It has been documented in a number of instances that after a feminist or women-only cyberspace forum was not vigilantly moderated, and had people of both sexes on it, the forum died, and active women participants migrated to other or all-women's lists and websites, and places controlled by women, or places where professional and other accountability mechanisms were at work to control hostile and personally aggressive behavior. Computer-mediated communications on the Net as presently generally practiced do, then, eventually inhibit most even well-educated and self-confident women from involving themselves actively. For women interested in disseminating and creating respect for and interest in 18th century texts by women: to develop women-friendly cyberspace, we must work for a progressive vision (socialism), transnationalization, antimilaritism (wherever violence is encouraged women are at risk), and the validation of women's experiential points of view.

I am very grateful to Mr. Pranav Gupta, Director of MD Publications Pvt Ltd, New Delhi, for his kind cooperation and support for this book.

D N Prasad

Contents

1

Reconceptualizing Learning for the Cyber-Classroom

COMPUTER TECHNOLOGY AND EDUCATION

Although much scholarship has considered the implications of computer technology in social, political, and economic arenas, critical reflection has predominantly dwelled on the consumption of new programs, software applications, or access to the Internet, both at an individual and an aggregate level, and has focused on the alterations of interpersonal and social interaction through this new medium. Since developments in digitalization and fiber optics technologies are still rapidly unfolding, literature documenting the impact of technologies in education remains on the forefront of an increasingly troublesome sociocultural debate.

In her book *Literacy in a Digital World,* Kathleen Tyner (1998) makes reference to some reviews of literature about the uses of technology for learning. Beginning in 1974, Peggy Campeau published an extensive report funded by the Council of Europe on the way media are selected for specific learning tasks in adult education. While the report sought to find the result of studies on "the instructional effectiveness of media under a variety of learner and treatment conditions" in order to construct a media taxonomy, the results of the literature search revealed less than twelve experimental studies.

Among the findings, it was discovered that instructional media were used extensively, under many diverse conditions, and that significant funding was spent to install expensive equipment. Interestingly, the report explains that instructional effectiveness has not been the determining criteria for the purchase and use of audiovisual technology. Rather, administrative and organizational considerations of cost, availability, and user preference have delineated the uses of technology in the classroom. As Campeau explains, this emphasis is not all that surprising given that current media research in postschool education "has not provided decision makers with practical, valid, dependable guidelines for making these choices on the basis of instructional effectiveness".

With no empirical studies on the effectiveness of learning through instructional media, Wilbur Schramm entered the scene in 1977, conducting a comprehensive literature review about learning with technology. Schramm assembled empirical applications in a range of media, including computer-aided education. His findings offer the following:

From the experimental studies we have plentiful evidence that people learn from the media, but very little evidence as to which medium, in a given situation, can bring about the most learning. We have hints that one medium may be more effective than another for a given learning task or a given kind of learner, but little systematic proof. Thus we can use the media with considerable confidence that students will learn from them, but, if we rely only on the experimental evidence, not with much discrimination.

Since Schramm's study, Tyner (1998) explains that even twenty years later "there is...a dearth of research about the use of digital technologies in schools". In fact, in 1996 a major study of computer networking conducted by a consortium of federal education and energy laboratories named Model Nets found "no large-scale studies of network use in schools that had tested the assumption that computer networking is a powerful tool that can both help students learn better and help teachers teach better".

As Tyner confirms, there are few studies that provide accounts of improved literacy skills through new computer technologies. Tyner is not alone in her findings. Many scholars and educators in the early 1990s realized that the literacy debates of the 1980s often ignored computers or treated them as obstacles. Myron Tuman explains in Literacy Online that we might expect to see in E. D. Hirsch's Cultural Literacy (1987) computer technology as a possible way to provide all Americans with ready access to the knowledge base about culture that he feels is essential for full literacy. Yet the single reference to computers offered by Hirsch is not favorable. Caught within an elitist, modernist assumption of culture that privileges some narratives, customs, and behaviours over others, Hirsch believes that "the more computers we have, the more we need shared fairy tales, Greek myths, historical images, and so on".

Tuman explains: Rather than representing a potential cure for our reading and writing ills, technology in the form of increased specialization is for Hirsch part of the disease, for which the "antidote...is to reinvigorate the unspecialized domain of literate discourse." Literacy and technological change are thus opposing cultural forces: "Advancing technology, with its constant need for fast and complex communications, has made literacy more essential to commerce and domestic life."

Unlike Hirsch, authors who situate themselves on the optimistic side of the fence contend that continuing progress in artificial intelligence may well relieve us of many of the traditional burdens entailed in transcribing and decoding texts, simplifying the literacy skills essential for commerce and domestic life. Accordingly, computers will reshape not just how we read and write and how these skills are taught, but will alter our very conception of basic terms such as reading, writing, and text. As Mark Warschauer (1999) explains, celebrants of new electronic literacies claim that they represent much fuller and richer ways to present and access information.

The decentered, multimedia character of new electronic media facilitates reading and writing processes that are more democratic, learner-centered, holistic, and natural than the processes involved in working with precomputer, linear texts. In their view, hypertext facilitates a critical and dynamic approach to literacy that is an extension of the best traditions of the print world and finally fulfills the visions of critical literacy to reconfigure the text, author, and reader.

New Zealand scholars Lalita Rajasingham and John Tiffin articulate their vision of education in an information society by radically reconceptualizing the roles of the teacher, the student, pedagogy, and the media. They imagine students using their PCs to both learn and teach themselves through an engagement with multimedia, computer-assisted instruction:

> The PC can take on the role of an automated teacher as well as being a source of knowledge and problems...thePCwill be portable so that the student can work with it anywhere...thePCwill automatically dial up the virtual educational network and identify itself. Once the system recognizes that it is talking to the PC of a registered student, a menu will appear that allows the student to select from the different kinds of services available in the virtual school or college.... These are asynchronous activities, so a student has the flexibility of time as well as space. Electronic libraries and computer-assisted counseling services never close.

Since the "telestudent" will be unrestricted by spatial or temporal dynamics, Rajasingham and Tiffin celebrate the autonomy of the learner through the use of a PC and modem, which allows for independent learning or participation through a virtual class at any time of the day or from any location. Although such a learning environment may increase possibilities for student participation, many questions remain about exactly how critical autonomy can be enabled solely by broader time and spatial parameters.

For educators Ruth Garner and Mark Gillingham, "the educational value for Internet access lies in global community-in McLuhan's [1964] global village". They are less concerned about Neil Postman's arguments in Technopoly that "new technologies are altering society in disturbing ways, that information is dangerous when it has no place to go, when it has no higher purpose, and when there is no theory to which it applies". Garner and Gillingham summarize the praise offered by technological proponents who celebrate the egalitarian nature of the Internet:

Young and old, brainy and not-so-brainy, ugly and handsome persons can participate as long as they have the mechanical tools (computer, account, and telephone access), and each can decide how many personal characteristics to disclose to communication partners. The Internet is not so hierarchical, so attentive to physical shortcomings and social status as, for instance, most high schools that we know. This lack of cliquishness means that Internet participants can learn from and about persons with whom they would have little contact otherwise.

Yet again, as with the celebrated telestudent, access to new communications tools is no guarantee that the means to learning will necessarily lead to fruitful outcomes. Although few doubt that computers change the terrain of communication and education, those situated on the pessimistic side of the fence, or somewhere in between, have provoked considerable debate about the "ubiquity and power of computers in the contemporary world". Communication scholar Stanley Aronowitz summarizes the debates between techno-proponents and opponents, explaining that "enthusiasts consider the computer a tool, a term that suggests a neutral social and political content," whereby the "versatility of the computer can provide the key to the historic dream that all work (including schoolwork) can become a vehicle of human creativity, that is, a form of play".

Meanwhile, "critics warn that human agency is irreplaceable, that computers cannot do more or less than those who create, program, and operate them". As Warschauer explains:

These scholars see net-based reading and writing as fulfilling not the best dreams of critical theory, but the worst nightmares of television, with readers surfing through catchy but vacuous material, never pausing long enough to read something from start to finish, much less critically analyze it. Writing, from such a perspective, would be reduced to searching for the snazziest graphics rather than attending to serious argument.

Despite their optimism for new models of learning, Garner and Gillingham are worried about unequal access to the Internet. Referring to work produced by Tony Scott, Michael Cole, and Martin Engel, they explain that there are inequalities in terms of gender, ethnicity, and class. For example, sons are more likely to have computers purchased for them by their parents than daughters. Moreover, they point out the problem of socioeconomic status, which delimits access to computers and telephone lines. Public libraries, such as those located in New York, are relegated to unequal data-transmission rates, which means they must limit services.

This poses inequity among economic status since it means that "middle-class and wealthy children in New York will be part of the information age, and poor children will not-an intolerable situation in a democratic society that espouses the principle of an informed citizenry".

Other forms of inequality raised by Garner and Gillingham include reports from the National Center for Education Statistics, which documents that funding is the major barrier to teacher and student Internet access. Citing from Henry Becker's survey data, they explain that it generally costs about $86,000 to do electrical work and classroom remodeling necessary to establish the local area network, there are additional one-time costs for Internet connectivity, and there are recurring costs of about $9,000 each year in access fees. Poor districts have tremendous difficulty in securing this level of funding without benefactor involvement.

This is because schools are funded almost exclusively by a combination of state and local taxpayers. In fact, in what Jonathan Kozol called "the arcane machinery by which we finance public education", the local property tax is the decisive force in shaping inequality of resources. These issues will undoubtedly impact the future of Internet and computer use in the nation's public schools and inform this study by considering the interconnections between political economy and private business initiatives to provide technology to schools philosophically and materially.

The final concern raised by Garner and Gillingham that deserves mention is their fear that the conservative ideology of vocal network opponents mistakes sexually explicit images on bulletin-board systems with children's classroom Internet communication. This poses another obstacle, as it directly impacts the approval of spending tax dollars to provide Internet access to schools. Going back to findings by Kathleen Tyner, contemporary studies still produce inconclusive results on the impact of educational technology in enhancing learning.

As Tyner explains, since little evidence confirms that student performance is improved by technology, "it is likely that the political call for more digital tools has more to do with issues of social justice and partisan economics than with an expectation in the actual improvement of student gains". She explains that "the quest for broad access to information has a particular cultural resonance in the United States that borders on the mythic":

> The equal access concept resonates with the conventional wisdom that information is the cornerstone of a participatory democracy and a healthy economy. Furthermore, multiliteracies that focus on access to electronic tools, in a technological determinist way, are often aligned with familiar modernist beliefs that equate literacy with progress.

Moreover, the important questions of what to do after schools have technological access are only starting to be asked. As Tyner documents, there is much confusion about the role of technology in the classroom curriculum:

- A 1994 study by the Educational Testing Service found that the uses of computers at home and in school were not clearly tied to focus curricular purposes.
- All students reported that they used the computer mostly to play games (87 percent of K–8 students and 77 percent of high school students).

- They also used the computer to retrieve information "to learn things" (82 percent of K–8 students and 71 percent of high school students) and to write stories or papers (68 percent of fourth-graders, 82 percent of eighth-graders, and 87 percent of eleventh-graders).
- About half of all students surveyed used a computer at home.

Unfortunately, this means that we still know little about the impact and objectives of teaching with new computer-mediated information technologies. However, since the establishment of a curriculum can help identify the learning goals within a particular subject area, we need to come up with effective ways to contribute to sparse research outlining how telecommunications technology can be conceptualized to maximize critical thinking skills and critical autonomy.

ENVISIONING CRITICAL PEDAGOGY IN CYBERSPACE

Encircled within scholarly debates about the pros and cons of computer and telecommunications technology in schools lays a body of literature, albeit modest in size that ventures toward the articulation of transformative possibilities within cyberspace. Among the first to conceptualize radical changes for the "virtual class" in the 1990s were Lalita Rajasingham and John Tiffin. In 1995 they articulated their vision of learning in their book In Search of the Virtual Class. Rajasingham and Tiffin provide a history of computer-assisted and computer-managed instruction that dates back to the 1960s; telecommunications has been used since the 1970s with audioconferencing, and efforts for instructional television have been going on since the 1950s.

However, their vision articulates "the coming together of computer and telecommunications technologies that could lead to the virtual class as the primary locus of learning in society". Through "telelearning," Rajasingham and Tiffin envision the reversal of trends toward big schools especially in the secondary and postsecondary levels, and a return to the village school and small rural college that caters to the neighborhood community. Although city schools have an advantage over small schools by catering to a wide variety of educational needs, "telelearning promises to make it possible to offer a variety of courses that no conventional school could match". Rajasingham and Tiffin explain that the number of courses that can be offered in telelearning is limitless.

In fact, they believe it provides new opportunities for the development of a global learning environment whereby individual learners can take classes from teachers in any country on subjects of their choice. Rajasingham and Tiffin are not the only ones who have searched for new paradigms of learning that displace conventional classroom learning and pedagogy. Critical pedagogue Henry Giroux proposes that educators should become border intellectuals by traveling within and among communities of difference and contends that educational projects need to examine the production and operation of new information systems.

Using this as a point of departure, Colin Lankshear, Michael Peters, and Michele Knobel examine the potential for critical pedagogy to expand and develop within cyberspace environments. They advance several supportive arguments for the utilization of cyberspace to transform classroom practices. First, they contend that cyberspace environments have the potential for making students aware of the historical and contingent nature of discourse.

This comes partly as a result of Net users' experiences as creators, refiners, and sustainers of social practices through the act of encoding and decoding symbols and images. Second, interactions, experiences, and information within cyberspace environments point to the complexity, diversity, and multiplicity of human subjectivities, the highly fluid nature of identity, and the enormous possibilities for creating personal identities (all of which challenge modernist notions of subjectivity). Third, conceptualizations of pedagogy can shift from teaching to learning within cyberspace.

These results from the fact that, in many instances, students know more about computer-mediated communications technology than do teachers, which displaces traditional power dynamics between educator and educatee. This does not mean that the teacher imparts irrelevant information or knowledge, but that student proficiencies in this area should be tapped into and considered integral aspects of the learning process. Furthermore, students can access a variety of information sources, which allows them to go beyond teacher and textbook knowledge and curriculum details.

As a result, learning can potentially become more collaborative between students and teachers. Without giving up claims to authority or valuable information, teachers can deploy knowledge by becoming interrogators, conceptualizers, and facilitators of student-generated questions and ideas. Lankshear, Peters, and Knobel go on to explain how critical learning can emerge within cyberspace through three interrelated areas of critical pedagogy, namely information, knowledge, and understanding.

Critical pedagogy questions: (1) the nature and role of information within cyberspace environments by problematizing information; (2) how knowledge is legitimated and regulated within cyberspace as it varies from other traditional spaces associated with the book; and (3) how students negotiate which electronically mediated spaces they will join and participate in by making judgments about what forms of information/knowledge make sense to them.

There are many educators who are beginning to realize the importance of combining computer information technologies with school reform. In his foreword to Garner and Gillingham's book Internet Communications in Six Classrooms, Bertram Bruce asserts that the purpose, use, and role of e-mail in the classroom must be associated with the teacher's pedagogical goals. For Bruce, a close look at technology, with an emphasis on the Internet, the World Wide Web, e-mail, and virtual communities, brings on the questions of teaching, learning, thinking, communicating, and caring:

The strengths and weaknesses of computer-mediated communication have little to do with technical features of the new technologies. It is true, of course, that being able to easily share texts across time and space creates possibilities for sharing across cultures that were not afforded previously. But the fascinating exchanges recounted here arose when teachers allowed students to write about things that mattered to them and when teachers worked hard to support students' learning.

Like Lankshear, Peters, and Knobel, Garner and Gillingham explain that the use of the Internet radically alters the role of the teacher in the classroom. Whereas the teacher usually responds to all speaking and writing assignments, in Internet discourse, writing topics are "chosen by the students, linked to their knowledge and interest rather than to an authorized textbook's contents or a teacher's chalkboard list". Moreover, the Internet allows other students to become the intended audience, rather than the teacher:

> When a topic really appeals, students many miles apart may write back and forth for weeks or even months, negotiating the difficult rhetorical territory of trying to figure out what their distant communication partners know and what more they should say on a variety of topics...on an international e-mail list, a handful of students may try to persuade the others of a particular point of view, responding to arguments, point by point, over a series of messages.

As such, the role of the teacher in this lesson is mainly advisory. Garner and Gillingham describe specific classrooms in which the main pedagogy is student-driven learning. They document several instances where the teacher's role as facilitator steers the learning process. The first case-in-point entails a fifth-grade teacher in Illinois whose main role in the classroom emerged at the beginning of the year when she introduced the writing revising process by using the overhead projector to have students look for problem areas in structure or mechanics. By the end of the year, most writing revisions took place on the computer as students composed their pieces.

The second case is of a high school teacher in Alaska whose students acted as peer editors when writing on the Internet. The third is of a teacher in Philadelphia who shared editing responsibilities with fourth-grade authors, other students, and word-processing tools. Despite the important uses of computers here, the end goal of the writing process has merely been enhanced by the means of technology. Like Garner and Gillingham, Mark Warschauer designed and conducted a two-year ethnographic study of the uses of the Internet in four language and writing classrooms in the state of Hawaii.

Warschauer believes that at the center of controversies over electronic literacies are broader societal struggles over the nature of literacy and schooling. He is equally critical of the technocratic paradigm of literacy that emerged after World War II and continues to dominate in U.S. schools today. While he does not believe that technologies necessitate a particular teaching method or approach, Warschauer believes, like Lankshear, Peters, and Knobel, that computers can be used for a variety of pedagogical purposes depending on the sociocultural context.

Although the body of literature calling for innovative pedagogies is limited, those scholars who do address the subject seem to be in unison in their call for action. As Todd Taylor and Irene Ward articulate, "to date, not enough effort has been invested in making sure that educational institutions are 'rebuilt' in ways that support effective pedagogy". Unless computers and the Internet are effectively integrated into the objectives and activities of the classroom teacher, they are unlikely to have a widespread impact on education. As Bonnie Bracey, teacher member of the National Information Infrastructure Advisory Council, explains, this means going beyond the use of new equipment by fundamentally transforming their institutional practices.

More Web-based lesson plans like those created by Laura Parker Roerden need to be designed and implemented if teachers are to transform their classroom pedagogy from dispensing all knowledge to serving as a guide. Roerden's development of Web-based instruction for the classroom is unusual because it focuses on curriculum development, asking teachers and administrators to carefully consider how and when the Internet might help them meet their curricular goals.

Consequently, further research is needed to document pedagogical innovations designed and utilized by classroom teachers and educational researchers as computer-mediated information technologies emanate in our schools. Once the potential of using Internet resources is realized, teachers can then evolve from "inculcators and deliverers of canned instruction and knowledge to learning facilitators, weaving a tapestry of support to their students".

Accordingly, more thought needs to go into the curriculum development phase of Internet and computer use in the classroom. Despite the broad initiatives we've encountered that are focused on access to communications technology within utopian virtual learning environments, the purpose of exploring cyberspace is obscured if the end goal of the learning venture is overshadowed by the means to get there. Likewise, it is not enough to seek out the destinations of our computer-based quests for knowledge.

As educators, administrators, parents, and students, we need to determine why we are undertaking new learning explorations in the first place, establishing the purpose and utility of our excursions so that we know what to do when we get there. The same is true with the production of Internet Web pages. Until we understand why we are creating them and how we can displace top-down models of mass communication through new voices and perspectives, the exciting prospects to be made with this new technology remain thwarted.

2

Beyond Literacy Theory

If we are going to adopt an appropriate model for learning excursions in cyberspace, we need to carefully examine the basic elements that make media literacy different from traditional literacy theory. Although the word literacy is not limited to one meaning, it describes the process of learning to read and write using language associated with print-based texts or alphabetic components. Synonymous with literacy are the terms literature, literary, and literate, all of which describe the extent of one's reading proficiency through written language. Oftentimes, literacy connotes a highbrow application of language so that it directly relates to one's level of education, familiarity with literature, and ability to write "polite," "proper," and/or "polished" essays.

Those marked as "literate" are well read in what usually consists of selected canonical works of literature. Due to the fact that literacy requires an understanding of the grammar, structure, mechanics, and playful usage of language, the process of "decoding" or interpreting the messages in a given text depends on one's comprehension of how language is organized, which oftentimes is arranged in imaginative and unusual ways.

Literary criticism has entailed a variety of approaches, such as understanding how a literary text functions, the effectiveness of the text in conveying ideas and values, both old and new, the capacity of the text to represent "reality" as associated with notions of "Truth," and the interrelationships between the text and the author's intent. Yet such approaches have been dismantled by new shifts in thinking that understand that the function and purpose of a text is contextual, historical, cultural, and personal. Moreover, "Truth" is not "out there" but is contingent on ideology and point of view inasmuch as "reality" is socially constructed. Thus the attempt to discover the author's underlying intent for a text is daunting and perhaps not as important as examining the effect or response evoked by the text.

When combining literacy with media, we begin to shift from a print-based literary sphere to a visual world whereby cultural texts are composed of a host of nonlinear signs and symbols that create meaning. Unlike the elite posturing of literacy within a privileged culture, the terrain of the popular is a crucial site of exploration and creativity so that the mediated "texts" that emerge from within the everyday are subject to critical analysis. The reason why media literacy is vital for today's generation has to do with the increasing deluge of visual, auditory, and multimedia messages that we're exposed to, from television programs and commercials, to newspaper stories, billboards, radio announcements, sales catalogs, and information acquired from the Internet.

Although literacy requires an engagement with a text in order to grapple with meaning, more often than not, the messages within multimedia are accepted without stopping to question and/or examine the ideas, values, or motives behind these messages and their producers. Inasmuch as the "intent" or "meaning" of the text is a focal point of literacy, comprehending the function and effect of a given visual text remains essential to media literacy. At the heart of a media literacy criticism is both a personal and a socio-cultural engagement with multimedia.

Criticism has been known to emphasize one's negative disposition in relation to a text; however media criticism involves an evaluation of our love/hate relationship with the media: for instance, we might enjoy specific television programs or magazines, but become annoyed with commercials or ads that suggest women must be extremely thin to be beautiful or must determine their success through stereotypical ideals. Although most of us are media savvy, it is important to go beyond cynicism and skepticism by becoming critical consumers of informative and persuasive media messages. We must also become critically engaged citizens.

When using the term critical, we're referring to the process of keeping a watchful eye on the mass media by using learned media literacy skills to detect bias, biased representations, inaccurate statements and falsities, and/ or the value messages of a text. Media "texts" include not only print forms of communication, but also broadcast and electronic media such as films, television, computer software products, and the like.

As officially defined in most national and international contexts, media literacy is the ability to (1) "read" media texts by analyzing, accessing, and evaluating communication in a variety of forms, and (2) "write" media texts by producing messages through personal experience, narrative, and point of view. By learning to critically "read" and "write" media, we can become an effective informed citizenry, making better choices and acting in the best interest of ourselves and others.

Before further discussing the "literacy" aspect of media literacy, it is important that we understand what we mean by "media." Media are vehicles that convey messages. There are print texts, such as newspapers, magazines, books, and catalogs; visual texts, such as television, movies, computers, billboards, and performing arts; audio texts, such as music and radio; and multimedia, such as computers, the World Wide Web, and the Internet. Most media messages use a combination of forms. For instance, television and movies use still and moving images, sound effects, and music. A person's individual style also sends a message. Body language, dress, makeup, hairstyle, tone of voice, and facial expressions convey meaning nonverbally. Thus there are many ways to send messages.

When we talk about the "mass media," we're referring to those industries and companies whereby control of the production and distribution of messages lies in the hands of a small number of individuals. Those messages are then disseminated to large masses of people. Newspapers and magazines are examples of print mass media. Television, radio, DVDs, video games, and online computer services are examples of electronic mass media.

Mass media have a powerful place and serve an important role in a democracy. The public's vision of the world, society, and self is shaped by words and images projected by the mass media. Much of the information we get about public business comes from mass media sources. Nevertheless, the exercise of democracy is affected by the constraints on mass media organizations. High production costs, advertising, and deadlines are just some of the components that affect media content. Since most print and electronic mass media are supported primarily from advertising, sponsors of a particular show or event can withdraw their support if they find the content displeasing.

For instance, sponsors have pulled their advertisements from television episodes of Ellen or Roseanne because they dealt with homosexual issues. Moreover, programs with low ratings have a difficult time attracting individual sponsors. Shows that have displayed strong female role models, such as Grace Under Fire, or intelligent female news anchors such as Connie Chung, have lost support from advertisers as a result of low ratings, or high ratings with the "wrong" demographic group (i.e., older, moderate-to low-income viewers). Likewise, newspapers and magazines need to maintain a high circulation to attract advertisers, and increasingly they need to be able to target their deliveries to particular segments of their subscriber lists in order to satisfy customers. Thus magazines such as Seventeen and Elle aim to attract young adolescent women through their advertisements and feature stories.

There are eight key media literacy concepts used by most media literacy educators and advocacy groups. These concepts are the result of many efforts to focus, narrow, and define the scope of media literacy since the 1980s. One of the overarching premises of media literacy is that reality is socially constructed. Accordingly, the first tenet of media literacy is that all media are constructions. Even though the media appear to be merely reflecting the world, they are carefully created through multimedia effects. With increased technological sophistication, the "seams" of most media texts are rendered invisible, making it difficult for us to see the media as manufacturers of reality, or manipulators of common sense. Our task, then, is to make visible the seams of the media that otherwise go unnoticed in our everyday lives.

The second principle of media literacy is that the media construct reality (reality is socially constructed). We discussed how literary theory has involved a preoccupation with the discovery of "Truth" as an enlightened intellectual process. Yet we now know that truth is not transcended, but is created in our daily lives.

The ways in which we come to understand how society functions and how we fit into society are based on our familial upbringing, schooling, and religion, as well as on our growing up in a certain community, region, and nation. Thus our ideas, values, and belief system-ideology-are formed from material conditions and our situatedness in the world. Like other institutional and sociocultural structures, the media provide us with certain viewpoints, opinions, and explanations of how the world works. Due to the fact that we're spending more and more time consuming media in all forms, we must carefully examine the media's influential role in packaging reality.

While the media construct reality, we do not necessarily see, experience, or relate to the same reality as the one projected in the media. Hence the third factor is that audiences negotiate meaning in media (audience analysis). Even though we all consume and engage with media, we don't all have the same experiences or interpretations. Our individual pleasures, desires, and fears will affect our understanding of media messages, as will our levels of education, gender, age, race, ethnicity, and sexuality. It makes sense, then, that no two people will interpret a given message in exactly the same way.

Differences in gender and generation can lead to varied aesthetic pleasures and interpretations of musical genres, soap operas, sports, computer games, and films, depending on what experiences, values, and belief systems we bring to these "texts." Put simply, meaning is "negotiated" in multiple ways. Expanding on earlier statements, the fourth principle refers to the commercial implications of the media. It is not enough to examine the meaning that emerges from a given form of media, as its meaning is contingent upon its economic function.

Consequently, media literacy involves an awareness and understanding of the interrelationships between the financial underwriting of production in the mass media and its resulting content, techniques, and distribution. Also known as political economy, we need to acknowledge that the mass media are part of a profit-making business, and as such are deeply political. For instance, the television industry uses audience ratings as a means to assess all programs-news, public affairs, or entertainment. Even an audience of twenty million viewers isn't large enough for most television shows to be kept on the air. In addition to the number of viewers, the demographic composition of audiences for certain media forms is vital in determining the "merits" of a given show or medium for advertisers. Thus media literacy requires a basic understanding of how audiences are divided into marketable groups and "sold" to advertisers seeking to profit from program content.

In addition to addressing advertising, we also need to examine the impact of corporate ownership of the media. Over the course of the last twenty years, large multi–billion dollar global conglomerates have emerged as powerful monopolies controlling both the production and the distribution of media with fewer independently owned and operated media companies, there lacks diversity in the types of media produced and disseminated to the public. Thus decisions to produce and not produce certain books, magazines, television shows, movies, music and computer games rest in the hands of a few powerful groups.

One serious effect of the concentration of ownership of the media can be seen in the newspaper industry. Whereas more than 60 per cent of U.S. cities had two or more competing newspapers in 1923, the number is now down to 2 per cent. Naturally, the point of view and story selection in news reporting are directly affected by the economic organization of the media. The fifth element of media literacy is that media contain ideological and value messages. We need to acknowledge that the media are disseminators of ideological material, and that they thereby promote some value and belief systems over others. More often than not, the media espouse belief systems that reinforce the existing social structure.

As such, ideas prevalent within dominant social structures-the business community, government, schools, religion-are strengthened within the media. Certain ways of life are explicitly and implicitly promoted in the media. This includes American ideologies that value freedom as an individual rather than social right, buying products as a way to gain happiness and success, competing with others to get ahead, affirming nationalistic superiority, reinforcing differences across lines of race, class, and gender, and adhering to authority.

Like fish in water, these basic ideologies are rendered invisible to us as Americans, until we find ourselves in new cultural surroundings or contexts. Media literacy requires that we challenge ourselves to continually think "outside the box"-the television box, film screen, radio box, and computer box-so that we can take apart the basic ideological messages and value systems of our society. In addition to reflecting the social needs and goals of powerful individuals, groups, a class, or a culture, media have social and political implications (cultivation analysis).

Accordingly, the sixth dimension of media literacy is an awareness of the broad range of social and political effects stemming from the media. For instance, television viewing has directly affected the nature of family life by replacing interactive family activities with inactive and isolated media consumption. Moreover, the media have directly impacted the use of leisure time in that people watch, on average, about four hours of television a day, while the television set is on for approximately seven hours in the average household. We could certainly argue about the extent of the media's role in creating values and ideas.

But rather than identifying whether or not the media are the ultimate determiners of social thought, we need to explore how the media legitimize and reinforce some ideologies over others. Shopping, for instance, has become the new national pastime in the United States, precisely at a time when the glut of advertised products in the media has reached a saturation point. In addition to affecting our use of leisure time, the media affect our understandings of ourselves and others by grouping us according to the consumption choices we make. Thus the media not only define our relationship to popular culture, but they also inform us of whom we are in relationship to our peers.

In a larger context, the media today are closely linked with the world of politics and social change (action). Because of television, we are much more likely to vote for our national leaders based on images and soundbites over policies and issues. Likewise, our exposure to politics is increased as we receive late-breaking news from local protests to international crises halfway across the world. Ironically, while we may feel more directly aware of certain political goings-on, we are often dependent on the media to tell us how we are supposed to interpret and react to political events, which usually involves sitting on the sidelines as spectators rather than directly playing in the "game."

The two final tenets of media literacy are that form and content are closely related in the media, and each medium has a unique aesthetic form. Canadian scholar Marshall McLuhan argued that each medium has its own grammar and classifies reality in unique ways. Consequently, even though various media will cover the same stories or events, our experiences, engagements, and interpretations of these events are directly related to the media form. To hear a ball game broadcast on the radio provides us with a uniquely different experience from watching it on television, as we have to use our imagination to make up for the lack of visuals present.

Unlike high and low cultural distinctions that may polarize the worthiness of literary works, media literacy is predicated on the assumption that we can enjoy as well as understand the different aesthetic forms of media texts. To "critically engage" with the media does not mean that one must take a negative oppositional stance toward all media. Rather, media literacy leads to a more complete appreciation and understanding of how meanings are produced and enhanced through media production.

Once we have applied all of these concepts through theory and practice, our ability to become critical consumers of all media is rendered possible. Accordingly, this process "enables us to establish and maintain the kind of critical distance within our culture that makes possible critical autonomy: the ability to decode, encode, evaluate, and (re)act upon the symbol systems that dominate our world".

THE GOALS AND APPROACHES OF MEDIA LITERACY

Having examined the basic elements of media literacy, we need to clarify some of the commonly used terms and objectives within media literacy. In Teaching the Media, British scholar Len Masterman stresses that the primary goal of media education is not to have students regurgitate the ideas, critical perspectives, or knowledge provided by the teacher. Nor should it simply encourage students to develop their own critical propensities. For Masterman, "the really important and difficult task of the media teacher is to develop in pupils enough self-confidence and critical maturity to be able to apply critical judgements to media texts which they will encounter in the future".

The acid test of any media education programme is the extent to which pupils are critical in their own use and understanding of the media when the teacher is not there. The primary objective is not simply critical awareness and understanding, it is critical autonomy.

This notion of critical autonomy is essential to media education if only in the fact that it stresses the importance of having a student-driven pedagogy that encourages learning beyond classroom walls and beyond the K–12 learning years.

According to Masterman, media pedagogy means that nonhierarchical teaching methods promoting reflection and critical thinking must be accompanied by lively, democratic, group-focused, and action-oriented teaching. Hence it is the teacher's responsibility to use pedagogical approaches that help students gain confidence through group dialogue, and in which students can make their own judgments, develop the ability to analyze those judgments, and take on the responsibility for their own learning, thinking, and action.

While many media educators and advocates understand and reference the principal tenets of media literacy, this is not to suggest that there is a general consensus about the movement's goals. Rather than providing Masterman's emphasis on critical autonomy, there are some media education programs that focus on providing students with marketable skills that will enable them to find jobs as future media workers, uncritical of current media structures or practices.

As David Sholle and Stan Denski explain, the practice of video, audio, photography, and graphics media in the United States is usually situated within schooling programs aimed at offering skill enhancement and/or career development. Other schooling initiatives encourage students to creatively express themselves through new media forms and aesthetic experimentation without a critical understanding of media systems. This has led to several debates between disjointed factions of primary and secondary school educators, academics, media artists, and media executives.

Most debates centered on the objectives of media education are divided over the balance between media analysis and production. As Deborah Leveranz and Kathleen Tyner explain, those favoring analysis believe that production is only important if it helps students understand how to analyze mass media products. Proponents of media analysis are typically school teachers and university educators who believe in a formal, structured approach to media education. Not surprisingly, many of these teachers have no training in production and are often not particularly comfortable with media technologies.

Production advocates are typically media artists who have observed the "power of student production to increase student self-esteem through self-expression and to offer a voice to those who have been marginalized by mass media". Media artists believe that a hands-on approach is the best way to teach the analytical component. Moreover, many have witnessed the demise of the arts in public education institutions and believe that media arts education can strengthen the arts.

Needless to say, the debates polarizing analysis and production are only part of the contentious circumstances surrounding media education. Although not all of the debates will be outlined in the purview of this study, a brief summary of some conceptual and application issues as outlined in the 1998 Journal of Communication edition on media literacy is useful in understanding the complexity of the subject. Scholars William Christ and W. James Potter explain that defining media literacy poses the central conceptual debate. Media literacy has been treated as

- A public policy issue,
- A critical cultural issue,
- A set of pedagogical tools for elementary school teachers,
- Suggestions for parents,
- McLuhanesque speculation, and
- A topic of scholarly inquiry from a physiological, cognitive (Sinatra, 1986), or anthropological tradition.

Some writers focus on several countries or cultures, while others focus primarily on one culture, such as

- American culture,
- British culture, and
- Chilean culture.

It is a term applied to the study of

- Textual interpretation,
- Context and ideology, and
- Audience.

The term is also used as synonymous with, or part of, media education. Moreover, in the Winter 1998 issue of the *Journal of Communication*, Renee Hobbs and David Buckingham explain how the terms media and literacy both present controversy. In contesting the term media, academics, teachers, and parents wonder which medium should be the focus of study (i.e., oral and written versus still and moving images, computers, or multimedia); regarding the notion of literacy are questions that ask: How broadly should literacy be conceptualized? Should it be regarded primarily as a skill, as an accumulation of knowledge, or as a perspective on the world?

The final conceptual issues concern the divergent educational models espoused through media literacy. As Christ and Potter summarize:

The two main theoretical views of media literacy, inoculation theory and cultural studies, bring with them orientations toward the subject matter and assumptions about the audience that impact not only interpretation but how the subject matter is taught.

As Buckingham explains, inoculation theory emerged from the work of literary critic F. R. Leavis and his student Denys Thompson. In their book Culture and Environment, Leavis and Thompson offered a framework for the teaching of mass media in schools. Yet their impetus was driven by cultural elitism and the conservation of a "distinguished literary heritage." For Leavis and Thompson, teaching about popular culture was not a radical pedagogical discovery, but a method of teaching students to learn to inoculate or defend themselves from the invasion of the corrupting influence of mass media.

CRITICAL PEDAGOGY

In his foreword "Critical Theory and the Meaning of Hope", Peter McLaren contends that the goals of critical pedagogy are "to empower students to intervene in their own self-formation and to transform the oppressive features of the wider society to make such an intervention necessary". Contrary to the banking metaphor, in which it is the teacher's task to deposit knowledge into "empty" students, McLaren asks: Do we want our schools to create a passive, risk-free citizenry, or a political citizenry committed to forms of public life and invested in advancing social and political equality?

In *Media Education and the (Re)Production of Culture* (1994), David Sholle and Stan Denski argue that critical pedagogy is about more than "teaching techniques." Rather, critical pedagogy is about the analysis of those processes that define what knowledge is important to know, how we should learn it, and how the production of knowledge creates social identity. Similarly, Henry Giroux and Roger Simon (1989) suggest that "any process which tries to influence the production of meaning is a pedagogical process". Thus the pedagogical can occur outside schools and within the family, public discourse, the church, the media, and so forth.

Despite the importance of the aforementioned definitions of critical pedagogy, critical pedagogues need to acknowledge the fundamental tension between a theory/pedagogy that on the one hand calls for a liberatory democratic classroom (a safe space where true participation can occur), and on the other hand views schooling as the institutionalization of dominant ideologies and cultural production (where teacher-as-critic is the primary role). Accordingly, we will explore a critical pedagogy of risk and articulation rather than a progressive pedagogy of emancipation and democratic participation.

In contesting modernist conceptions of "equality," "social justice," "democracy," and "emancipation," we find ourselves in accordance with critical pedagogues whose philosophical pedagogical approaches are advanced through postmodernism. In Issues and Trends in Critical Pedagogy (1997), Barry Kanpol argues that critical pedagogy should be situated within a critical postmodernism that questions those worldviews that uphold and perpetuate "absolutes" and "universal truths." As critical pedagogues, we need to ask, accordingly: Whose knowledge or worldviews are we teaching? How is identity constructed? How many ways of learning are there? How many realities are there?

Moreover, Kanpol argues that a critical postmodernism is politically aligned with unraveling the processes that define social, cultural, and human difference, with an eye toward a shift of consciousness to challenging and transforming unequal relations of power and overcoming oppression, subordination, and alienation. Such goals are commensurate with Paulo Freire's work (1989), in which oppressed people can undertake to transform their lives by understanding those structures of power that set them up as unequal members of society.

One of the lauded goals of critical pedagogy has been its concern for diversity, multiculturalism, and democracy. Yet again there are many issues to be raised in light of the ways critical pedagogues and media literacy advocates have theorized these concepts. First, as Kanpol argues, critical pedagogy should foster a critical multiculturalism founded in understanding "difference" versus "diversity." In other words, it is not enough for school personnel to state that "we accept diversity." Multiculturalism must move beyond once-a-year celebrations of diversity, "international foods night," or a chapter on Asian American history.

Rather, difference must be thought of both at the level of the subject/individual and at the group level through race, class, sex, age, and so forth, whereby structures of identity and power are historically connected and interrogated. Such an approach does not have to essentialize difference, but should approach power as relative. One approach toward demonstrating the relativity of power is by encouraging students to see difference through similarity.

This can be done through the following examinations: (1) the cultural differences and similarities of student investments in cultural forms, such as rock music; (2) struggles over identity and representation within television and cinema, moving beyond the analysis of the media's hegemonic influences; (3) disapora and home/homelessness-how "minority" or "marginalized" students create and find homes within and outside the dominant structures, becoming "border crossers"; and (4) deconstructing whiteness-taking apart a multiculturalism rooted in a "democratic imaginary".

In accordance with critical postmodernism and multiculturalism, the goals of critical pedagogy should transgress progressive pedagogical approaches. As Lawrence Grossberg describes in his introduction to Between Borders (1994), there are three philosophical models of a progressive pedagogy, all of which deserve critique. First, there is the hierarchical model, in which the teacher's goal is to teach "truths" to students. This is the model that most critical pedagogues have critiqued. Second, the dialogical model of pedagogy aims to encourage silenced students to speak. For example, Shor situates critical pedagogy through personal empowerment whereby the goal of education is geared toward the self and social change as "the self and society create each other" through voice and dialogue.

Unfortunately, the problem with this model is that it assumes students aren't already speaking in ways teachers can understand or demand, or that there aren't serious material and social conditions that disenable students from speaking at particular moments in particular forms. Third, the praxical pedagogy is one (previously defined through the theorists above-namely McLaren, Giroux, and Shor) in which students are to intervene in their own history and fight for public spaces that encourage democratic participation.

The problem with this model is that it assumes that students aren't already invested in transforming their own history and that the teacher has the right knowledge and skills through which to make such transformations and emancipation possible. Consequently, given these critiques, a new model of critical pedagogy should be conceptualized. It is through Grossberg's pedagogy of risk and articulation that the goals of critical pedagogy should be retheorized philosophically and pragmatically. First, pedagogy of risk and articulation begins by arguing that teachers must go beyond traditional notions of intellectual authority without dismissing claims to authority.

Additionally, the teacher needs to acknowledge her/his role within the institutionalized power structure of schools as well. Teachers should not assume to know in advance the necessary knowledge, language, and skills of students; rather, through the contextual, teachers should take risks by interrogating forms, drawing lines, mapping articulations between discourses, domains, and practices. Accordingly, theory and politics, or theoretical and political correctness, cannot be determined in advance (Grossberg).

Moreover, within pedagogy of articulation and risk, the goals and outcomes of the learning process cannot be known in advance. In other words, students should be encouraged to determine for themselves their futures in unimagined and unimaginable ways. This may mean going beyond illusory goals or notions such as "democracy" and "emancipation." Chantal Mouffe realizes that common interests, consensus, and unanimity are illusory goals. For her, "a healthy democratic process calls for a vibrant clash of political positions and an open conflict of interests".

It might make more sense, then, to reconfigure altruistic goals like democracy through "a political framework that can accommodate difference and antagonism to sustain what Mouffe calls an 'agonistic pluralism'". Through this paradigmatic pedagogical shift, students need to define for themselves "the political" through the intersections of their locations, experiences, and concrete practices with historical and/or social representations of experience.

Hence the goal of teachers (and critical pedagogy) should not be to move students from one location or position to another, encouraging them to submit to or accept the political notions, ethics, and ideals espoused by the "radical" teacher. Rather, the goals of critical pedagogy should be to encourage students to identify their practices and complicitness in the political, popular, and cultural realm, allowing them to create new possibilities and new organizational spaces for their future. This approach can be associated with Masterman's notion of critical autonomy.

While Ira Shor's notions of Empowering Education (1992) advance a dialogical pedagogical model preoccupied with modernist ideals of "democracy" and "empowerment," his model of "problem-posing" versus "problem-solving" is extremely useful in applying the goals of critical pedagogy within a model of risk and articulation. Rather than privilege simple solutions to complex problems by asking students to spit out "the correct answer" as determined by the teacher, problem-posing allows students use their experiences and diverse perspectives to address those social issues that concern them and their communities.

This allows for new organizations of spaces to emerge as students travel and explore new possibilities and ways of understanding society, culture, identity, and knowledge. By connecting problem-posing with media literacy theory and production, students can best address the issues that directly affect their lives and futures. We will return to problem-posing when we critically engage with information in cyberspace, as it requires comparing and contrasting mediated "reality" with personal and experiential-based reality.

In this final section, the central theoretical tenets of critical cultural studies and the study of popular culture in order to examine how the use of new telecommunications technology in schools perpetuates a hegemonic force in which the business community defines the curricular uses of computer skills rather than educators committed to a liberal arts education examined. Just as Stan Denski and David Sholle (1994) argue that the use of video equipment in most liberal arts programs creates a hegemonic influence that normalizes the dominant production methods and predefines career needs, we will see how the current use of computer/online technology in schools perpetuates or reproduces a similar cultural hegemony.

Furthermore, the theories articulated here will make it possible for us to look at how information available on the Internet is affected by graphic design elements and advertising that naturalize and predetermine the possibilities of Webpage design and our understanding of how information can be sought, organized, and retrieved through a decentralized form of technology. As with all communications technology, capitalist interests have defined the content and structure of the media soon after its inception.

But since there is no intrinsic formula defining the content and structure of the Internet, it is vital that classroom curriculum and pedagogy take learning in a new direction by teaching students to venture into otherwise unknown enclaves located within this predominantly commercial terrain. Students need to differentiate between various sources of information using critical thinking skills and an understanding of political economy in order to keep in play the contest and struggle over meaning.

This is not to suggest that students are uncritical thinkers or that the Internet as a medium is completely invested with the politics of commodification. Rather, through a pedagogy of risk and experimentation, our goal will be to articulate how teachers and students can together inform what questions and investigations need to become part of critical learning, and what actions need to be taken upon such exploration. Although cultural studies is a disciplinary field without a uniform definition, methodology, approach, or practice, I will attempt to discuss some of the important and relevant themes within the field as they have been conceptualized by the Birmingham School of British Cultural Studies.

Within the study of mass communication comes a long history of various approaches to media or popular cultural forms that ask interesting but impractical questions about the "effects" of the media on our views and perceptions of the "culture" or the world. Unlike most traditional approaches to the analysis of the media (effects research, uses and gratifications, textual analysis, etc.), research stemming from Dr. George Gerbner's cultural indicators project (1978) poses and addresses three important core questions, namely:

1. Who gets to tell the stories of our culture? This allows for the study of the institutional analysis of the media or popular forms or the political economy of the media.
2. What is the content of these stories? (textual analysis).
3. How do these stories impact audiences? (audience analysis).

Through an analysis of Antonio Gramsci's notion of hegemony (1971) and Louis Althusser's conception of ideological state apparatuses (1971), cultural studies goes beyond an orthodox Marxist approach by expanding Marx's conception of capital as the ultimate determinational force of culture. It seeks to examine the many "cultures" that exist within society and within various groups and variables (e.g., race, class, gender, etc). But although cultural studies goes beyond the notion of capital as the ultimate determination of ideology, it nevertheless retains a vested interest in examining the institutional forces that limit and "encode" our culture through capital and ruling ideologies.

This area of cultural studies examines how the conglomeration of media through mergers and monopolies serves to delimit a plurality of voices and/or cultural forms and expressions. Cultural studies are concerned with issues of power and struggles over meaning within media, history, culture, art, and so forth. Without imposing a high culture/ low culture distinction, cultural studies treats all cultural forms as "texts," so that the production of meanings is studied and examined within and among all cultural forms of expression.

Whereas other approaches toward the study of culture have downplayed the importance of popular forms, cultural studies understands culture as those aspects that are part of everyday life; as Paul Willis (1977) describes, culture refers to our everyday practices-"the bricks and mortar of our most commonplace understandings". By defining culture through everyday life, cultural studies allow us to examine the production of meaning as articulated within particular contexts and practices. Through "deconstruction," textual analysis allows us to take apart those taken-for-granted "stories" or narratives that give us our commonsense knowledges of how the world works and what our roles within it are.

Through poststructuralism, cultural studies allows us to debunk the "canons" that have traditionally accorded ruling-class ideologies and aesthetics a privileged place within culture. Questions of identity-how it is produced, "articulated, experienced and deployed"-remain central within cultural studies, as evidenced in studies on race, ethnicity, and postcolonialism. Likewise, feminism has informed cultural studies by raising questions about subjectivity, gender, politics, and desire. Cultural studies as an approach recognizes that the hegemonic or ideological forces that aim to foreclose meaning and understanding are not without their limits.

Culture is transacted between consumers and producers, not simply laid on people from above. However, the more Marxist the approach, "the less emphasis is placed on the active role of consumers in determining cultural meaning". Accordingly, cultural studies examine how audiences are active rather than passive agents who can challenge and resist mediated messages about culture. Despite their political and/ or economic ties, the media (or the "culture industry," as Theodor Adorno and Max Horkheimer [1972] would conceive them) do not impose their "values" or ideological positions onto "dupes" who are unresponsive or uncritical consumers.

Consequently, in understanding how popular meanings are produced cultural studies moves beyond a theory of hegemony through Hall's theory of articulation, which allows us to examine "the continual severing, realigning, and recombining of discourses, social groups, political interests, and structures of power within society". Hence "the meaning of popular cultural forms can only be ascertained through their articulation" within a set of practices or as "historically specific contextual relations" that determine political meaning and ideological interests. As Hall reminds us, what is important is not the intrinsic or historically fixed object(s) of culture, but the state of play within cultural relations.

Although Hall, Laclau, and Mouffe's theory of articulation moves beyond Gramsci's notion of hegemony, we need to address the importance of hegemony as a concept in the study of popular culture, pedagogy, and media literacy. First, unlike theories of "domination" or "power" that understands the imposition of ideology or power through overt force and/or punishment, hegemony works within the terrain of everyday life and requires the consent of audiences/citizens/the masses.

Hegemony raises a number of theoretical questions about how power, as a cultural, economic, political, and pedagogical force, aims to define, organize, and legitimate particular conceptions of common sense. In Gramsci's view, the process of reaching consent through common sense is achieved through the continual (inter)play between the cultural and ideological domain of subordinate groups in order to sanction the interests and authority of the ruling block.

Yet unlike Adorno and Horkheimer's analysis of the culture industry, in which capital prevails as the dominant ideological force, hegemony allows us to study how power is continually struggled for/over. As in critical cultural studies, the dual concepts of hegemony and ideology function concurrently to substantiate the need for critical pedagogy. According to critical pedagogues Giroux and Simon, Gramsci's concept of hegemony is both a political and a pedagogical process:

> Moral leadership and state power are tied to a process of consent, as a form of practical learning, which is secured through the elaboration of particular discourses, needs, appeals, values, and interests that must address and transform the concerns of subordinate groups. In this perspective, hegemony is a continuing, shifting, and problematic historical process. Consent is structured through a series of relations marked by an ongoing political struggle over competing conceptions and views of the world between dominant and subcultural groups.

It is through this struggle for consent that the task of critical pedagogy merges with cultural studies in its objective to unmask hegemonies and critique ideologies with the political and ethical intent of helping to empower students and, more generally, the social groups to which they belong: by fostering awareness of conditions that limit possibilities for human becoming and legitimate the unequal distribution of social goods; and by unveiling the origins and the historical contingency of these ideologies/hegemonies and the social relations and practices they simultaneously beget and sustain.

Hence the struggle for power is never about "pure victory or pure domination...it is never a zero-sum cultural game". It is always a struggle over the balance of power within/

between cultural relations. Thus, in accordance with analyses of hegemony as a political and pedagogical process, we will also look at "alternative" Web sites, in order to observe the state of interplay between cultural forces.

3

The Exploration of Cyberspace

The face of Thomas Paine, rendered in yellow and pink, graces the cover of the first British edition of Wired, a successful magazine from the United States devoted to proselytizing the benefits of computer networking. For the technophile devotees of this subject, it is far more than a tool; rather it will usher in a complete transformation of every facet of our lives, no less than a mental and eventually a material revolution. On the cover, too, appear the words, 'We have it in our power to begin the world over again', the recast 'digital revolutionary' being summoned up to defend the global Net from threats of restriction, governmental and commercial.

Yet networking alone is an insufficient peg on which to hang a visionary future in which all human relations are forever changed. The environment in which all digitized media promise to combine and be exchanged has been called cyberspace. It is a curious subject for discussion, because as yet it hardly exists, but this has not hindered previews of its concepts and ideals being constantly played out in theory and fiction. These writings, which look to an unbridled technology to fulfil their wishes, visions and nightmares, can tell us much about attitudes to information, identity and the future.

The component parts of cyberspace-virtual reality and computer networking-are already with us; the first, in a crude form, can already be seen in the video arcades, while the second forms a rapidly growing global infrastructure. Until now, however, the heady marriage of the two, which is the ideal of cyberspace, has only been described in theory and science fiction. The typical vision is as follows:

From vast databases that constitute the culture's deposited wealth, every document is available, every recording is playable, and every picture is viewable. Around this: a laboratory, an instrumental bridge; taking no space, a home presiding over a world...

The user is immersed in a world of data which is present either as we would normally see it (perhaps a simulation of a printed page), or represented graphically (a dynamic three-dimensional graph of financial movements on the stock exchange). The massive number of sites or specialisms which this data comprises could be presented as different geographical areas between which the user would virtually travel.

A number of old bourgeois dreams are encompassed in the promise of this technology: to survey the world from one's living room, to grasp the totality of all data within a single frame, and to recapture a unified knowledge and experience. It also holds out the vision of a total and eternal archive which will persist long after the physical objects from which it was taken have crumbled; paintings may crack and photographs fade but digital records permit their colours and surfaces to remain forever pristine, while the exact trajectory of the actual object's decline is plotted.

Artifacts and even species which have been lost may be reconstructed; in a computer simulation, at least, we can wander about the Acropolis in its prime, or see dinosaurs stamp the virtual earth. Of course to write about the culture's 'wealth' assumes a community of interest among users before this process starts, and that cultural riches are simply out there to be grasped and codified. Yet this is in fact widely assumed: to the renewed liaison between technology and culture, the developers of cyberspace bring both a charming naivety and much commercial acumen. Microsoft is buying up the digital rights to what its founder, Bill Gates, calls the million most fascinating images in the world.

The ideal of cyberspace takes in more than just the sum of all human knowledge. It is also an electronic agora in which isolated, anomic but presumably rather well-informed individuals may once more come together, without risk of violence or infection, to engage in debate, exchange information or merely chew the fat. Both data and conversation are potentially accessible from anywhere; to be able to 'chat' instantaneously with a neighbour on the other side of the world certainly changes notions of distance and locality. Cyberspace seems to offer simultaneously the advantages of privacy and cultural wealth, self-sufficiency and opportunities for sociability.

Yet despite all the attention it has been receiving, cyberspace as a technological development has a strange status, not only because it has not yet been realized, but also because it is a concept which has its origins in fiction, particularly in the cyberpunk novels of William Gibson. Programmers and engineers are acting on fictional blueprints and, since these are naturally extremely vague, the very concept and the details of its implementation are up for grabs. The whole affair is even more curious because the fictional vision of cyberspace and the world which surrounds it is hardly positive: what has been taken up so enthusiastically is not so much a technical proposal as a dystopian vision of the future.

Of the very term itself, Gibson admits that he: 'Assembled word cyberspace from small and readily available components of language. Neologic spasm: the primal act of pop poetics. Preceded any concept whatever Slick and hollow-awaiting received meaning.' In Gibson's books cyberspace is a dizzying, dangerous 'place', where such intense experiences may be had that they exceed anything likely to be encountered in real life. It is dominated by leviathan corporations for whose operations it exists, but the system has exceeded them, producing mysterious creatures of mythical abilities, and encompassing such enormous complexity that there are many opportunities for daring Net frontiersmen, who make money by breaking security systems and copying confidential information.

Above all, cyberspace is a visual environment in which, while deception is occasionally a feature, things generally look much like what they are: large databases look large, corporations look powerful, military complexes look remote and dangerous, electronic countermeasures look threatening and as they operate their workings are graphically represented. There is, as we shall see, some sense to this. The transparency of meaning in cyberspace, the absolute match between concept and appearance, is a utopian feature which stands in marked contrast to the real world, of meaningless detail and redundant matter.

These descriptions should be contrasted with the reality of computer networking today where there are certainly opportunities for hackers, but where the interface is largely text-based and highly technical. Visceral experiences and reactions are absent. If computer networks are eventually to present themselves through graphical systems, there is no particular rule to say that there will be any resemblance between 'what they are' and what they look like (although there will no doubt be a tendency to link looks and the image an entity wishes to project).

Yet links between data and its representation cannot be entirely arbitrary, because the major advantage of cyberspace is that everyday perceptual skills are employed in understanding and manipulating complex information; people are generally much better at picking up an anomaly in a visual representation of data than from a raw mass of figures. The development of computer systems is also certainly running in the direction of Gibson's vision as Michael Benedikt points out, the 'evolution' of systems, from typed command to menu to Graphical User. Interface (for instance the Macintosh operating system copied in Windows) is that of making implicit navigation data visible and marrying it to content. The idea of an apparently immersive, three-dimensional cyberspace is another step in this direction.

DEVELOPING DYSTOPIA

What, then, are the details of this fictional vision to which many technicians, parts of the mass media and a portion of the public have subscribed? There is little common agreement about the definition or extent of cyberpunk. However, its main features are easy to characterize, as Istvan Csicsery-Ronay Jr, a writer about science fiction, rather wearily demonstrates:

> how many formulaic tales can one wade through in which a selfdestructive but sensitive young protagonist with an (implant/ prosthesis/ telechtronic talent) that makes the evil (megacorporations/ police states/ criminal underworlds) pursue him through (wasted urban landscapes/ elite luxury. enclaves/ eccentric space stations) full of grotesque (haircuts/ clothes/ self-mutilations/ rock music/ sexual hobbies/ designer drugs/ telechtronic gadgets/ nasty new weapons/ exteriorized hallucinations) representing the (mores/ fashions) of modern civilization in terminal decline, ultimately hooks up with rebellious and tough-talking (youth/ artificial intelligence/ rock cults) who offer the alternative, not of (community/ socialism/ traditional values/ transcendental vision), but of supreme, life-affirming hipness, going with the flow which now flows in the machine, against the spectre of a world-subverting (artificial intelligence/ multinational corporate web/ evil genius)?

Despite all this, he goes on to argue that the genre suggests links between four levels of information processing: the individual's biological processes and personality, the totality of social life, nonliving artificial intelligences and finally new, 'living' entities, created out of these A1's. Cyberspace jockeys in fiction do not just wear virtual-reality headsets but have had their physiology surgically altered to interface directly with the Net. There is an air of telepathy 'about the way they experience, if not understand, the sublime complexity of the world's data, and the most fortunate may hope for mystical contact with artificial super-beings.

In the connection of the individual and the social, there is a dialectical move in which opposed qualities find resolution in a higher unity, and we shall see that this is typical of writing about cyberspace in fiction and non-fiction. For the moment it is important to note the strange combination of high-tech and grunge, of the laboratory and the street (or at least a suburban boy's idea of the street), of social critique and unreconstructed heroism. Cyberpunk sports a Gothic technophilia.

The cyberpunk vision is not simply negative, but it is not a happy one. Gibson's first novel, Neuromancer, which was a great success and the book which, more than any other, defined the genre, is set in the wake of a world-wide nuclear conflict. After, the reconstruction, the rich are fabulously so, while everyone else survives on their wits in an environmentally degraded world of drugs, violence and conspiracy, aided by bizarre mental and physical prostheses. The hero: slept in the cheapest coffins, the ones nearest the port, beneath the quartz-halogen floods that lit the docks all night like vast stages; where you couldn't'see the lights of Tokyo for the glare of the television sky, not even the towering hologram logo of the Fuji Electric Company, and Tokyo Bay was a black expanse where gulls wheeled above drifting shoals of styrofoam. Behind the port lay the city, factory domes dominated by the vast cubes of corporate arcologies. Port and city were divided by a narrow borderland of older streets, an area with no official name....By day, the bars down Ninsei were shuttered and featureless, the neon dead, the holograms inert, waiting, under the poisoned silver sky.

The real world is in perhaps terminal decline, and threatens to bury its inhabitants in obsolete consumer goods, an ever rising tide of trash. People turn their backs on reality, into drugs, into cyberspace, or, for the less active, into an enveloping form of television which imparts the sensory experiences of its stars. Cyberspace is at once an ideological inverse image of this world, and what helps to maintain the power of those who govern it. Nevertheless, for those who regularly inhabit it, even the real world comes to seem like cyberspace, as the virtual takes on a reality which often has material effects, and the material acquires an unreal virtuality.

Given this scenario, the question arises, why does anyone want to develop dystopia? Among,the reasons which immediately spring to mind are its supposed technical inevitability coupled with dissatisfaction with currently fixed identities and activities, and also that there might be a career in it. Most of all, perhaps, because fictional cyberspace has a fascination as a glossy, technophile's dystopia which contains some curiously utopian elements. In cyberspace-as it appears in novels, at least-the world seems to make transparent sense, if only for the godlike entities that haunt its highest margins. Yet beyond this, there is a resolutely positive vision of cyberspace, very much at odds with its face in fiction, which is at once highly congruent with current intellectual fashions and with powerful commercial interests.

HI-TECH HEGELIANISM

A phone book is a material object containing data; this data is abstract and can only be understood by those who know how to read it; the book itself is a piece of matter and has to be put in the appropriate place and sometimes moved around. In cyberspace both of these conditions may be changed: data is extracted from its material support and purified so that it can be in many places at once, and sent at near the speed of light. Cyberspace also promises to restore a sensorial form to data without its losing utility or fungibility. The system may still work with phone numbers but the regular user would never need to deal with them.

The representation of data within cyberspace is generally thought of as visual and strictly organized in space. Michael Benedikt, a professor of architecture, writes of 'cyberspace architects' who will visualize the 'intrinsically nonphysical' and so give 'inhabitable visible form to society's most intricate abstractions, processes, and organisms of information'. Cyberspace then will be a unified field in which the real is abstracted and the abstract solidified, in which data, extracted from real processes, is refrozen into solid, immediately comprehensible forms, stripped of all actuality. Within this neat schema, the status of representations is equivocal.

As data gains physicality, representations in cyberspace lose it, floating free in the digital environment, but as pieces of data which already have a form, they are not manipulable in quite the same way as, say, numbers. They are hard nuggets of discrete information among a shifting mass, manipulable by position and presentation, but not so much (except on the whim of the individual) in terms of form or content, nor changeable in response to shifts in the values of external data. Old, fixed representations, then, might be an important anomaly within the dematerialized visual arena of cyberspace.

To leave this issue aside for the time being, the simultaneous dematerialization of data and its transformation into readily understood visual forms has been used as the basis for much metaphysical speculation on the nature of cyberspace. At times this has amounted to a hi-tech Hegelianism. It is often presented as a new realm between the material and the mental: 'Cyberspace becomes another venue for consciousness itself. And this emergence, proliferation, and complexification of consciousness must surely be this universe's project.' Its materialization of information, the gift of form to data, is a Platonic dream comes true:

Cyberspace is Platonism as a working product. The computer recycles ancient Platonism by injecting the' ideal content of cognition with empirical specifics. The computer clothes the details of empirical experience so that they seem to share the ideality of the stable knowledge of Forms.

Rather than see cyberspace simply as a halfway house between various pre-existing concepts, the temptation is to view it as a Hegelian synthesis. If for Hegel the real was ideal, in cyberspace the ideal is made virtually real. Very often theories about cyberspace encompass a grand historical sweep, taking on a Hegelian tone as the technology is seen as the means of achieving a sublation of previously opposed fundamental forces or qualities.

Cyberspace becomes the conclusion of a wondrous and harmonious historical pageant, a story of human technical and cultural evolution sweeping forwards from cave-painting to computer science. So Benedikt, for instance, argues that it ushers in a 'post-literate era' which unites the advantages of pre-literate physical activity with literate symbolic activity. Or it may be seen as the sublation of the monadological body and the community, body and mind, art and science-and no doubt quite a few other combinations. Two selfproclaimed, networked media philosophers, Mark Taylor and Esa Saarinen spell out the nature of the attraction clearly:

According to Hegel, the concept is actually embodied in time and space. In different terms, objectivity is actually conceptual or the real is the idea. In the society of spectacle, the idea becomes the image and the real is imaginary. For Hegel, it is concept all the way down; for the society of the spectacle, it is image all the way down. In the twentieth century, the Hegelian concept becomes real in electronic telecommunications. The net wires the world for Hegelian Geist.

The Hegelianism of the cyberphiles is not one of process, a form of becoming-in fact there is a general assumption that what is technically possible will inevitably be socially implemented. Rather, it is a fixed state in which the end of history and the total realization of mind is finally achieved: in this way it is a fixed Platonic form. Yet data, which must be handled in the visual arena of cyberspace, like numbers on the stock market, has already been abstracted from the real world and made fungible. Its particularity has already been stripped away in its reduction to number.

In cyberspace, where it is given an apprehensible form, this data must be constantly animated, as if in a movie. Given that the function of virtual representation is tied to movement, a fixed perfection like that of architecture will certainly elude these forms. Yet even these clean, mobile cyberspace forms can never show the material suffering behind a row of financial figures, for this has been stripped away long ago in the very collection of the data. When a form is restored to this data, the 'reality' it adopts is utterly cleansed of anything that cannot be exchanged.

Perhaps we should try to stand Hegel on his head for a while. 'Empowering technology' is the new buzz phrase of the informatics enthusiasts, and it has a revealing ambiguity to it. The cyberphiles have generally had an easy time of it in a media which is owned by the very companies which are buying up rights to data for virtual distribution. Fundamental questions about the direction in which the technology is being taken are rarely asked.

A basic assumption behind the acceptance of cyberspace underlies that of the information society as a whole: Andrew Ross has rightly argued that 'the technical fact of communication itself is celebrated as an inherent good', without any discussion of the 'resulting shape of the community that is wired up in this way'. New Age dreams of universal, seamless networking are oddly congruent with features of a modern corporate communications ideology.

Cyberspace is also allied with an unashamed consumerism: 'We are present at the apotheosis of commercial culture. Commerce is the ocean that information swims in....the means of exchange in commercial culture is now pure information.' Vivian Sobchack has analysed the mix of New Age spiritualism and New Edge technophilia in which sixties political activism and social consciousness has been resolved into 'a particularly privileged, selfish, consumeroriented and technologically dependent libertarianism', which fulfils 'the dreams of "mondoids" who, by day, sit at computer consoles working for (and becoming) corporate America'. It is cyberspace which will allow this becoming to complete itself.

In this light, cyberspace appears as less the end of history than the ultimate business environment, being stock market, warehouse and shopping centre all in one. Aside from commercial interests, there is also an unholy alliance of postmodern disintegration theorists and wide-eyed New Agers, producing a ludicrous image of the world immersed in a great, shifting sea of data, each person jacking in and finding exactly what they want, in their own personalized order and format. People will live intensely in this digital utopia, forgetting their grosser material needs in an affective, intellectual search for companionship and knowledge.

In this ostensibly democratic forum, a chairman of some Western conglomerate and an impoverished peasant in Central Africa will both use a device, much the size of a Walkman, to communicate by satellite with a panoply of open information systems. As soon as this utopian vision of global information-sharing is baldly stated, its stupidity becomes obvious. It is not a matter of doubting the capabilities of the technology, which has already been developed and is becoming cheaper all the time.

One should be deeply sceptical, however, about who will control the information, how much it will cost, and to whom it will be sold. Technological revolutions of the past parade their many broken utopian promises. As Herbert Schiller has shown, similar arguments have been rehearsed about all manner of new technologies in order to prepare for their acceptance, and in all cases the liberatory effects have been negligible. Desktop publishing is one example, as is cable television which, Schiller notes, although it was much touted as the guarantor of pluralism, has rapidly succumbed to homogeneous corporate dominance.

Domestic computer technology provides another striking example of the marketing of a rapidly improving technology. Computers have indeed become much cheaper, but only in a certain sense. Average systems still cost a considerable amount of money and, while they are far more powerful, their basic price has not fallen for many years; in fact it may be that the average system has got more expensive in real terms. Software developments which do not always develop in a strictly functional manner push the minimum acceptable machine ever upward into new areas of speed and sophistication. Below a certain price level, there is little money to be made selling these goods, unless they can be shifted in vast amounts.

There is no interest in selling electronic commodities at the price the world's poor can not afford, nor is there likely to be. The idea that high-band global networking will become truly universal in a world where only a fifth of the population currently have even telephones is laughable. Even in the highly improbable event of the hardware price sinking to that of a can of Coke, there are still insuperable obstacles for the impoverished. The technology requires that end-users are connected by satellites or a network of specialized terrestrial cabling, the 'Information Super-Highway' in which the United States government is currently investing much money.

Already there is awareness that the placement of the cables may be another means of discriminating against the less wealthy. Without the cabling, and without expensive, advanced modems to receive the data, transfer is much slower, to the point of being either impractical or, since online charges are like telephone calls, too expensive. Then there is the whole vexed issue of copyright, which will certainly add further charges for the access of 'intellectual property'. Large companies are active buying the digital rights to all kinds of data, from financial records to pop records; they are not doing this to distribute them free of charge.

The emergence of Cyberspace as the main information channel is worrying because it will not necessarily be seen as complementary to existing media. If the Net becomes the only way of receiving certain kinds of information, it may be more restrictive than current systems. Schiller puts the broad issue clearly:

Transforming information into a saleable good, available only to those with the ability to pay for it, changes the goal of information access from an egalitarian to a privileged condition. The consequence of this is that the essential underpinning of a democratic order is seriously, if not fatally, damaged.

Now of course, access to certain kinds of information has always been difficult and time-consuming, and what appears in the mass media has always been strictly controlled; in one sense, and perhaps as it exists today, networking can provide a minority with the means to receive information and opinions from diverse sources, yet in another, pay-as-you-go cyberspace threatens to add another powerful disincentive on top of the controls which already exist.

VIRTUAL COMMUNITY

Far from closing down access to information, cyberphiles have generally seen the Net as evolving into an open, global forum to which anybody can contribute, in which information and data are shared and weighty issues discussed. Communities, often sundered in the real world by traffic, the threat of violence or the self-sufficiency encouraged by modern domestic appliances, will be reborn in the ether, as people with the same interests but who are perhaps geographically distant, virtually meet. Roy Ascott, for instance, has stressed the dialogic nature of the new telematic media:

Interactive telecommunications-telematic technology speaks a language of cooperation, creativity and transformation.

It is the technology not of monologue but of conversation. It feeds fecund open-endedness rather than an aesthetics of closure and completion.

This is not to forge the way for a society of the kind described by Habermas, in which agreement is founded on reasoned conversation, but something far more fractured and postmodern; not so much dialogue as a cacophony of separate, atomistic voices. For Ascott, and this is a very common association, it has its philosophical basis in the writings of Nietzsche, Bateson, Weiner, Derrida and Rorty. Ascott, speaking now of art on the Net, continues:

Art is no longer seen as a linear affair, dealing in harmony, completion, resolution, closure-a composed and ordered finality. Instead it is open-ended, even fugitive, fleeting, tentative, and virtual. Forming rather than formed, it celebrates process, embodies system, and embraces chaos. On the face of it there would seem to be some contradiction between building a community, which must have a basis in some agreed terms, and the supposed ever-shifting fluidity of postmodern discourse. Yet people on the Net, despite their differences, have managed to build something of a community, though as we shall see, it is of quite a particular kind.

Until very recently, many of the advantages of networking were derived from its very exclusiveness: it was open only to people who had access to a computer and a modem, and using these was quite a technical matter. In Britain especially the social composition of participants on the Net was very narrow (in part because of high telephone charges), being dominated by young computer professionals and academics, usually scientists, who gained access through the free university network. In all countries, the restricted social make-up of those on the Net, and the fact that they were all technically competent, encouraged solidarity.

The great increase in the number of new users, however, has led old hands to complain that the pleasures of discovery are being obstructed by the high number of learners and 'party-goers'. Theodore Roszak, writing of Bulletin Board

Systems where people can post computer messages, describes part of the problem:

Even those who are enthusiastic about the potential of the Net have to admit that most bbs discussion is 'mundane or puerile or esoteric', having something in common with homemade fanzines. Net conversations are often theatrical, featuring well-known regular participants who are thoroughly informed about networking; etiquette, and are greatly outnumbered by silent listeners. Various intellectuals hang around this world, in the hope that a little of its street cred might rub off. Some have cultivated a cool but apocalyptic mode of writing, replete with neologisms and oxymorons. This is a passage from Arthur Kroker and Michael Weinstein's aptly named book, *Data Trash*, in which the authors are careful to parade their pretensions in detail:

I am sitting in Foufounes Electrique, an underground cyberpunk music bar in Montreal. I've a shooter in my hand, copies of Bruce Sterling's Crystal Express and Nietzsche's Will to Power in my data bag, and my cyber-flesh is taking direct hits from the sound forcefield of Fuzzy Logic, a group of digital music hackers...

And so it proceeds interminably. Aside from the danger that meaningful discourse can be buried by trivia (and increasingly advertising), there is a postmodern dilemma which the Net faces, and which is very much linked with the philosophical work of Rorty and others. Howard Rheingold, who has been very active in building a local network in San Francisco, notes that the diversity of dialogue and porosity of boundaries on the Net'might be an artifact of the early stages of the medium-fragmentation, hierarchization, rigidifying social boundaries, and single-niche colonies of people who share intolerances could become prevalent in the future.'

The idea that there is a 'true' structure of information is one of the most pervasive myths of cyberspace, notes Erik Davis, and it is likely to be eroded as people begin to disagree about what constitutes trivia, or how special-interest groups are structured and represented. The consensual environment of cyberspace must try to satisfy many competing demands. These incipient communities also have to face active vandalism. This may take the form of hacking into the operating system to cause disruption or bypass security measures in order to read private mail. Beyond this, forums may be attacked merely by the content of the messages. Rheingold notes:

> One of the great problems with the atmosphere of free expression now tolerated on the Net is the fragility of communities and their susceptibility to disruption. The only alternative to imposing potentially dangerous restrictions on freedom of expression is to develop norms, folklore, ways of acceptable behaviour that are widely modelled, taught, and valued; that can give the citizens of cyberspace clear ideas of what they can and cannot do with the medium, how they can gain leverage, and where they must beware of pitfalls in the medium, if we intend to use it for community-building.

He gives one example of a community Bulletin Board System which was destroyed by a group of young males choking the system with obscene postings. Such tales point to a fundamental problem: the virtual community demands a real one prior to it in order to function successfully. That communities can for the moment flourish is due to the still relatively closed and technophile nature of the Net, which is just what gives it its coherence, and means that it is hardly the identity-free utopia that some claim. People are defined at least by the fact that they are there.

Postmodern critics who praise Netspeak for its diversity are reluctant to raise questions of judgement about its quality. The central argument of Roszak's book, The Cult of Information, is that there is no necessary connection between the mere amount of data available and the quality of thought brought to bear on it. There is a further question of whether the computer itself has any 'effect on the quality of thought produced in its presence. The computer is a universal machine, in that it is capable of simulating the action of any other machine, but just because of this, it need do little to change our previous habits and predilections. Yet the form which it has taken is highly specific, and very much determined by the fact that it must be marketed and sold to businesses and consumers, and this particular form does seem to encourage certain types of relationship to its content.

In part, this may be to do with the system of navigation; effortless and unlimited jumps lead to skimming, while the lack of hierarchy in presentation and the equality of access give the impression that all pieces of information are equivalent. There is a propensity to travel but never to arrive. Benedikt is aware of the difficulty:

> If instant access to people and information were to become endemic to cyberspace, gone would be the process of progressive revelation inherent in closing the distance between self and object, and gone would be a major armature in the structuring of human narratives: the narrative of travel. Destinations would all be certain, like conclusions foregone. Time and history, narrativity and memorability, the unfolding of situations, the distance between objects of desire and ourselves-the distance, indeed, that creates desire and the whole ontology of eroticism would be collapsed, thrown back, to existing in this physical world only, and only as lame, metaphorical constructions, here and there, in that one.

This is not mere speculation. Theodore Roszak has commented on the diminished attention span encouraged by 'edutainment', arguing:

> There is something about all computerized activities that is worrisome in this respect, something built into the physical posture, emotional affect, and perceptual action of sitting at a video terminal, entering data, scrolling through, revealing snippets of this and that.

If this seems exaggerated, it may be because we have already been affected: Adorno wrote of the abbreviated thought which takes place with pencil in hand, so what would he have made of the insistently flashing cursor? Even the best multimedia programs encourage constant flicking from screen to screen, partly because the options for moving on are always marked and await the mouse click, but mostly because of the paucity of the material presented. One might gaze at a painting by Poussin for quite some time, but not at the little images in 256 colours provided in Microsoft's cd-romArt Gallery. There is a tendency for different kinds of information and representation to become flattened into a single field in which all things seem equivalent. The consequence and significance of the unusual tends to be eroded in such circumstances.

DISEMBODIED IDENTITIES

The greatest freedom cyberspace promisis is that of recasting the self: from static beings, bound by the body and betrayed by appearances, Net surfers may reconstruct themselves in a multiplicity of dazzling roles, changing from moment to moment according to whim. From being restricted to a single time and place, the Net being may distribute itself over the wired-up globe and make its acts and statements eternal. The new technology offers us freedom of the most fundamental and necessary kind, from identity itself:

> The technology of these transformative systems fulfils a profound human desire: to transcend the limits of the human body, time and space; to escape language, to defeat the metaphors of self and identity that alienate and isolate that imprison the mind in solipsistic systems. Our need is to fly, to reach out, to touch, connect-to expand our consciousness by a dissemination of our presence, to distribute self into a larger society of mind.

As it currently exists, this utopian anonymity has been founded on text, in fact on the technical crudity of an interface. Identity can be fluid in virtual communication where accent, looks, wealth, posture and gender are screened out in text-only dialogue; this is not likely to last long, and in fact the degree to which it happens even now may be exaggerated. Such playing of roles goes back to Alan Turing's gender game where a man and a woman in separate rooms conversing only with written messages would each try to convince the other that they were women.

Turing of course also devised a similar test for machine intelligence. When video rather than text is exchanged, the conventional boundaries of identity may be re-established. Images could be modified, of course, but only by deliberate falsification. On the other hand, representations of the self in cyberspace may be thought of as deliberate fictions, and gender swapping seems to be one of the most demanded, to the extent that in the Lucasfilms virtual world, Habitat, there is a 'Change-o-matic' object which switches the virtual gender of its user. The Humean kit form of identity change is likely to be the most open to most users: true fluidity being beyond all but the independent programmer.

Yet the extreme mutability and multiplication of identity possible in cyberspace collides with the desire to build communities based upon honest communication with people of diverse backgrounds and interests. Role-playing, and the potential for dishonesty which goes with it, militates against community. The potential flexibility of cyberspace does not extend merely to the presentation of identity, but also covers a personal tailoring of how the virtual environment is experienced. It might form the ultimate solipsism, because space and perception are infinitely malleable to the user:

Liquid architecture is an architecture whose form is contingent on the interests of the beholder; it is an architecture that opens to welcome me and closes to defend me; it is an architecture without doors and hallways, where the next room is always where I need it to be and what I need it to be. Liquid architecture makes liquid cities, cities that change at the shift of a value, where visitors with different backgrounds see different landmarks, where neighborhoods vary with ideas held in common, and evolve as the ideas mature or dissolve.

The next room is indeed always where you need to be, but this is only half the problem. Such schemes amount to a materialized phenomenology, a realization of the postmodern dream in which we create reality itself. Benedikt tries to rule this out with his 'Principle of Indifference' which states that 'the felt realness of any world depends on the degree of its indifference to the presence of a particular "user" and on its resistance to his/her desire' Such pre-emptive restrictions on the freedom of identity, its multiplication, and the speed and latitude of travel are imposed by the requirements of a consensual space. Of representations of objects and people in cyberspace Benedikt writes:

> These malleable data representations, worlds, and selves, seemingly so desirable, instantiating (at last!) our much-vaunted individual subjectivity and the late-twentieth-century notion that reality is nothing but a projection'of that subjectivity, are, in fact, as much laid against each other as into each other. While the temptation to narcissism and deception are dismaying, the risks to rational communication are staggering.

Immediately, then, and just as in the real world, personal freedoms are restricted by the demands of a consensual environment; cyberspace enthusiasts may want completely fluid identities and organic communities, but they cannot have both at once-at least not within a unitary environment. The propensity for trying to make virtual communities is comment enough on the debility of real ones, but also on the need for them.

Politics and commerce are as closely linked in the emergent medium of cyberspace as they are in any, other mass-marketed cultural form- television for instance. Again, however, political advances are supposed to be founded on this new technology. The unrestricted exchange of information is supposed to make life difficult for totalitarianism, and to augment the power of citizens in democracies.

Networks have indeed often been employed for radical purposes: Green organizations use them to maintain contact with remote areas where rapid responses to, say, new logging operations are necessary. News can be passed on quickly to activists internationally who can 'then mobilize opposition. More generally, however, and when we consider not specific radical activities, but the idea of universal data access as a whole, as Roszak has argued, this optimism is based on a strange diagnosis of our social ills: 'It assumes that the body' politic is starving for lack of information and that only the computer can make good that shortage', while obviously politics has hardly exhausted the information already available.

The idea that networking has a politically radical aspect has not, however, just been invented out of the blue by cyberphiles. It has a basis, especially in the early idealism of those who established the popular use of computer networks. The utopian and politically progressive moment of networking lies not in its future but in its anti-commercial origins, when enthusiasts established an exclusive counter-culture based on the free exchange of information and programming tools. For those wealthy enough to be consumers, the personal, digital world provided and perhaps still can provide an escape from the ubiquitous mall that the world has become.

The key programs that made amateur computer communication possible were distributed for free or at a nominal cost. Furthermore, the Internet is remarkable because it requires so little administration; while it has its origins in military computer communications networks which were designed to be robust and flexible enough to survive the destruction of a large number of their nodes, the result is a modular and largely self-regulating system.

The hope is that the shiny new world of cyberspace will be a free, public space where the environmental depredations and commercial white noise of the real world can be avoided. In the United States, it is often described as a new frontier. For those rugged, libertarian individuals who dare to venture there, the realm of cyberspace will reactivate the lost magic of a mythological past. For Timothy Leary, who has retired from recommending designer drugs to take up proselytizing the benefits of computer networking, cyberpunks are the strong, stubborn individuals who have inherited the mantle of the early explorers, mavericks, ronin and freethinkers everywhere.

Certainly some of the hackers and legitimate explorers of the networks as they currently exist do understand their experience in this way: they can do so because the networks are still difficult to navigate. These informational spaces are relatively private and crude, and are largely 'inhabited' by like-minded initiates. When and if this space really does become as public and immediate as television, what is to say that it will not become as cluttered and full of commercial garbage as anywhere else? There is little, except the protests of the users, to protect the virtual world from this fate. Within the past few years the previously unsullied world of computer games has succumbed to 'product placement'.

Two descriptions of cyberspace skies elucidate this situation: for Gibson they are a 'monochrome nonspace where the only stars are dense concentrations of information, and high above it all burn corporate galaxies and the cold spiral arms of military systems'. A bleak vision of some frozen frontier, then, forbidding but at least not crass.

For Benedikt, by contrast, the skies are alive with the images of its travellers, hurtling through space, and 'alive with entities licensed to inhabit this public realm, floating like ribbons, hot-air balloons, jellyfish, clouds, but in wonderful, unlikely shapes, constrained only 1) to represent information systems in the public interest, and 2) to be mostly transparent. There would be a thousand words and images, a din of voices and music (and, yes, advertisements are possible)...They are far more than just possible. Benedikt also recommends that travel in cyberspace have a monetary cost, and speculates about various sources of cyberspace profit, from virtual 'real estate' in cyberspace which might be leased to advertisers to connection charges for the system.

NET BUSINESS

So the radical and exclusive position of the Net is fragile. Howard Rheingold correctly argues that the Net offers liberatory potential just because it is still largely outside the control of the mass media. Using Ben Bagdikian's analysis of the media monopoly, he argues that the 'new media lords are not likely to encourage their privately owned and controlled networks to be the willing conduits for all kinds of information that unfettered citizens and nongovernmental organizations tend to disseminate.' The commercialization of the Net will raise questions of pricing, access, censorship and copyright, of 'intellectual property' in short, which the owners will take action to protect.

In 'Operation Sun Devil', FBI agents arrested hackers not for causing damage but merely for gaining free access to information. Here the open-door ideology of the network founders collides with the commercial ethos of the society in which they live. The United States government's support of the networking infrastructure is founded on connecting supercomputers, and gaining advantage in international technological competition, rather than on some experiment in networked democracy. Rheingold, analysing this process of commodification, warns that 'this transition might render moot many of the fantasies of today's true believers in electronic democracy and global online culture.' Commercialization and political control are entangled issues.

Cyberspace will be highly complex so people will need guidance through it, and this is where corporations step in, providing regular and assured channels of access. In an industry where common standards are usually of more importance than quality, the big players have most of the advantages. The nineties have' seen various powerful mergers and alliances between large companies which are trying to dominate this technology, including the agreement between Microsoft, Tele-communications Inc. (the largest cable television company) and Time-Warner. Such corporations are limbering up for the control of a medium which could serve as a substitute for movies, newspapers, magazines and even shops.

The virtual world is also the ideal arena for public-relations exercises: 'Perhaps the most dramatic opportunity cyberspace provides for a corporation is a dynamic and exciting public face. Public visits to the corporation will provide intimate interactions with company products either simulated or real.' Best of all, the information flows both ways for, as the potential customer gathers information about the product, the corporation will gather data about its customers 'for instant measurements of acceptance'.

A great benefit of cyberspace for producers of information is its dematerialization of the 'soft' commodities which they sell (whether it be books, images, music or software). Marx argued that the status of the commodity was dependent upon movement:

> Circulation proceeds in space and time. Economically considered, the spatial condition, the bringing of the product to the market, belongs to the production process itself. The product is really finished only when it is on the market. This locational movement could be more precisely regarded as the transformation of the product into a commodity.

In making a virtual space in which soft goods may be replicated and moved around at little or no cost, cyberspace becomes a perfect marketplace. Those commodities which are not marketed primarily on their merits as objects may be launched in cyberspace with no material basis; this involves little outlay and great potential for distribution. Holding 'stock' will cost almost nothing. Unwanted 'goods' will be dematerialized and immediately disposable. Without the material substratum restraining them, commodities may respond instantly to the fractal climate of fashion. Most of all, the support structure for all this, cyberspace itself, becomes the grand universal commodity. The virtual environment is marketed and put on a meter. As one commentator put it: 'Experience will become a substance and a commodity.'

What effect might this dematerialization have on 'soft' data commodities? The pieces of plastic, paper and metal which serve as vehicles for games, music or images currently receive a little aura, some small affective charge by way of association. Covers and styling aid this, and although these may be simulated in the computer, these immaterial adjuncts will no longer have any rigorous distinction from their contents. While it is unlikely that such developments will stop people wanting to collect objects, it may affect our view even of the soft commodities which continue to be sold.

The world of commodities and the world of things will become more manifestly separate, as will the disjunction between notions of value and the material purchased (most people know that compact discs are very cheap to produce, but at least they look expensive). This may produce a more obvious separation of use-value and exchange-value, something which is already apparent in attitudes to the pricing and illicit copying of software.

COMPUTER HEAVEN

Although misgivings about the economics of cyberspace are rarely expressed, there is certainly little agreement about its likely cultural effect. From the overview given so far, it is obvious that there is a basic contrast between utopian theory and dystopian fiction, a fundamental difference over whether the new technology will bear us to heaven or send us to hell. Despite this, both are agreed on the magnitude of the effect, and often express it in quasi-religious terms. Brenda Laurel describes her 'conversion experience' on first being introduced to a computer:

> A friend of mine worked at a large think-tank where he was head of a new department in computer graphics and imaging. Late one night he asked me if I wanted to see a computer. We went through three security checks and up an elevator and through a maze of cubicles to a workstation where images were materializing on a little screen. I think it was Mars we were looking at. All I remember now is that I saw a portal to a new world, a million new worlds. I fell to my knees and said, whatever I do, I have to get my head into this stuff.

Many of the elements of myth are here: the mystery of the dead of night, the hazardous pilgrimage followed by the revelation of another world. Many enthusiasts of cyberspace let its propensity for dematerialization transport them into the realms of spiritual discourse. For Michael Benedikt:

> Cyberspace: The realm of pure information, filling like a lake, siphoning the jangle of messages transfiguring the physical world, decontaminating the natural and urban landscapes, redeeming them, saving them from the chain-dragging bulldozers of the paper industry, from the diesel smoke of courier and post-office trucks, from jet fuel fumes and clogged airports, from billboards, trashy and pretentious architecture, hour-long freeway commutes, ticket lines, and

choked subways from all the inefficiencies, pollutions (chemical and informational), and corruptions attendant to the process of moving information attached to things-from paper to brains-across, over, and under the vast and bumpy surface of the earth rather than letting it fly free in the soft hail of electrons that is cyberspace.

The reality of the computer industry is of course far from the image of rarefied immateriality in which it likes to pose, but nevertheless the message is clear. Humanity, freed from the effort of moving material around, will be raised to a purer, ethereal domain, leaving Nature to its own devices-and a good thing too.

Cyberspace does not stop at dematerializing a part of the world's transport. In a fulfilment of the dreams of modernists, it offers the hope of eroding the boundaries between high art and the cultural environment as a whole:

We may, at last, have broken the stranglehold of the gilded frame and bypassed the parasitic high-priests and culture vultures to establish an egalitarian art of, for, and by the people. Not the constrained and hierarchical social realism of totalitarianism but a hetrarchial and streetwise cyber-grafitti, an art from the grassroots of democracy that, like urban spraycan walls, will impinge upon and possibly integrate all our diverse consciousnesses.

The apparent freedom and lack of structure within cyberspace comes to affect its contents, letting everyone have access to the world's cultural riches, and initiating a golden age of universal, radical creativity. It promises also to let us enter behind the screen, to embrace us as participants in new worlds. There we will be dematerialized and made eternal: 'Forget about Andy Warhol's petty promise of fame for fifteen minutes. We will all become angels, and for eternity! Highly unstable, hermaphrodite angels, unforgettable in terms of computer memory.

Every statement, eventually every thought, is recorded, unchanging even though we change, persisting even when we have passed away. In this dream of immortality, of a fairytale land where the mind's every blip has a permanent place and meaning within a vast collective dream, there is also a clear sense that computers have exceeded us, outgrowing their merely practical uses and militaristic origins to become an embracing, eternal spirit.

The concept of cyberspace attracts a breathless, hyperbolic writing which, whether positive or negative, tends to sport a proliferation of lists, as though the prose were trying to suggest the vast connected catalogue that the virtual world should become. It also encourages writing of a quasi-religious nature, the better to suggest the escape from the taint of material and flesh that the technology offers, and the disinterestedness of its purveyors. Benedikt again consider: Where Eden (before the Fall) stands for our state of innocence, indeed ignorance, the Heavenly City stands for our state of wisdom, and knowledge, where Eden stands for our intimate contact with material nature, the Heavenly City stands for our transcendence of both materiality and nature; where Eden stands for the world of unsymbolized, asocial reality, the Heavenly City stands for the world of enlightened human interaction, form and information....

The Heavenly City, though it may contain gardens, breathes the crystalline gleam of its own lights, sparkling, insubstantial, laid out like a' beautiful equation. Thus, while the biblical Eden may be imaginary, the Heavenly City is doubly imaginary: once, in the conventional sense, because it is not actual, but once again...because it is information, it could come into existence only as a virtual reality, which is to say, fully, only 'in the imagination'. The image of a Heavenly City is, in fact...a religious vision of cyberspace.

Again sublation is in evidence, this time between innocence and knowledge. Here cyberspace is a modernist vision of light and insubstantial form, the pure stuff of dreams. Now, as we have seen, its image in fiction is quite different: for Gibson cyberspace and its surroundings (which sometimes appear congruent) is tawdry, hybrid, even filthy:

The architecture of virtual reality imagined as an accretion of dreams: tattoo parlors, shooting galleries, pinball arcades, dimly lit stalls stacked with damp-stained years of men's magazines, chili joints, premises of unlicensed denturists, of fireworks and cut bait, betting shops, sushi bars, purveyors of sexual appliances, pawnbrokers, wonton counters, love hotels, hotdog stands, tortilla factories, Chinese greengrocers, liquor stores, herbalists, chiropractors, barbers, bars....These are dreams of commerce. Above them rise intricate barrios, zones of more private fantasy.

This fantasy is little more than a description of some downmarket Las Vegas, the dream of a middle-class boy losing himself in a cheesy display of street decadence (and Gibson is no doubt aware of this). For the rebellious kid, this is a grubby, fascinating heaven; for the mature academic, paradise takes rather the form of a kingdom of information, whose palatial halls we might wander without fear, chaos, dirt or darkness. The contrast between these scenarios, and more specifically between the fiction and those who come to recommend its vision, has certainly struck Gibson, who has commented on the endeavours and the propaganda of the technophiles: '[I]t never occurred to me that it would be possible for anyone to read these books and ignore the levels of irony.'

The dichotomy between utopian prophecy and dystopian fiction must be qualified, for there are phenomena which take in both; the technophile magazine Mondo 2000, for instance, happily embraces heaven and hell, covering them with an irony which allows it to take neither seriously:

> There's a new whiff of apocalyptism across the land. A general sense that we are living at a Very special juncture in the evolution of the species. This magazine is about what to do until the millenniumcomes. We're talking Total Possibilities....Flexing those synapses! Stoking those neuropeptides! Making Bliss States our normal waking consciousness. Becoming the Bionic Angel....But things are going to get weirder before they get better. The Rupture before the Rapture. Social and economic dislocation that will make the cracked 80's look like summer camp.

This is not the sudden catastrophe of nuclear annihilation

or alien invasion, but something more internal, slower, and perhaps already here. The revamped apocalypse might creep up on you. The 'post-human' aspect of cyberpunk writing with its prostheses, genetic tinkering, and computer augmentation of the brain, which is most evident in the work of Bruce Sterling, carries postmodern identity politics to the last degree. Being merely human is a poor and obsolete thing which only the latest technological commodities from the smartest companies can fix, although again these tales are inflected with some ineffectual irony, to divert criticism.

This fiction revels in the dangers of unleashed technology, in the possibilities of dehumanization, a taking of apocalypse for apotheosis. This is premissed on the apparently unlimited power of technological development and the simultaneous debility of the current authorities to face the dangers of the situation: the apotheosis of the system takes place when it is pushed to its logical limits, triggering a strangely familiar apocalypse. The very utopianism of the early netheads produced a belief in the apocalypse, for in part their resistance was founded on the idea that the system could not survive.

Cyberpunk is part of a coopting and marketing of apocalyptic visions as entertainment; on one level there is nothing frightening about these tales, even if they do pose as an extrapolation of current tendencies. Rather the idea that one is participating in headlong, dangerous scientific progress imparts a frisson to the mundane use of today's technological equipment. Real apocalyptic tales are out there in profusion, but generally do not affect those who write these stories or read them.

The current system, as seen in fiction, is corrupt but all encompassing, unsustainable but inescapable-or at least the only apparent way out is a mystical solution in which poor, deluded humanity is itself superseded. Gibson is utopian about the experiential aspect of the technology (its slickness, speed, definition and the experience of immersion and freedom from the body), if not about its overall effects; his dystopia is made necessary as a field for the heroic actions of the cyberpunk cowboys who ameliorate it. The morality-play aspect of much science fiction disarms its dystopian scenarios.

Beyond fiction, in technophile writing, the mix of apotheosis and apocalypse is perfectly illustrated by the supposed emergence of a transcendent, inhuman Net mind. The individual computing and human units of the network will become neurons participating in a collective, worldwide mind of incredible power. As one enthusiast puts it, arguing that any system going beyond a certain complexity must evolve selfawareness, 'I believe that we can think of this globalNet as a potential neural network in its own right....' Furthermore, the linking of an artificial intelligence with the information on the network should produce 'an ultra-fast learning curve.

Very soon after it has evolved, machine intelligence will eclipse human facilities and the new sis [superintelligences] will begin to inhabit the Net. A growing number of researchers are suggesting that by facilitating this process we are, in fact, fulfilling the dictates of our own dna and creating a more rugged intelligence that will become our evolutionary successor.' The link with science fiction here is obvious, particularly with Wintermute, the shackled a1 of Neuromancer.

Again, there is a decidedly religious aspect to such glimpses of super-intelligences and emergent identities across the Net, as though what was being born or perhaps merely accessed was the mind of God itself. In Gibson's writing, especially in Count Zero, an alliance is established between a1's and the 'Other' of voodoo gods, black magic and mysticism' against the material forces of technocracy, rationalism and utilitarianism. Again this is an extrapolation, but a utopian one, from a tendency which, as we shall see in looking at computer art, is already present in the computer, the sense of an inhuman presence with its own volition.

REPRESENTING CAPITAL

The paranoia about super-intelligences and multinational intrigue is not only found in fiction, but in a whole shadow world of, conspiratorial literature; there is a rational basis for this at least in the sense that corporations certainly protect their interests by nefarious means. Its expression in this writing, however, takes the form of myth-making, encouraged by the complexity and immateriality of the capitalist system, which resists representation. In science fiction, corporations are generally presented as powerful, but are nonetheless themselves governed by the impetus of the technologies they have created.

In one sense, though, the activities of corporations are straightforward enough, and: make good sense when they are considered in the light of what these institutions are set up to do. If these actions are sometimes hard to spot, it is only because corporations own the mass media. Super-intelligences are hardly needed to work out that corporations support friendly governments, undermine unfriendly ones, employ (at some removes) people to dispose of their unprotected enemies, push for favourable legislation, and so forth. Their activities are mundane in practice, if not in terms of ethics and long-term consequences.

In a well-known passage of his book Postmodernism, Fredric Jameson linked such high-tech paranoiac literature with the representation of capitalism itself:

I want to suggest that our faulty representations of some immense communicational and computer network are themselves but a distorted figuration of something even deeper, namely the whole world system of a present-day multinational System.

Most evidently, in cyberpunk:

The circuits and networks of some putative global computer hookup are narratively mobilized by labyrinthine conspiracies of autonomous but deadly interlocking and competing information agencies in a complexity often beyond the capacity of the normal reading mind.

It is a degraded attempt to grasp the impossible complexity of the worldwide capitalist system: 'Gibson's cyberspace is an image of a way of making the abstract and unseen comprehensible, a visualization of the notion of cognitive mapping.' Or rather, any attempt to grasp the actual complexities of the workings of global capital is abandoned to a literary spectacle of the sublime phenomena of complexity itself. Now the development of cyberspace is actually meant to address this issue of a complexity beyond normal human capacities to comprehend; the lack of a complete picture of the working system is quite as worrying for capitalist enterprise as it is for literary theorists. We should look at the form of cyberspace to see if there is anything substantive to this idea of it representing the entire operation of Capital.

Cyberspace is above all conceived as a visual environment. While it does not yet exist except in crude prototypes, and while users may be given the choice of a number of options determining how they see it, we may look to computer art for a preview of its form. A particular and remarkably constant aesthetic has emerged out of the relationship between art and computer science, and it is likely that its preoccupations will be carried over into the design of cyberspace.

Although there is no necessary requirement for it, virtual spaces are always described as Euclidean, at least in the way that they are experienced, and as hierarchically structured (usually on a vertical axis). The connection between discrete areas might be non-Euclidean, as might the overall shape of the virtual universe (which could take the form of a hypersphere) and there could be a nesting of worlds within worlds. Movement from one part to another could be instantaneous. Michael Heim has noted that jumps, not steps, are typical of movement in hypertext, and suggests that the same will hold for cyberspace.

Such broad considerations do not give much idea of what cyberspace might actually look like; for this we need to turn to the way artists have arrived 'at an aesthetic' which they consider to be appropriate to the computer. For at least twenty-five years computer art has been in its infancy. Just as promises, of a technical utopia, of free power or plentiful food for all, are constantly being made and then postponed (just over the temporal horizon), so the hope of a techno-cultural utopia is also constantly deferred. The old predictions of a radical computer art are still being made, with the addition of a new set of buzzwords.

In 1968 Jack Burnham predicted the end of sculpture, which was to be superseded not by an as yet undreamt-of virtual space, but by the development of cybernetic systems, dominated by artificial intelligence: 'In retrospect we may look upon the long tradition of figure sculpture and the brief interlude of formalism as an extended psychic dress rehearsal for...intelligent automata . . .' Similarly, in an early article about computer art, Robert Mallary made bold claims about artificial intelligence systems which he thought would develop an aesthetic sense, eventually producing art without the aid of humans.

The idea was that figurative sculpture had prepared humans for the advent of a breed of autonomous, intelligent robots upon which future artistic talents would be lavished. Now these beings have appeared in abundance, although for the moment they are fictional and seen only on cinema, television and computer screens, and they are certainly much less friendly than those which Burnham envisaged. These biological robots (such as Terminator or Robocop) are computer-controlled or assisted, both in fiction and in fact. If they have a particular aesthetic, it is of a slick, elitist and deadly modernism: they form a pre-emptive: counter-claim to the optimists of cybernetics and cyberspace.

When virtual objects are visualized within the computer, they do not necessarily exhibit any of the qualities of conventional objects. They do not have to be three-dimensional; higher-dimensional shapes may be indicated, while fractal forms provide a visual expression of fractional dimensions. Some of the images produced from these virtual forms may be thought of as the shadows of higher-dimensional forms, their insubstantiality and complexity resulting from their materialization in a form that humans can appreciate.

Their apparent scale and material are purely arbitrary. Viewpoint, lighting, colour and texture are totally independent of the structures depicted. As digital forms, nothing about them is fixed and they provide the possibility for the viewer to interact with or even virtually become the 'sculpture'. Computer art has often been associated with idealist aesthetics, using explicitly Platonist models relating number and beauty.

Claims are frequently made by adherents of computer art that objective progress in aesthetics is now possible. Brenda Laurel simply states that 'art is lawful', thus thinking that the persistent opposition between art and science can be definitively eroded within the rationalist silicon frame. Another strand, which goes back to D'Arcy Thompson's famous book On Growth and Form, has been to study the structure of natural forms and write programs which generate similar shapes. It is visual rather than structural essence that is involved in such programming, since it is hard to tell whether the look alone has not been produced by reverse engineering. Computer artists sometimes fake the look, for instance by using randomization to modify over-precise forms.

In 1990, when an issue of the *Art Journal* was devoted to computer art, the editor remarked upon the contributors' optimism, based on the flexibility of the computer as a universal tool. There is often a gung-ho, unashamedly masculine ethos to writing about computer art, which alongside talk of pioneering, returns us to the heyday of modernism. Carl Eugene Loeffler, for instance, assures us that 'Electronics was and continues to be the true new frontier for contemporary art'.

Whether in high art or in the more popular manifestations of computer culture, an unreconstructed sexism is frequent in this male-dominated world, whether blatantly, in the covers of Mondo 2000, which 'tended to feature women's heads floating somewhere in the ether of an erotic wet (ware) dream', or simply in the whole notion of the free navigation, penetration and manipulation of a feminine sublime. Computer art exhibits a curious combination of great technical sophistication and uncritical theory. In part, this may have a sociological cause, of the kind explored by Pierre Bourdieu in his book *Distinction* which looked at how taste strictly conforms to income and education.

There is a snobbery attached to any kind of machine work which forbids it contact with the heights of fine art and rarefied theory. Those committed to the computer are more likely to look at fine art from the outside and in an over-idealized fashion. Equally, they are likely to be interested in forms of popular culture which high-art practitioners shy away from, or only approach with the intent of ironic appropriation. Computer art forms, then, feed off cyberpunk fiction, and the hip apocalyptic visions of sci-fi film.

THE DEMON WITHIN

Something different happens, though; when artists cease to confine themselves to using the computer as a drawing or animation tool, and let the processor itself contribute to the design of form. One way to do this is to simulate the evolutionary process, allowing the machine to breed forms over generations. Like mutating computer viruses and other forms of artificial life, evolutionary programs are to some degree autonomous. In this way forms of an inhuman complexity and alien appearance may be produced.

If we find such images disturbing, this is because of our habit of reading intention into complicated images, and here there is a feeling that, while an intention is certainly at work, it is not entirely human. The computer takes on the guise of an allegorical being, the program being the unstoppable ghost in the machine and the image its mere materialization. Some are keen to embrace this presence.

If there is a deep sense of identification with the allegorical image of a being wholly devoted to the service of a single principle, it is because it is expressive of a more general reification in which living beings take on the guise of objects, and objects seem inhabited by living spirits. In cyberspace the two are likely to attain total elision.

When we see the operation of another sort of intelligence in computer art, we become aware of a power which is hard to define or hold steady in the mind, yet which is perceived as a presence, like the fleeting, protean artificial minds of Gibson's novels. Goethe wrote of a force of nature which is:

> Both animated and inanimate, both souled and soulless, something which manifested itself only in contradictions and could not therefore be formulated in concepts, let alone in words. It was not divine, for it seemed irrational; not human, for it had no understanding; not diabolical, for it was beneficent; not angelic, for it often betrayed Schadenfreude. It was like chance in its inconsequentiality; like Providence in the interrelationships it revealed. Everything that has limits for us seemed to it penetrable; it seemed wilfully to recombine the most necessary elements of our existence, eclipsing time and extending space....This being, which seemed to interpose itself between all the others, to sunder or unite them, I called the Demonic.

Goethe's natural force is surely what we now call emergent order, that force which somehow forges pattern from unthinkable complexity, a force which we have begun to know only through computer simulation. It is notable that it is described as demonic, notable that it is harnessed now to control real or virtual robots, or artificial life. Such order is not merely apparent in nature, but in many complex systems; if in computer forms we find a disturbing recognition of some alien order, then it is of the operation of economic markets, of apparently obscure and inhuman forces which control each detail of our lives. The computer can, then, in one sense act as an 'analogue' of these forces, showing us an image of the demon of Capital.

Although most descriptions of cyberspace stress its dizzying complexity, they also emphasize the empowerment of the user, who flies through the virtual sky, or swims through its depths. The fantasies are always the same:

> Sometimes I linger on a pattern for the sake of its strangeness, and as it becomes familiar I grow into another self. I wonder how much richer the patterns I can recognize can become, and surprise myself by scanning faster and faster regions in times shorter and shorter. Like a bird of prey my acuity allows me to glide high above the planes of information, seeking jewels among the grains, seeking knowledge.

New Agers make computer simulations of flying through fractal landscapes at great speed which are transferred to video and marketed as 'cyberspace' experiences. The question arises, about this new sea of Capital in which millions of punters swim; aside from their own personal experience of immersive travel, what will be their relation to the Leviathan corporations, and how will they treat each other?

Horkheimer and Adorno argued that at the heart of the Enlightenment there was a secularized version of the belief that God controlled the world. People thus confronted nature as an inferior, external other, a world of lifeless, fungible atoms, open to manipulation, and without conceiving of an interpenetration of subject and object. In one sense, then, cyberspace might be seen as the final act of the Enlightenment, in which the interface of nature disappears, replaced by a more evidently divine other. Although subject and object are most certainly entwined, the subject's attributes become definitively open to exchange.

Long before the age of intelligent machines, Aldous Huxley described virtual reality pornography, his 'feelies': '[T]hen suddenly, dazzling and incomparably more solid-looking than they would have seemed in actual flesh and blood, far more real than reality, there stood the stereoscopic images . . .' While each solipsistic user may feel empowered, every other being is prepared for use. Cyberspace is an ideal realization of Lukács' 'second nature', entangling the subjective and objective, and since, unlike the transformation of the real world by Capital, it evolves without direct material destruction, the speed of development (and mental destruction) can be all the more dizzying.

Cyberspace is also likely to be, in flagrant contradiction to its postmodern apologists, the embodiment of the totalizing system of Capital. Again, Adorno and Horkheimer are relevant here: 'For the Enlightenment whatever does not conform to the rules of computation and utility is suspect...Enlightenment is totalitarian.' It aims at a principle of scientific unity in which the 'multiplicity of forms is reduced to position and arrangement, history to fact, things to matter.' If we replace 'matter' with 'data' then this is all directly relevant to cyberspace.

Douglas Kellner notes that: 'Such quantitative modes of thought presuppose an identity between concept and object, word and thing,"and privilege mathematical logic as alone capable of grasping the essence of things.' The invention of cyberspace is, then, the attempt to create a world where to perceive is the same as to understand, where 'objects' are entirely adequate to their concepts, and are even, through their dematerialization, identical with them. Despite the sport of fictional demons within cyberspace, the impetus of the system is towards the reduction of everything to the calculable; 'the Net' is indeed an apt name.

Technophiliac enthusiasts are stitching up a totalizing, brave new world based on an Enlightenment paradigm but defended by postmodern theory. Adorno, and others following him, have been much concerned to argue that there is a negative and liberatory charge in objects exceeding their concepts. It is this which cyberspace promises to abolish. This virtual space threatens to form the ultimate illusion of a unified understanding, not by surmounting contradiction, but by remaking the world in specious harmony. As a universal system of data, however, cyberspace will have to contain representations of pictures, texts and photographs.

While these will have lost all materiality, at least their fixed forms will challenge the homogeneity of the system. History and its representations will become resistant islands of unchangeable data, reminders of the other of reality, of process, history and finally of humanity. In the extraordinary situation in which a new technology of profound importance is being created, there is a curious parallel between the associated confusion, bloated claims, predicted utopian dystopias and vice versa, and what Benjamin described in his analysis of Germany during the great inflation of the twenties. He noted that within accounts of widespread decline, accommodations were always made to justify specific personal positions and activities:

A blind determination to save the prestige of personal existence, rather than, through an impartial disdain for its importance and entanglement, at least to detach it from the background of universal delusion, is triumphing almost everywhere. That is why the air is so thick with life theories and world views, and why in this country they cut so preposterous a figure, for almost always they finally serve to sanction some wholly trivial private situation.

For just the same reason the air is so full of phantoms, mirages of a glorious cultural future breaking upon us overnight in spite of all, for everyone is committed to the optical illusions of his isolated standpoint. This passage illuminates the solipsism of cyberspace, which is merely a literal expression of the situation of the individual in contemporary society, and more specifically of business people and their camp followers (engineers and intellectuals) spinning universalizing fantasies out of their desire to ride the next commercial wave.

This wondrous but specious technology threatens to act as another curtain between those who consume it and the condition of the world: as the poor are excluded from cyberspace, and will appear on it only as objects, never as subjects with their own voices, there is a danger that they recede even further from the consciousness of the comfortable. As the real world is left to decline, the air once again becomes full of phantoms, this time digital, promising at the last moment to pluck utopia from apocalypse.

4

The Diary on the Internet

The diarists adopt self-reflexive and self-deprecatory perspectives about their online lives, and acknowledge their personal and textual shortcomings with tongue in cheek. Though my own life has little in common with the diarists' daily life experiences, all are my age or older, and share similar political views and other values.

Certainly, literary and aesthetic snobbery informs my dismay at many online diaries. They have not been properly "vetted," properly shaped for a reading audience, before being made public. But Web diarists do not need to prove the marketability of their lives and stories in order to be "published," and Web diaries, though the contemporary equivalent of the vanity press, nevertheless have a potential readersh ip of millions. These sires often reinforce the stereotype of the diary as a genre for unbridled narcissism, and indeed, since all these diarists write for a public readership, they "super-size" the narcissism factor.

And yet, if online diarists presume that their lives and their narratives merit our interest, attention, and time, in terms of readers' responses and in terms of the theoretical issues their texts raise, their presumptions are nor unfounded. Some diaries receive thousands of visits, and many diarists have become famous amongst the cyber-community, even parlaying their diaries into commercial success in "real life."

In their immediacy and accessibility, in their seemingly unmediated state, Web diaries blur the distinction between online and offline lives, "virtual reality" and "real life," "public" and "private," and most intriguingly for auto/biography studies, between the life and the text. I am particularly intrigued by the fact that the diary, this centuries-old practice associated with the spiritual, the therapeutic, and the strictly private, has become one of the genres of choice for Internet life-writers. But why has this form in particular made the transition from print to online culture so successfully? What does the Internet bring to the diary genre, and the diary genre to the Internet, that has made this pairing of form and media so felicitous?

No longer considered the domain of adolescent girls, the diary has been embraced by thousands of cyber-citizens, from crackerjack HTML writers to Net neophytes who have only recently mastered the word processor. In fact, services such as Diary/and, Blogger, or LiveJournal provide journal templates that allow today's Internet diarists to flourish without needing to know HTML coding or to have any significant software knowledge. To the computer-literate (and those with access to a computer), then, creating an online diary has become as easy as "putting pen to paper."

The result is an unparalleled explosion of public life writing by private citizens. By March 2002, more than 800,000 blogs were registered on the Net; in July 2002 an average of 1.5 "Blogger blogs" were created per minute. This phenomenal proliferation of life writing spaces on the Internet marks an equally unprecedented interest in the lives of ordinary individuals who, before the Internet, had few opportunities to publish their life stories on such a wide scale.

Bypassing the commercial, aesthetic, or political interests that dictate access to traditional print media and that decide whose life stories deserve to be told, online diaries can be read as assertions of identity, and arguments for the importance of an individual's life. Even as their authors retain a degree of anonymity, these texts make very personal connections to a reading audience that recognizes and confirms these individual life assertions.

Given the conventional understanding of the diary as a private form, a public online journal seems to many people an abomination, or at least a contradiction in terms. In "Cher ecran ..., "his self-reflexive analysis of online diaries, Philippe Lejeune notes his initial prejudices against these texts and their writers. In considering the impact of "la revolution de l'Internet" on the development of the personal diary, he sees two possible reactions.

At the same time that one could revel (s' extasier) in the possibilities for the genre that online production presents, one could also perceive the Internet environment as "totalement oppose aux conditions de developpement du journal intime, fonde sur une autre conception du temps (le delai, la maturation, l'accumulation) et de la communication (differee ou exclue: le secret)" [totally opposed to the conditions for developing a journal intime, based on a different idea of time (waiting period, maturation, accumulation) and of communication (differed or excluded : secrecy)].

Lejeune's second reaction, one natural response to the idea of the online personal journal, reflects the long-held popular assumption that the diary is a private, for "oneself alone," genre. Web diaries' public nature but private-that is, personal, often intimate-content confounds traditional distinctions between public and private writings and functions. Such texts therefore can create confusion for the reader, as well as for the critic. As texts that do not fit cleanly into generic categories, they may be misread or dismissed altogether.

Despite having been a part of the World Wide Web since 1995, and despite the astonishing number of journals presently being written, apart from Lejeune's early explorations in "Cher ecran ..." (2000), Web diaries and blogs have received little academic attention. The ramifications of online production for the diary genre, however, need to be addressed, for as Suzanne Bunkers argues, "time-worn assumptions that the diary is kept only for the diarist and that it is an intensely secretive and private enterprise are unworkable when exploring the phenomenon of the online diary".

These texts therefore demand a reconceptualization of the diary genre, and in this chapter examination of the diary's transformation from print to online practice, considering the implications of this reformatting for the diary as a literary genre and as life writing and explore the challenges the online diary represents to traditional concepts of the genre as private and monologic, investigating how online diarists use their texts to attract readers, build communities, and construct identities in cyberspace.

Though such issues are beyond the scope of this discussion, these texts also invite reconsiderations of what "private" and "public" mean when we look at "living online." My ambivalence about online journals, my confusion about "how to bring one's 'literary opinions' to bear" on texts that may not be traditionally literary are, as Joanna Gill has described, standard responses to confessional texts. In its functions as a spiritual journal and a private space to tell secrets, the diary has a long association with the confessional mode in both its private and its public forms. Indeed, the pleasures of reading these journals may lie partly in their potential for confession: readers expect self-exposure and the telling of secrets.

Like the confessional memoirs that Gill discusses, then, online journals cast their readers in the role of "listener/reader/confessor", who must be in place in order to absolve the teller. In a contemporary print diary, that confessor would typically be an imagined or projected addressee; in cyberspace, however, he or she actually receives the confession, and often responds. The reader of an online diary therefore actively participates in c onstructing the text the diarist writes, and the identities he or she takes on in the narrative. Though active and even intimate, however, that participation remains virtual disembodied.

The confessor stays behind the "grille" of the Internet, allowing the diarist-and the reader-the illusion of anonymity necessary for "full" self-exposure. Janet Murray notes that "some people put things on their home page ... that they have not told their closest friends. The enchantment of the computer creates for us a public space that also feels very private and intimate". Diarist Jane Pinckard suggests that the "enchantment" of anonymous intimacy is one of the most compelling features of the online diary. "What I love about online journals and diaries," she comments, "is the paradoxical combination of complete anonymity and a startling level of intimacy."

Though "complete anonymity" may be in fact impossible, even undesirable, for Web diarists, the illusion that identity can be secret or shrouded online contribute s to writers' sense that they are free to, or perhaps required to, tell all. Online diarists combine a traditionally confessional genre, the diary, with a medium that makes confessions widely available but still anonymous, impersonal, separate from diarists' offline lives and identities. Though some writers do eventually meet their readers in "real life," the majority of their audiences remain virtual, a part of only their online existences.

COMING TO TERMS

Virginia Woolf's famous description of the diary as a "capacious hold-all" (I:266)-a catch phrase both the online and print journaling communities have taken up with zest-gestures towards the genre's elasticity and multiple forms, incorporating among other genres the letter, scrapbook, family history, and travelogue into "diary" narratives. The diary's arrival on the Internet raises new questions about generic distinctions and practices, and their consequences for autobiographical acts.

Though the interchangeable use of the terms "diary" and "journal" has become acceptable in diary studies, my use of the new and distinct terms "online journal" and "blog" needs some explanation. While such quibbling over definitions may seem to be splitting hairs, it does point out the confusion that surrounds these texts-what they are supposed to be, what they should be doing, and for whom.

In attempting to explain the phenomenon of Weblogs, which postdate the appearance of online diaries, the popular media has further mudd ied the waters, defining the blog as a "kind of spontaneous online public journal", a "sort of hybrid diary/bio/community/bulletin board", or as a "chronological diary" that is a "descendant of the personal homepage". Recognizing that "a lot of people are quite insistent" that journals and blogs are different forms, however, blogger Jane Pinckard discusses her decision to create separate pages for her "journal" and her "blog."

Anticipating her readers' confusion about "what's the difference between a journal and a weblog," she explains that for me the weblog and the journal have very different functions. The weblog is sort of my "instant fix" for when I feel like I just have to write about something, even if I don't necessarily have a lot of time. Since it's the front page of my site, it's also meant to be a quick peek for the casual browser at various things I find interesting.

The journal is where I sit down and think, "now I will write in the journal." That doesn't mean the quality of writing will be any better, mind you, but it's different. It takes me longer to write, I think about it more, and it tends to be much more rambling, introspective what have you.... I tucked it away in a place where people don't have to read it if they don't want to.

Pinckard's quasi-reverent approach to the act of creating a diary, suggested by her phrase "now I will write in the journal," is a long-standing response to the diary genre. Journal writing, as described by Pinckard, is an activity requiring time, thought, and meditation-a characterization that reflects traditional uses of the diary as a spiritual exercise, personal therapy tool, and literary production. Despite the public nature of the online journal, it is still focused on the personal and introspective, and consequently may not be to her "casual" readers' tastes.

Her characterization of the blog as off-the-cuff, capturing her thoughts in the instant of writing, however, is a style also popularly associated with the diary genre. While the term "online diaries" clearly connects these texts to the print world, to the traditions of the diary and the generic rules and expectations that come with them, the expression "blogs" invites a reading of these writings as a new artform" (Schalchlin), one without the cult ural baggage of an existing (print) genre. In reality, though, even the scantiest of blog narratives incorporates "trademark" diary features, with regular, dated, entries that focus on the diarist/narrator's experiences and interests. Few practitioners separate their writings as Pinckard do, making instead texts that do a little bit of everything.

Since the diary component, then, seems essential to the Weblog, perhaps we can read the blog as simply another kind or function of the diary genre, one particularly well-suited to perform the social actions desired by contemporary diarists. Online participation in this genre allows writers to carry on diary conversations that will no longer be monologic, where the response will not be just imagined but actual. These conversations may be in-depth discussions, as in Pinckard's journal, or simply chats, as in her blog, with varying degrees of personal disclosure and intimacy.

Since the diary genre, whether in its avatars as an online journal or as a Weblog, showcases the daily and the (seemingly) trivial, and seems to require no particular literary skill to create, its online writers have generic permission, so to speak, to produce texts that meet these standards. Because anyone with access to and some familiarity with a computer can create a Web diary, readers will not be expecting texts or lives that are lite rary, exceptional, gifted, or even particularly thoughtful. As Pinckard's comments point out, Web diaries respond to the needs and interests of both writer and reader, making the online diary "totally interactive".

Unlike a novel, the writer of a diary doesn't always know what's happening in his head. The reader has to pick u clues and figure it out.... It's like a real life serial being played out be ore our es with the author making it up as he goes along. Was this ever even possible before the internet? Are we talking about this being a new artform altogether?

Are Internet diaries, and their generic relations, the Weblogs, a different form from diaries in traditional print media? Or have Internet users simply adopted the traditional diary genre and adapted it to the public realm of cyberspace? Despite Steve Schalchlin's belief in the Internet diary as a "new artform," its practitioners in many ways reproduce the traditional diary, upholding instead of resisting the genre both in form and content. As Lejeune observes about this latest evolution of the already elastic diary genre, "Seule Ia maniere change" ("Cher ecrran ..." 12).

Often almost absurd parodies of the stereotypical diary, many online diaries are fragmented narratives that jump disconnectedly from topic to topic, recording in mundane detail the diarist's daily life. They focus on the quotidian and the personal, foregrounding the diarist's experiences and emotions. Their narratives follow the generic convention of starting in medias res, with the most recent entry appearing as the diary site is visited (though, as I discuss below, Web technology allows diarists to uphold this generic feature at the same time that they subvert it). Entries ate organized chronologically, though their regularity may range from several a day to one every few months.

While online diaries may not be a "new artform," as Schalchlin suggests, they do bring to the genre new possibilities for autobiographical acts that change or expand the functions it can perform. Diarists can incorporate the instruments of the Internet to enrich their diary narratives, turning textual self-portraits into three-dimensional virtual experiences that allow the reader to take a guided tour of the diarist's "life."

Diarists now add audio or video files to their texts alongside still photographs, building on the diary-as-scrapbook tradition. Using hypertext, diarists can create links between relevant entries, allowing readers to put events in context and get the whole story without the diarist having to explain again. Both new and old readers will therefore grasp the significance of what the diarists describe as it unfolds. In contrast to the lag between writing and publishing that exists for offline public diaries, new entries in online journals can be uploaded as soon as they are finished. This immediacy heightens the reader's sense of identification with the writer, since the reader can experience vicariously the events in the diarist's life almost in "real time."

Diarists may also supplement their biographical material in respon se to real or imagined queries from readers with a separate page for "FAQ" (frequently answered questions). These prefatory pages enable a potential audience to make quick decisions about whether to read this diary, or move on to a diarist with whom they share more interests.

Such capsule biographies also act as waivers or disclaimers, devices not generally needed in diaries published by traditional methods, which package texts and subjects, identifying them for the appropriate audiences. Having confessed in these introductory biographies their foibles, beliefs, and attitudes, diarists have told readers what to expect, and do not have to apologize in their narratives for attitudes that may be unpopular or offensive.

On his "Welcome" page, Johnny Reb, a Civil War aficionado, anticipates negative reactions, and defends his position: "The things you you [sic] see and read in here are my thoughts, if you have a problem with that, to be honest, I really don't care. I'm not a racist, I am a Christian. I do tend to vent a little bit about some racial things that upset me, but once again, this is my diary, not yours."

Johnny Reb's apologia suggests that he does not feel accountable for whatever he says in his online journal; they are only his (private) "thoughts" expressed in his dia ry, which he contends is still a private medium even online. His sense that this excuse is adequate highlights the tension between simultaneous and competing definitions and functions of the diary, between offline and online perceptions of the genre and its roles.

Because Johnny Reb brings contemporary print culture readings of the diary as a private space to the public forum of the Internet, he can argue that the diary form itself provides him with carte blanche for free expression. Though not every visitor to his site will agree with his politics, or in his right to discuss "racial things," they have been forewarned. This stance serves as a reminder of both the online diarist's freedom from the external censorship inherent in the traditional publishing process, and of the implications of that freedom for online readers and writers.

The role of the (active) reader is a new wrinkle in studies of the diary. As Jane Pinckard's, Johnny Reb's, and Steve Schalchlin's comments have demonstrated, online diarists are acutely aware of their readers, whose desires, expectations, and reading practices shape the texts that bloggers produce. Of course, writing a text to suit an imagined reader is hardly a new concept, even for the diary. Before the online diary community came such public personal diarists as James Boswell, Anais Nin, and May Sarton.

Nin's diaries in particular shaped contemporary stereotypes of the journal intime in English as private, a "secret box" even though they were published while she was still writing them. But the accessibility of the diarist and the diary, their invitations for input, their sense of responsibility to respond to and address readers' concerns, are practices not possible before the technologies and media of the online diary. For the online diarist, having readers means that the diarist has bot h joined and created communities, acts that inform the texts he or she will produce.

The online diarist, in the complex position of writing to the self and to others, for readers both imagined and actual, employs multiple strategies to construct communities. Johnny Reb writes diary entries during shifts at Wal-Mart, chronicling the tedium of life during and after work: "last night when I got home, I hopped on line for a while, messed around there. I ate a nice juicy 9 oz steak that I brought home the other night, it was still pretty good had a bud light, and watched behind enemy lines again, it has to go back to hollywood video in a few days, and I wanted to watch it again".

In Dreams of Glass, diarist Nora notes, "tonight i found a new Asian convenience/grocery store in the east village (at 11th

and third aye), its called Morning to Midnight.... bought a green iced tea, a regular pocky, and these choclaty wafer cookie type things that they had samples of" (15 Aug. 2002). Such entries fulfill the diary's traditionally personal functions of logbook and memoranda, but when written on the Internet, diarists give these functions a public purpose, presuming that others will want to read these records, and even comment on them.

Johnny Reb's and Nora's attention to the particular details of their daily routines and landscapes invites readers who share their interests, values, backgrounds, even neighborhoods, creating insider/outsider roles for readers. Outsiders, who lack the background knowledge necessary to understand these entries, presumably do not belong. A reader from or visitor to New York may feel a sense of identification with Nora because he or she also frequents the "Morning to Midnight" store, or is familiar with "11th and third ave." These diarists' use of proper nouns, place names, presuppositions, and explanatory asides are traditional strategies by which both on- and offline public diarists create intimacy.

Web diarists, though, also have the option of adding links to external sites to help the reader feel a part of their personal lives. These links act as community builders by constructing a virtual world for the diarist, peopling her autobiographical landscape with the friends and family, restaurants, shops, and sch ools that the diarist invokes, or the movies, music groups, or causes about which she is passionate. By following the links, readers can in a sense share the diarist's experiences, see as he or she does, rather than relying on the diarist's textual descriptions, and thus these links foster a greater sense of intimacy between writer and audience.

They also, arguably, add to the reader's sense of the diary's "authenticity," because the narrative is anchored in "actual" places and people that members of the audience may also recognize, making them feel part of the narrative, as "insiders" who are part of the community the diarist addresses. From the first utopic visions of cyberspace and its possibilities, "community" has been a key concept, explored and defined in

Howard Rheingold's The Virtual Community: Homesteading on the Electronic Frontier.

Though much of Rheingold's theorizing, along with the early idealism that surrounded the advent of the Internet, has been challenged and expanded, his emphasis on "community" as comprised of the "webs of personal relationships in cyberspace" does point to the centrality of communion as well as communication, the desire to make (personal and virtual) connections, that online diarists project. Challenging the enduring view of diary-writing as a solitary activity, online diarists have made community-building a major component of their texts.

In addition to joining other diarists through Webrings, writers can provide links to fellow diarists on their diary home page, constituting themselves and their readers as part of multiple communities. This "recommendations" section, often called "Friends," is a built-in feature of fill-in-the-blank online diaries like LiveJournal, Diary/and, and Diarist net. These often reciprocal links between diaries not only connect readers and diarists, but also act as legitimating forces-the online diary community's version of print-culture practices of celebrity endorsements or book-jacket blurbs, "selling" readers on other personal journals and their diarists.

These alliances form the basis of what John Swales calls discourse communities: groups united by their commitment to similar rhetorical goals. Though members may be geographically isolated, and may never meet each other in person, or "real life," Swales argues that they still form a community linked by shared identifications and values. To remain a community member, one has to participate actively in the group, and acknowledge one s allegiance to the community. For the print diarist, full participation in discourse communities will be hampered by her inability to share her text publicly, or to receive and respond to feedback on what she has written.

The online diarist, on the other hand, makes this community conversation a part of the process, often incorporating readers' responses into the diary itself, thus creating a dialogue between herself and her readers. When the conversation between diarist and reader takes place on the diary site's feedback page, in the form of discussion boards, forums, or comments pages, other readers can join in, addressing their comments directly to fellow respondents. The diary then becomes a meeting place and starting point for further discourse among previously disconnected readers.

Many diarists design their sites to continuously accommodate new readers, including a jump-button that links to the first entry, and pages such as "About me," "FAQ," "Cast," or "First time?" that provide first-timers with the background to the diarists' stories. New readers who lack the community knowledge but wish to acquire it can therefore quickly be made part of the community. Diarist Nora's concept of self-policing readers/communities, who recognize when they are welcome and invited, reflects the communal nature of online textual identity practices.

By aligning our values, goals, and discourse with a community, Roz Ivanic theorizes, we construct an identity that reflects our association with that group. She argues that we "negotiate an identity within the range of possibilities for self-hood which are supported or at least tolerated by the community", possibilities that represent the community's values and norms. As Carolyn Miller points out, a rhetorical community, a "site where centrifugal and centriperal forces must meet," mediates its members' disparate motivations and actions through their participation in genres, which "structure joint action through communal decorum".

Diarist Tracy Lee's experiences with the fledgling Web diary community of the mid-1990s illustrate the problems in trying to base community membership on generic participation alone. Her 1995 diary, which featured explicit entries and erotic photographs, brought disapproval from other online diarists. She recalls, "I got the impression from a few journalers who considered their pages to be 'Serious Writing' by 'Serious Writers' that I was dragging them down merely by being associated in the same category on Yahoo" ("Personal Recollections").

Lee had deviated from the online diary community's codes for decorum; her online persona as an "intelligent person who also happened to be involved in erotica" ("Personal Recollections") addressed different audiences than did the other diaries that a search engine had grouped together by genre. Other readers, however, did identify with Lee, and her diary created new discourse communities that were perpetuated by positive reader response.

Lee's sense that she had "sullied" the Yahoo diary category highlights the different strategies online diaries adopt to get readers. As Jane Pinckard's design, which distinguishes between casual browsers and serious readers, and Johnny Reb's warning about his Confederate-friendly political views remind us, Web diarists want to attract readers-real, live readers. Certainly both print and Web diarists write to audiences who may be real as well as imagined, as Boswell's diaries meant for John Johnstone, Dorothy Wordsworth's diaries written to her brother, and, less publicly, multiply-authored family diaries demonstrate. But online writers extend the invitation to read not only to intimates but also to the reading public at large.

They post their diaries in the hope of reaching a wider audience, an imagined community who, by reading and responding. will become an actual community. Writers who create online diaries express their desire for acknowledgment, perhaps praise, for their life or their writing-some ass urance that their voice is being heard. Johnny Reb ended his first diary entries on August 15, 2002, by begging readers for feedback: "drop me a comment or something so that I know somebody reads these!"

One of the first things he wants to add to his site is a counter that records how many visits his diary receives, a feature prominently displayed on the majority of diary sites. Journals on diary servers such as Diaryland include links where readers can vote for their favorite diaries to receive awards; on Diarist. net the diaries with the most "clix" are featured in a weekly "Top Sites." For "Yellowrose," Johnny Reb, and thousands of other diarists, to be valid and worthwhile, the assertion of identity that the online diary performs demands a response, a witness for the confession to be enacted. Readers who follow the diary but who do not join in by signing the guestbook, posting in the forums, or contacting the diarist, are known as "lurkers," or more accurately, "blurkers," as one blog respondent suggests.

Calling such passive participants lurkers, a term used in IRCs and forums to represent users who eavesdrop on conversations without adding to them, denotes new roles for diary readers. "Read-only" audiences for online journals may be seen as inappropriately voyeuristic, since they take in the personal stories of the diarist without revealing anything of themselves, and without accepting the community membership being offered them. But, as Michele Willson argues in "Community in the Abstract," simply making a community space does not mean that a community will infact develop, a fear that seems inherent in these diarists' use of counters and appeals for feedback.

Building a site "does not mean that interaction will automatically take place, "Willson notes," or that a community will form, since people cannot be forced to participate. Even if you build it, then, they may not come. For online diarists, who write explicitly to be read, the absence of an (active, responsive) audience would be a significant blow. To attract and maintain engaged readers, online diarists must anticipate and meet audience expectations. But since bloggers write in a familiar genre that predates the Internet, they must also satisfy that genre's requirements even though they have taken the genre into a new forum.

The diary written for a public readership is a concept at odds with popular contemporary beliefs about the diary as a private text not meant for other eyes, in which the diarist can reveal his or her "true self." But even while Web diaries confound the concept of the personal diary as a private and therefore "authentic" space, they seem to uphold other expectations of authenticity. Since diarists can post entries immediately after writing them, they have less opportunity to "tamper" with their texts, less time for hindsight to "alter" the "true" version of experiences. Of course, the ability to make seamless emendations to entries, or even delete them altogether without the telltale signs of a ripped page, can undercut readers' co nfidence in the "stable" text. In his initial entries, longtime Web diarist Steve Schalchlin struggled with how to handle the fluidity of the online diary.

After looking back at the previous month's entries, which he feels painted an overly optimistic view of his life, he wonders, "Is it fair or practice to go back and insert things like that upon reflection? I mean, I've gone back and inserted details I've since remembered but left out. But is it fair to add or change the way you felt at any given time? I just don't know". On September 12, 1997, he records the impulse to change an old entry in which he had been extremely angry, but concludes, "My diary page from yesterday will stay as it is (because readers have now laid down the law about me changing a single word of anything I write)." To Schalchlin's audience, his going back and changing entries that cast him in an unfavorable light would be "cheating"inauthentic, inaccurate. His readers seek a text that cannot be altered after the fact, a "finished" version that would most resemble the fixed nature of the entries in a published diary.

Even in a public diary, Schalchlin extends the promise of total and unmediated honesty: "Part of the 'deal' we have together-as diary writer and diary reader is that I do not hide the times when I am an ass or a fool". Despite his readers' awareness that he writes for an audience, they have bought into this contract. Schalchlin's "deal," so reminiscent of Lejeune's autobiographical pact, underlines the popular concept of autobiography as requiring some kind of participation from, or even communion with, the reader, who accepts the writer's claims of identity and facticity, and believes in the autobiographer as a "real" person.

For Schalchlin's readers, this deal extends beyond readers' faith in the "truth" of his existence, and his claims to encompass their demand for full disclosure, almost to the point that Schalchlin should have no life outside the written version. To some diary readers, the division between the online/written life and the offline/lived life becomes obscure or nonexistent.

After admitting in April 1998 that he had not written online about the breakup of his long-term relationship, Schalchlin received an angry email from a reader: "Ibegan to really question whether you had really been honest in the diary all along and I quit reading your diary except to catch up once a month or so I began wondering if all the things you'd written about all along were not-as-they-seemed".

By inviting readers into his personal, or "private," life, Schalchlin sets up reader expectations not just of honesty but of total exposure. Writing in an era that begat the reality television show, in a medium that introduced the Webcam, Schalchlin encounters audiences who bring expectations of "Truth," confession, and revelation from both the "old" media-the diary-and the "new" non-print, "unmediated" forms. Such expectations also suggest readers' belief in these online diarists as real people, despite the possibilities for total identity deception on the Internet.

Even in online diarie s that do not provide the proper name that Philippe Lejeune once hailed as the defining element of the autobiographical pact, readers seem to accept the diarist's identity claims-a faith arising again, perhaps, from popular conceptions of the diary as unmediated, artless, and therefore honest, and somehow less manipulative than other autobiographical forms. Though the majority of personal online journals are accessible to anyone surfing the Net, some diary servers, as Joel Haefner observes, do allow writers to password-protect their diaries, meaning that only a select group can read them.

This control over circulation, this ability to limit access to only the readers the diarist desires, distinguishes the online diary from print forms. Traditional print diarists who publish their texts relinquish any power over who can read them, while such "public-yet-private" Web diaries allow the diarist to be a public presence on the Internet without going "all the way." The presence of these "secret diaries," none of which I can access, upholds the reader's sense of a "private" self who exists behind the public figure, a "true self" exposed only to a chosen few. In her latest diary entries, Tracy Lee writes for anyone on one page, but creates others with "all of the good stuff" that are accessible only to "the 70 or so people that I've decided I can trust" (LiveJournal, "User Info").

"Not everyone in the entire LJ [LiveJournal] land needs to know all my secrets," she concludes (emphasis added), and although only an intimate community can read these "secrets," their promised presence casts a tantalizing shadow of the "real" Tracy Lee, who does "tell all" in her diary. Lee's decision not to bare all to everyone marks a change in attitude from her first online journal, "I am becoming," which she began in September 1995. She recalls her original concept of the role of the diary: "What would make my site different from the other journals out there already would be that I wouldn't hold anything back.

Good times, bad, arguments, sex-whatever was happening in my life that I'd normally write about in my personal journal would go up on the website" ("Personal Recollections"). Once people from her "real life" began to read and comment on the journal, however, she felt that she had lost her anonymity and therefore could not write freely; she ended that journal and began others that incorporated the dual public and "private" modes.

Lee's sense of intimacy through anonymity marks one of the key ingredients of the popularity of online journals. The virtual space of the Internet, with its possibilities for role-play, identity performance, and consequence-free fantasy lives, can bear lit tle relation to the "real" world. Much has been made of the possibilities for multiple, even duplicitous identity performances on the World Wide Web. But Web diarists, whose intensely personal narratives and acts of total self-exposure would paradoxically suggest the desire for greater anonymity, seem to insist on the "reality" of their self-representations.

Though thousands of people may read their journals, in which they tell secrets and intimate details, bloggers still post photographs of them, use their real names, and give out their email addresses. Unlike the players in MUDs and MOOs, who rake on the identities and characteristics of characters in a larger game, diarists play "themselves," but in a venue that seems disconnected from, if based on, their offline lives. Though these readers neither do nor know the diarist outside of the context of her text, they believe her textual representation is "real," the flesh made digital.

LIVING ONLINE

Diarists as well as their readers experience this confusion of the textual and lived life-one of the hazards, perhaps, of inhabiting the unmapped and unprecedented realm of cyberspace, that "consensual hallucination" William Gibson so aptly described. The intersections of the offline and the online, and by extension, of the represented and the real, can have a range of implications for both the diarists and their texts. I want to close by looking at one online journal where these intersections have been an integral part of the journal's functions and forms.

Steve Schalchlin's Living in the Bonus Round is one of the earliest Web diaries to appear, debuting in March 1996: his diary banner boasts that his site is "historically the 28th internet diary they say" (Schalchlin, "First Time?"). Unlike other Web diary pioneers such as Tracy Lee, Justin Hall, and Carolyn Burke, Schalchlin has continued his diary in more-or-less the same form, under the same name, at the same address. His site has garne red several awards and attracted thousands of readers over its six years of development; as he explains in his introduction to the diary, Living in the Bonus Round played an integral role in the critical success of his musical The Last Session when it debuted off-Broadway ("First Time?").

Through his diary, Schalchlin has moved from being a "'somewhat famous' songwriter living with AIDS" (Schalchlin, "Index") to a "cyberlebrity" (Senft 191), whose site fosters an international readership and multiple communities who connect at his site, and frequendy, in "real life." The online diary, in which the writing and the written subject seem to occupy the same moment as each other and as the reader, already creates a sense of congruency between the lived and the written.

By allowing Schalchlin's readers to receive the diary serially, reading each entry as it is posted, a process not possible or at least rare in print diaries, the Internet further seems to break down the division of textual and lived lives and selves. Without the delay or explicit mediation of the traditional publishing process to remind readers and writers of this difference, Schalchlin appears to be living-or, in the diary's opening entries, dying-online. Living in the Bonus Round began as a "goodbye letter to the world" ("First Time?") when Schalchlin was near death from AIDS.

Though the site originally served to record his symptoms for his medical doctor, and to keep his out-of-town family upto-date on his condition, it quickly attracted other readers, strangers who were drawn to his narrative. As Schalchli n's diary began to take shape as a public record of what he thought were his last days, it became a way for him to live as he could not do offline. Reflecting on the journal's genesis, Schalchlin recalls, "When I began this diary six years ago, I could barely function in the 'real' world. But in cyberspace, I was a superhero". Though his diary identity, for very particular personal and political reasons, was as the representative "man with AIDS", and his diary consequently foregrounded the physical toll AIDS was taking on his body, his online presence compensated for these offline disabilities.

As Schalchlin's health improved, however, the distinctions between life and text became literally harder to distinguish. He gave his journal its snappy title, explaining that "[i] n the Bonus Round time goes faster and the prizes are better" ("First Time?"). He separated entries into books, and eventually volumes, noting, with some gallows humor, "its multi-volume cuz I wasn't supposed to last this long" ("Index"). The diary has an annotated index for ease of access, along with the usual biography and other introductory pages. His online life therefore turned into a book, packaged in ways familiar to readers, who responded enthusiastically to this unfolding story.

Many of his readers began to think of Schalchlin as a literary character, the protagonist of what one calls "a Living Novel". A few entries into a new book of his diary, Schalchlin anticipates readers' confusion about the narrative, asking, "Are you still waiting for something to happen? Something dramatic? ... I could look for some foreshadowing ... but then, I don't exactly know what's coming".

Though his readers' narrative expectations, expectations brought from both print culture and from fiction, cannot be met in the actual online diary, Schalchlin is acutely aware of how he and his life are read as text, a reading his diary format suggests and perpetuates. Schalchlin has also started to think of his life in narrative terms, musing in April 1998 that dividing his diary into books has affected the way he lives.

"This simple act had a profound effect because it changed the way I perceive life itself," he notes: "Now, instead of thinking of life as this long highway without end, I see it [as] little segments of time in which I can accomplish great things....But more importantly, I look forward to each new book, wondering what will come but fully knowing that it's totally up to me to generate the life that will come". In the course of creating his online life, a textual/virtual self meant to compensate for and outlast the embodied/actual person, Schalchlin begins to live his life like a stoty. He makes the transition, outlined by Paul John Eakin, from "writing autobiography" to "living autobiography, performing it in our daily lives". For Schalchlin, the textual has come to shape the lived life; as his comments demonstrate, Schalchlin is now both producer and product of his autobiographical narrative.

While the "life as book" trope is a traditional diary metaphor, Schalchlin's sense of living in as well as creating a "real life serial" becomes more significant when his story is played out before thousands of readers who echo his sentiment. By April 1996, Schalchlin began to receive emails from people who had discovered his online diary and felt compelled to contact him. With the online diary still a novelty, Schalchlin's site provoked questions about the nature of such a text.

He records that "Someone (a stranger) sent me an e-mail last week and asked me how I could 'put my whole life' out on the net for everyone to read. Isn't it embarrassing, he asked? I hadn't really thought about it before." Schalchlin muses about what he really is doing with his online diary, what he hopes to accomplish by turning his life into an Internet serial:

> Perhaps I'm like a bug some kid has rolled over onto its back. Perhaps this is me kicking my legs up in the air begging him not to squish me. I just have this weird feeling that if I cry loud enough and long enough, if I make people care...maybe it will make some scientist work that much harder to find a cure for us all. (Maybe it'll make them slow down just to get me to shut up!)

From his initial self-construction as powerless and insignificant, even inhuman, Schalchlin moves to a position of agency, offering himself and his personal life up to the public in order to enact change, a role made possible by the accessibility of the Internet, and its openness to the narratives of "Every-man." Constructing himself as the representative "man with AIDS," Schalchlin hopes to help educate the reading public about people society would rather ignore. Through sharing his life/story, he invites readers to think of themselves as part of a connected community, a group that now, through him, all "know" someone with AIDS, and therefore have a personal interest in the fight against the disease.

For Schalchlin to accomplish these purposes, however, he has to forego the partial anonymity that most Web diarists enjoy, and emphasize his reality, even his corporeality. To make the personal political, to put a face on AIDS, or on the other causes he champions, he must represent himself as a real person. Less philanthropically, his online and offline identities need to be contiguous enough in his readers' minds to encourage their financial and commercial support of his forthcoming musical and his compact discs, which are available for sale through his site.

Though both the framing of his diary as a book and the drama of his story invite associations with fiction, his generic choice of the online diary, a non-fiction form, grounds his narrative in the "real" world. While his fans may read his story like fiction, they seem to accept him as real. Schalchlin's offline career as a speaker at campuses and churches further enhances his readers' feelings that the "character" from the "LIVING NOVEL" has come to li fe, stepping out of the computer screen and into many people's own personal lives, seemingly obliterating the boundary between representation and reality.

As the site and its creator became somewhat of a cause celebre, the diary evolved from its original roles of goodbye letter and illness narrative. With scores of eager fans that demanded-literally-daily updates, living in the Bonus Round grew into an entity, and even a career in itself. This constant pressure to produce strained Schalchlin's enthusiasm for, and ability to seem as if he were, living online. By 1997, he wonders, "Is this diary a never-ending story? ... Am I now committed to doing this the rest of my life?"

During the show's 1998 Laguna Playhouse run, the diary "morphs temporarily [into] a backstage fan notebook" ("Index"), and focuses on promoting and selling the show and its souvenirs. Pictures of merchandise and links to purchasing sites usurp the daily personal narrative, reflecting both Schalchlin's vested interest in keeping his musical financially viable, and his lack of time to devote to the diary. The play had become the diary subject, not Schalchlin, whose own person al story, apart from his role as actor and songwriter, became secondary and at times nonexistent. His decision to continue the diary even in this truncated form reflects his sense of responsibility to his readers, for whom he fulfills multiple public as well as personal roles.

When Schalchlin posted Part 5 in 1998, he announced that he was taking a "hiatus" from the diary in its present form, thereby ending. "The Bonus Round will continue," he reassures his readers, "but it will evolve". The "new diary" will be a combination of posts to the discussion board and emails; "in other words," he explains, "the diary is now totally interactive." His decision comes after a bad blood test and a "backbreaking schedule" of touring. Rather than quit the diary entirely and let down the many communities who congregate and mingle at this site, rather than dismantle his online life even though its maintenance and ongoing construction threaten to disrupt his offline life, Schalchlin expands the elastic borders of the genre to include other writers in his personal diary.

His diary, then, becomes "totally interactive" not only in the sense of providing links to follow, audio files to hear, and photographs to view, but also in the sense of being collaborative. Throwing open the construction of his diary to his reading public, inviting them to contribute to his personal story, ensures that the diary will continue. He can therefore give the readers exactly what they want: they still get the diary, and, even better, they can write its contents so that it reflects their own desires as well as his. In this interactive form, the diary's textual representation thus becomes representative, reflecting the online diary's function as a public document built to serve its writer and its communities.

Schalchlin's blurring of the life and text, of virtuality and reality, of public and private, accumulates over hundreds of entries, as his online identities take shape, and communities begin to form around and participate in his diary. The cumulative nature of online diaries and Weblogs makes their autobiographical projects distinct from such other forms of online life writing as the personal home page or the chat-room persona, genres to which readers bring from print culture fewer expectations of both texts and writers. Since Schalchlin's journal was one of the earliest on the Internet, it was for many readers their first experience of this "new artform" that, though similar in many ways to offline diaries, challenges traditional generic definitions and reading practices.

Reading online diaries can be a frustrating and discomfiting experience for a reader-and a researcher-accustomed to published print materials. In an online diary, I do not know what will come next, and I cannot jump to the last entry or glean the final outcome from the summary provided by the book jacket; I may even find one day that the diary has disappeared entirely. Since online diaries incorporate the familiar alongside the strange, they are unsettling narrative territory-uncharted, with the potential for both thrills and peril for writers and readers.

As a text that consciously bridges both print and Internet cultures, Living in the Bonus Round helps new audiences negotiate the forms of, and develop expectations for, online life writing and its producers. Concerned to a much greater degree than traditional diarists with creating texts that serve themselves and their readers, online diarists write with an awareness of and a desire for a reading public. Carrying over to the Internet such expected features as dated, distinct entries, a confiding if not confessional tone, and a concern with the everyday details of one's own life, Web diarists reassure readers of the print diary that their narrative expectations will be met.

But these diarists also expand the form to fit new uses and users, adding counters, email addresses, links, and discussion boards, supplementing the solo voice of the diarist with a chorus of respondents in conversation. For online readers and writers, the diary becomes a site for communities to work their values, language, and membership, by reading, writing, or responding. Participating in these conversations that she has initiated or entered, the online diarist creates a text that is at once both personal and public.

Even as they throw open the diary genre and their lives to the Internet, though, Web diarists retain a measure of anonymity, writing to readers they will for the most part never meet in real life. Bloggers' simultaneous verisimilitude and immateriality account for readers' conflicting impulses to accept them as real people even as they read them as characters in a life fiction.

As an emerging form of life writing, online diaries serve as fresh reminders of the tenuous division between "life" and "art," between virtual and actual, realms that these texts seem to straddle more explicitly than traditional written autobiographical forms. Their interstitial status, which makes it harder for audiences, and even authors, to distinguish the represented from the real, contributes, perhaps, to my own concerns about how to read these texts, how to approach these narratives as a genre and as life writing. Web diaries challenge not only our notions about whose lives should be written, but how they should be written, forci ng readers to examine their own aesthetic, cultural, generational biases.

5

Social Implications of the Internet

By "Internet" we refer to the electronic network of networks that links people and information through computers and other digital devices allowing person-to-person communication and information retrieval. Although the late 1960s saw the inception of an ancestral network dedicated to scientific (and, after 1975, military) communication, the Internet did not emerge until 1982; it began its rapid ascent only in the early 1990s, when graphical interfaces became widely available and commercial interests were allowed to participate. Access to and use of the medium diffused widely and swiftly.

The number of Americans online grew from 25 million in 1995 (when only 3% of Americans had ever used the Internet) to 83 million in 1999, with 55 million Americans going online on a typical day in mid-2000. The amount of information available on the World Wide Web has also risen exponentially, from fewer than 20,000 Web sites in 1995 to over 10 million in 2000, representing over two billion Web pages, with as many as two million pages added daily.

Our focus in this chapter is on the Internet's implications for social change. The Internet presents researchers with a moving target: Agre (1998a) describes it as "a meta-medium: a set of layered services that make it easy to construct new media with almost any properties one likes." We use Internet to refer both to technical infrastructure (public TCP/IP networks, other large-scale networks like AOL, and foundational protocols), and to uses to which this infrastructure is put (World Wide Web, electronic mail, online multiperson interactive spaces).

We focus primarily on general, public uses. Among the topics we do not address systematically are the use of digital technologies for communication within formal organizations, the technology's potential contribution to the conduct of social-science research and scholarly communication, or the much broader topic of social antecedents and consequences of computerization. Many observers allege that the Internet is changing society. Perhaps not surprisingly, given the novelty of the new digital media, there is little agreement about what those changes are.

Our purpose here is to summarize research by social scientists about the Internet and to encourage more sociologists to contribute actively to such research. We believe that it is important for sociologists to address these issues for three reasons. First, the medium's rapid growth offers a once-in-a-lifetime opportunity for scholars to test theories of technology diffusion and media effects during the early stages of a new medium's diffusion and institutionalization. Second, the Internet is unique because it integrates both different modalities of communication (reciprocal interaction, broadcasting, individual reference-searching, group discussion, person/machine interaction) and different kinds of content (text, video, visual images, audio) in a single medium.

This versatility renders plausible claims that the technology w ill be implicated in many kinds of social change, perhaps more deeply than television or radio. Finally, choices are being made-systems developed, money invested, laws passed, regulations promulgated-that will shape the system's technical and normative structure for decades to come. Many of these choices are based on behavioural assumptions about how people and the Internet interact. We believe such assumptions should represent more than guesswork.

THEORETICAL CONTEXT

Sociology's major theoretical traditions emphasize different aspects of electronic media. For Durkheimians, point-to-point communications media like telephones reinforce organic solidarity, while broadcast media like radio or television yield powerful collective representations. Marxists focus upon exploitation of communications media to enhance elite control of both politics and production through cultural hegemony and enhanced surveillance. Weberians attend to the ways in which point-to-point media advance rationalization by reducing limits of time and space, and broadcast media provide the elements of distinctive status cultures.

Other traditions also offer perspectives on the digital media. Technological determinists suggest that structural features of new media induce social change by enabling new forms of communication and cultivating distinctive skills and sensibilities. In the 1960s, students of social change suggested that in the face of new developments in communications technology, industrial society would yield to the "information society," with consequences in every institutional realm. Critical theorists problematize the effects of technological change on political deliberation and the integrity of civil society.

Daniel Bell appears to have been the first sociologist to write about the social impact of digital communications media themselves. Bell predicted that major social consequences would derive from two related developments: the invention of miniature electronic and optical circuits capable of speeding the flow of information through networks; and the impending integration of computer processing and telecommunications into what Harvard's Anthony Oettinger dubbed "compunications" technology.

Anticipating the democratization of electronic mail and telefaxing, as well as digital transmission of newspapers and magazines, Bell explored the policy dilemmas these changes would raise, calling "the social organization of the new 'compunications' technology" the most central issue "for the postindustrial society". More recently, Manuel Castells has argued that the world is entering an "information age" in which digital information technology "provides the material basis" for the "pervasive expansion" of what he calls "the networking form of organization" in every realm of social structure.

According to Castells, the Internet's integration of print, oral, and audiovisual modalities into a single system promises an impact on society comparable to that of the alphabet, creating new forms of identity and inequality, submerging power in decentered flows, and establishing new forms of social organization. The comprehensive visions of Bell and Castells, like the other theoretical traditions we have described, suggest a range of empirical questions one must answer to understand the Internet's influence upon society. From the Marxian and Weberian traditions come concerns about power and inequality in the access to the new technology.

The Durkheimian perspective sensitizes us to the new media's impact on community and social capital. The work of Habermas and Calhoun leads us to ask how the Internet may alter the practice of politics. The Weberian tradition raises the question of the effect of Internet technology on bureaucracy and economic institutions. Critical theory raises important questions of how the Internet may affect the arts and entertainment media.

We address each of these five topics in turn, summarizing the results of research undertaken by social scientists and other investigators. In most of these areas, the research literature is limited, and many questions remain. But there is a pattern: Early writings projected utopian hopes onto the new technology, eliciting a dystopian response. Research on each topic yields two conclusions. First, the Internet's impact is more limited than either the utopian or dystopian visions suggest. Second, the nature of that impact will vary depending upon how economic actors, government regulation, and users collectively organize the evolving Internet technology.

Enthusiasts predicted that the Internet would reduce inequality by lowering the cost of information and thus enhancing the ability of low-income men and women to gain human capital, find and compete for good jobs, and otherwise enhance their life chances. By contrast, cyber-skeptics suggest that the greatest benefits will accrue to high-SES persons, who may use their resources to employ the Internet sooner and more productively than their less privileged peers, and that this tendency would be reinforced by better Internet connections and easier access to social support.

As in other areas, early research results suggest that the outcome is more complex than either of these predictions, and that the Internet's effects on inequality will depend on the social organization of its use. In this section, we examine research on individual-level inequality among users, as well as cross-national differences in Internet penetration and inequality in effective Internet access for content producers.

The "Digital Divide" in the United States Anderson et al (1995) were among the first to highlight the potential of inequality in Internet access to limit people's opportunities to find jobs, obtain education, access government information, participate in political dialog, and build networks of social support. By "digital divide," we refer to inequalities in access to the Internet, extent of use, knowledge of search strategies, quality of technical connections and social support, ability to evaluate the quality of information, and diversity of uses.

Although some speculate that current intergroup differences will evaporate as the Internet diffuses, Schement (1999) points out that inequalities in access to information services (e.g. telephone, cable) tend to persist in contrast to the rapid diffusion of information goods (e.g. radio, television, VCRs) that reach near saturation relatively quickly. This is because the former require ongoing expenditures, whereas the latter are based on one-time p urchases. For example, although 94% of all American households have telephones, this figure drops below 80% for the low-income elderly and female-headed households below the poverty level.

Because sociologists have conducted so little research on the digital divide, to chart the dimensions of inequality we must rely primarily on studies reporting bivariate statistics. Reports of the National Telecommunications and Information

Administration documented differences in Internet access favoring the college educated, the wealthy, whites, people under the age of 55 and, especially in earlier years, men and urban dwellers. Interestingly, despite the focus of early reports on income differences, the impact of educational attainment on Internet use is twice that of income after multivariate controls.

Research has also found that Internet non-users report as reasons for not going online that they are not computer users, they do not want their children to have Internet access, they lack time or interest, or they cannot aff ord it. There is some evidence that measures of access reflect resource control, whereas measures of intensity of use are driven more by demand. Thus teenagers are less likely to report Internet access than adults between the ages of 25 and 54; but when homes have Internet access; teenagers are online much more than adults.

Patterns of inequality are likely to reflect such changing factors as public connection availability, private subscription price, services available, and the technology necessary to access them effectively, as well as the diffusion of knowledge and the evolution of informal technical-support networks. Therefore, it is crucial to examine change in inequality over time. Three surveys conducted between 1996 and 1998 found that the gap in access between whites and African Americans had increased over time, but NTIA surveys (1998, 2000) found that divide diminishing between 1998 and 2000.

Wilhelm (2000) reports that significant differences persist in Internet use among racial and ethnic groups, with socioeconomic status held constant, and he argues that access to telecommunications tools and lack of easy access to Spanish-language content explain lower usage rates among Hispanics. By contrast, broad evidence suggests that two gaps, the advantage of men over women and of the young over the old, have declined as the technology has diffused and become more user-friendly. Other evidence suggests that late adopters have less formal education and lower incomes than earlier cohorts.

Several exemplary studies go beyond description to analysis. In a study notable for its use of multivariate analysis and multiple outcome measures, Bimber (2000) found that the gap between men and women in access to the Internet reflected male/female differences in income and other resources; but that women with access used the Internet less frequently than did otherwise similar men, a result he attributed to the fact that full-time employment had a significant effect on frequency of use for men, but not for women. In a study exemplary for tying individual-level inequality to institutional arrangements, Strover (1999) compared dial-up Internet connectivity in four rural US counties, concluding that low levels of commercial investment in telecommunications infrastructure in sparsely populated areas limits use by generating less choice among service providers and higher connection fees.

Other research has focused on public settings that provide Internet access for pesons unable to reach the Internet at home or work. A national survey of public libraries reported that urban libraries are almost three times as likely as rural libraries to offer high-speed Internet connections; and that because many urban libraries serve high-poverty areas, access to high-speed connections is relatively available to the urban poor.

An evaluation of Internet access programs at two public libraries and two community centers indicated that effectiveness was a function of the extent to which staff were trained to assist Internet users and potential users found the atmosphere welcoming and nonthreatening. Research on schools, another key site for public access, indicates that the proportion of US public schools offering Internet access rose from 3% in 1994 to 63% in 1999 (US Department of Education 2000), but that training and support staffing necessary for teachers to inco rporate the technology effectively in instructional plans has lagged behind.

Much research and policy assumes that people can convert Internet access into other valued goods, services, and life outcomes. Researchers have not yet tested this premise for Internet access, but research on general computer use sustains its plausibility, while leaving much to be done. Krueger reported a substantial wage premium accruing to workers who use computers. Attewell & Battle found that home computer use was significantly related to students' test scores m mathematics and reading, with higher returns for boys, whites, and the well-to-do.

THE GLOBAL DIGITAL DIVIDE

The number of Internet users globally skyrocketed from 16 million in 1995 to almost 360 million by mid-2000. Despite this rapid diffusion, this number represents just 5% of the world's population. As is the case with other communications devices, access across countries is very uneven, with 97% of Internet host computers located in developed countries. With respect to content, US producers dominate the Web, creating and hosting a large percentage of the most visited Web sites and so establishing English as the Internet's dominant language.

Studies of cross-national variation in levels of Internet connectivity and use are few. Most reports on global Internet diffusion present little more than descriptive statistics, emphasizing correlations with national wealth and education. Cross-national differences reflect differences in the availability of local-language programming, but not that alone. Hargittai (1996) called attention to institutional factors, reporting that in 1995 three quarters of highly developed countries, but only 10% of LDCs, had commercial access providers (an indicator of private-sector involvement and thus additional impetus for diffusion). Although data quality constrains generalization, the divide between developed and less developed nations appears not to have lessened as the Internet has diffused.

Better data make it possible to analyze Internet diffusion in OECD countries in more detail. Using multivariate analyses of OECD nations, Hargittai (1999) demonstrated that national wealth and competition in the telecommunications sector (and regulatory environments fostering competition) were the strongest predictors of connectivity.

Wilson (2000) distinguishes between "formal access" (physical availability) and "effective access" (affordable connectivity and diffusion of skills people need to benefit from the technology). In-depth cases studies help develop this distinction. Rao et al (1999) suggest that lack of local content in native languages in South Asia discourages use. Based on a detailed review of statistics and case reports, Norris (2001) concludes that the Internet is reproducing cross-national inequalities in use of newspapers, telephones, radio, and television because diffusion largely depends on economic development and research and development investments that are unequally distributed across societies.

Yet a case study of Trinidad reports that by 1999 penetration was deep (approximately 30% of households had at least one regular user) and, while stratified by income, relatively broad. The authors attribute this both to Trinidad's comparatively strong communications infrastructure and healthy economy, and equally important, to the premium placed on email by residents of an island nation that exports its most successful young people abroad. Technologies shape themselves to the contours of local priorities and ways of life: Just as some less developed countries were vanguard adopters of sound cassettes and cell phones, some may embrace the Internet relatively quickly, especially as wireless transmission creates convergence between Internet and cell phone technologies.

Inequality in content providers' access to attention Sociologists should be concerned not only with inequality in access to the Internet, but with inequality in access to the attention of those who use the Internet. By dramatically reducing the cost of the replication and distribution of information, the Internet has the potential to create arenas for more voices than any other previous communication medium by putting product dissemination within the reach of the individual.

Information abundance creates a new problem, however: attention scarcity. Content creators can only reach large audiences if online gatekeepers-Web services that categorize online information and provide links and search facilities to other sites-channel users to them. Yet Internet traffic is highly concentrated: 80% of site visits are to just .5% of Web sites. As was the case with broadcast media, the growth and commercialization of the Internet has been accompanied by a commodification of attention.

A rapidly evolving mosaic of search engines and point-of-entry sites compete for dominance, playing a pivotal role in channeling users' attention toward some contents and away from others. During the late 1990s, entrepreneurs developed comprehensive and strongly branded "portals"-Web sites containing search engines, category guides, and various shopping and information services-to match users and content. Such sites now account for one in four of the most visited destinations of the Web. The search engines they feature are often biased in their identification and, especially, ranking of sites in response to user queries.

The effects of bias are compounded by the tendency of engine users to employ simple search terms and to satisfice by terminating searches at the first acceptable site. [A 1998 analysis of almost one billion queries on the Altavista search engine revealed that 77% of sessions included but one query and 85% of users viewed only the first screen of search results]. Thus, Web destinations that are displayed prominently on portal sites or ranked high by search engines are likely to monopolize the attention of all but the most sophisticated and committed Internet users. Understanding the processes by which such display opportunities and ranks are awarded is an important research tack.

Research on inequality in access to and use of the Internet-among individual users, groups, organizations, countries, and content creators-should be an important priority for sociologists. At the individual level, the priority should be on using multivariate methods to explore the determinants of different measures of inequality: not just whether or not one has "access," but inequality in location of access (home, work, public facilities); the quality of hardware, software, and connections; skill in using the technology; and access to social support networks. Because inequality reflects the technology's organization, not inherent qualities, special priority should be placed on studies of how inequality is affected by such factors as government programs, industry structure and pricing policies, and approaches to the provision and organization of content.

SOCIAL ISOLATION OR SOCIAL CAPITAL FORMATION

Initial enthusiasts anticipated that the Internet would boost efficiency, making people more productive and enabling them to avoid unnecessary transportation by accomplishing online tasks like banking, shopping, library research, even socializing online. The results (less stress, more time, and new online contacts) would make individuals more fulfilled and build social capital for society at large.

More recently, two studies have suggested that the Internet may induce anomie and erode social capital by enabling users to retreat into an artificial world. In this section, we explore research on what Internet users do with their time, how the Internet affects their well-being, and how the Internet influences communities, both real and virtual.

TIME DISPLACEMENT

Much of the debate over social capital is about whether the Internet attenuates users' human relationships, or whether it serves to reinforce them. Experience with earlier communications technologies suggests that Internet users may substitute time online for attention to functionally equivalent social and media activities. Thus, when television appeared in the United States, it had rapid impact on use of other media: Audiences abandoned their radio sets, movie theaters closed, and general-interest magazines stopped publishing fiction and eventually folded.

Early studies documented reductions in time spent going to the movies, listening to radio, and reading fiction as television viewing time increased. Subsequent research replicated these results cross-nationally and also documented significant declines in out-of-home socializing, in-home conversation, housework, personal care activities, and even sleep. If television, a unidirectional mass medium, displaced so many activities, then it stands to reason that the Internet, which permits interactive as well as one-way communication, might substitute for even more. Observers have expressed particular concern that Internet users may reduce the time devoted to off-line social interaction and spend less time with print media, as well as with television and other media.

The functional-equivalence model that described the effects of television thus far appears not to fit the experience of Internet users. Analyses of 1995 and 1998 national surveys by the Pew Center for the People and the Press, which asked respondents about activities "yesterday," have found Internet use to be unrelated or positively associated with social interaction.

Moreover, analysis of 1997 data from the federal Survey of Public Participation in the Arts indicates that Internet users (with appropriate controls) read more literature, attended more arts events, went to more movies, and watched and played more sports than comparable nonusers. A more recent study based on 1998 Pew Center data indicates intriguing changes associated with the Internet's diffusion: Among users who had been early adopters, Internet use was associated with greater use of print media. Among new Internet users, however, this relationship had disappeared. No significant decline in TV viewing was found after demographic controls.

Overall, then, these analyses provide scant support for time displacement due to functional equivalence with respect to other media. The situation with respect to social interaction is more complicated. Two well-publicized studies reported indications that Internet use substituted for other interactions. Kraut et al (1998), who used a rare longitudinal design to study 169 Pittsburgh-area families who were given computers and Internet connections over a two-year period, reported that higher levels of Internet use were "associated with declines in communication with family members, declines in social circles, and increased loneliness and depression."

The authors inferred that heavy users substituted interactions with weak ties on the Internet for time spent with close friends and relatives. Yet as the researchers followed their sample they discovered that, except for increased stress, negative psychological effects decayed to statistical insignificance and some positive outcomes emerged. They attribute these changes to increases in experience and competence and, more speculatively, to the Internet's greater utility in the later period and to a change in sign of network externalities from negative to positive as more of these users' friends and family went online.

An innovative study that used special use-logging software to compare the online behaviour of experienced and novice Web users reinforces the notion that the effect of Internet use may vary with user competence. Compared to experienced Internet users, the novices engaged in more aimless surfing, were less successful in finding information, and were more likely to report feeling a souring of affect over the course of their sessions. Their negative reactions reflected not the Internet experience per se but the frustration and sense of impotence of the inexperienced user without immediate access to social support.

Nie and Erbring (2000) surveyed four thousand Internet users online and asked how the Internet had changed their lives. Most reported no change, but heavier users reported declines in socializing, media use, shopping, and other activities. By contrast, analyses of national (off-line) sample surveys (from both 1995 and 1998) using more fine-grained activity measures indicate that Internet users are no less likely (with controls) to engage in social visiting or to call friends on the telephone.

More recent surveys (online and off) have revealed that Internet users have higher levels of generalized trust and larger social networks than nonusers. Results from survey analyses also suggest that Internet use serves to complement rather than substitute for print media and offline socialization. Indeed, a detailed time diary study also found Internet users to be no less active media users or offline socializers than nonusers, though they did do less housework, devote less time to family care, and sleep less.

COMMUNITY

Wellman (2001) argues that the Internet has contributed to a shift from a group-based to a network-based society that is decoupling community and geographic propinquity, and thus requiring new understandings and operationalizations of the former. Consistent with this insight, Katz et al (forthcoming) report that Internet users visit friends more and talk with them by telephone more frequently, but that they also travel more and have fewer friends in their immediate neighborhoods. To some extent, whether one views the Internet as corrosive to or supportive of community depends in part on how one evaluates the things people do with it.

For example, Nie & Erbring view moderate to heavy-users' self-reported substitution of email for telephone contact as part of their loss of "contact with their social environment." By contrast, Lin (2001) regards online communication, including email, as markedly expanding the stock of social capital. Indeed, an increasing body of literature suggests that the Internet enhances social ties defined in many ways, often by reinforcing existing behaviour patterns.

A report on a national survey of users (Howard et al forthcoming) revealed that the Internet puts users in more frequent contact with families and friends, with email being an important avenue of communication. This study also suggests that research on Internet use and social capital should distinguish among different types of Internet use: The Internet seems particularly unlikely to corrode the social capital of women, more of whom than men employ the medium as a complement to other channels of social interaction. Similarly, a longitudinal study by Kraut et al (forthcoming) found that Internet use increased interaction with family members and reported closeness to friends, especially for users whose perceived social-support networks were strong before they began using the Internet.

The Internet is unique among media in making it easy for people to assemble (at a distance) and communicate with many others at the same time in such settings as chat rooms or online discussion forums. "Online communities" come in very different shapes and sizes, ranging from virtual communities that connect geographically distant people with no prior acquaintance who share similar interests, to settings that facilitate interactions among friendship networks or family members, to community networks that focus on issues relevant to a geographically defined neighborhood. Research on "online community" should distinguish among these forms, lest results appear contradictory and confusing.

Early studies tended to focus on online role-playing games [e.g. multi-user dungeons or MUDs (Turkle 1995)] and newsgroups. These were among the first online communities and are still popular research sites, in part because researchers can obtain full transcripts of discussions and events. Such "online ethnography" has provided useful insights into issues of identity formation and the status and concerns of particular groups. But as the technology matures, ever smaller percentages of Internet users participate in online games and newsgroups. Increasingly, researchers must follow users into newer kinds of online communities based on shared interests or (physical) community networks.

The number of case studies of online communities is large and growing. Participants value such online settings for making it easy (and inexpensive) to communicate across large distances, providing opportunities for participation by the homebound aged or infirm, and enabling people with minority interests or lifestyles to find companionship and counsel unavailable in their communities of residence. Rheingold's (1993) classic study of an online community emphasized the capacity of online networks to provide their members with social support.

And other researchers have noted that, compared to real-life social networks, online communities are more often based on participants' shared interests rather than shared demographic characteristics or mere propinquity. Nonetheless, issues related to racial, gender, and sexual dynamics do permeate and complicate online interactions [e.g. requiring communities to establish norms for dealing with intimidating or offensive langu age].

Whereas some studies focus on "virtual" communities, others explore the impact of the Internet on geographic communities. An exemplary study of a highly wired residential community underscores the importance of examining online interactions in the context of offline everyday life. It revealed that Internet users maintain community ties through both computer-mediated communication and face-to-face interaction. Although they maintain more long-distance relationships than do non-Internet users, they communicate even more with their neighbors-and are acquainted with three times as many of their neighbors as are their unwired peers.

A study of a similar community revealed that residents make much use of the Internet for "social-capital building activities," but that individual-level community involvement and attachment increased only for residents who were already very active at the experiment's inception. Similarly, a study of scholarly networks found that although the Internet helps maintain contact over long distances, most email contacts are between people who also interact face-to-face. In other words, research suggests that the Internet sustains the bonds of community by complementing, not replacing, other channels of interaction.

SOCIAL CAPITAL

Many scholars believe that the Internet facilitates the creation of social capital and other public goods by making information flow more efficiently through residential or professional communities. Yet Putnam (2000) reports that, after demographic controls, Internet users are no different than non-users on measures of civic engagement. He notes, however, that it is premature to project this result onto future user cohorts, and he is agnostic about the Internet's contribution to social capital at the community level.

Putnam calls attention to the need to understand qualitative differences between mediated and face-to-face interaction and to explore a tension between the technology's potential and the dangers of unequal access and "cyberbalkanization". Other studies indicate that, under some circumstances at least, Internet use may enhance social capital. In a longitudinal study of Pittsburgh residents, Kraut et al; (forthcoming) found

Internet use associated with greater participation in community activities and more trust (though less commitment to remaining in their community), with the positive effects greater for more extroverted participants.

An analysis of online survey respondents from the United States, United Kingdom, Canada, and Australia found that increased Internet use tended to have a direct positive effect on social capital (operationalized as participation in community networks and activities) and a positive indirect effect (through social capital) on political participation. There is much anecdotal evidence that the Internet provides significant benefits to people with unusual identities or concerns (e.g., rare medical conditions). But there is some evidence that "social capital" produced by less focused networks is rather thin.

For example, a survey of users of Amsterdam's "Digital City," a multi-use space created to encourage Internet access and public-spirited interaction, found that, despite soaring membership figures, most users participated relatively infrequently and for recreational purposes. It has also been argued that the Internet builds social capital by enhancing the effectiveness of community-level voluntary associations, but little research evaluates this claim. The Internet has also been described as an inexpensive and effective means of organizing oppositional social movement.

Lin (2001) describes the fascinating case of China's Falun Gong organization, which used the Internet to establish a powerful, hierarchical religious movement under the noses of an authoritarian regime. Whether similar movements will follow suit will depend on the success of states in monitoring and controlling such activities. We draw five morals from the research to date. First, the Internet has no intrinsic effect on social interaction and civic participation.

This nonfinding should challenge scholars to understand the circumstances under which different effects are produced, which will doubtless lead them to distinguish different profiles of Web use and different orientations of users. Second, Internet use tends to intensify already existing inclinations toward sociability or community involvement, rather than creating them *ab initio*. Third, we need to know more than we do about the qualitative character of online relationships.

Fourth, we know that virtual communities exist in large number, but we know relatively little about their performance. Research on how virtual communities address problems of commitment and trust (like Kollock's [1999] innovative study of institutionalized reputation on E-Bay and Usenet barter sites) is necessary to understand the limits and possibilities of community online. Fifth, we need more systema tic studies of how civic associations and social movements use the Internet, so that we can move beyond single cases to understanding the institutional conditions that encourage or discourage successful exploitation of this technology for collective ends.

IMPACT ON POLITICS: RENEWED PUBLIC SPHERE OR ELECTRONIC BATTLEGROUND

In the political domain we again find utopians and doomsayers at odds. Enthusiasts find early evidence of a re-engaged, more deliberative, more equitable political community. Skeptics foresee the re-emergence of an unresponsive commercial sphere dominated by the usual corporate players-but with an increased capacity to invade the privacy of individual citizens. Most research suggests that effects thus far have been mixed and modest.

Drawing conclusions at such early stages of technology diffusion before the emergence of stable norms is risky because it is difficult to disentangle: 1) the unique characteristics of early adopters from the characteristics of the medium in question; 2) the primitive limitations of the early Web from the technology's mature characteristics; and 3) the Web's explosive growth from other political trends. As with other topics, the literature about politics on the Internet has progressed through three stages: unjustifiable euphoria, abrupt and equally unjustifiable skepticism, and gradual realization that Web-based human interaction really does have unique and politically significant properties.

AN INFORMED PUBLIC

Empirical research on mass political knowledge in industrial democracies, and particularly in the United States, has drawn heavily on the 'information cost' perspective of Downs and Schumpeter to explain why the public is so poorly informed. Because it takes time and energy to seek out, interpret, and remember political information, it may be rational to free-ride on the civic attentiveness of others. The political promise of the Internet is that it significantly lowers the behavioural costs of finding, storing, and communicating specific and personally relevant political information at convenient, timely intervals.

The literature reveals, however, that after controlling for education and political interest, there is little evidence of an effect of Internet use on political knowledge. Those who seek political information online are generally well informed to begin with, politically oriented, and heavy users of other media. At present, the Internet supplements and complements rather than replaces traditional sources of political information.

A June 2000 survey revealed that 33% of US adults (and 46% of those under thirty) go online for news at least once a week, compared to 20% in 1998, and 15% they say do so every day. About half say they seek out political news, fewer than report that they look for weather, technology, business, and sports news (Howard et al forthcoming). In some cases they access news not readily available through print or broadcast media, but often the Web is a supplementary medium through which conventional news organizations distribute information available through other means.

AN ENGAGED PUBLIC

The economic and psychological dynamics of Web-based human communication, however, are potentially distinct enough from those of traditional print and broadcast news media that in time we may see evidence of an Internet effect. For example, news sites often provide interactive links that encourage users to "send a copy of this chapter to a friend or colleague." The capacity for horizontal interpersonal communication, to rebroadcast a news article with personal commentary, enhances the capacity for discussion, engagement, and the two-step flow that serves as the critical antidote to anomic mass communication.

Evolving third-voice technologies would permit users to unilaterally convert every mass-medium Web site into an open public discussion. Discussion groups on the Web at present lack the selective, highly edited character of letters to the editor and citizen op-eds. But though they may not achieve the ideal of deliberative discourse envisioned by Habermas, they would appear to be a step in that direction.

There is great concern about the political malaise and disengagement presumably reflected in low voter turnouts in US national elections. Will reduced costs of gathering political information produce higher voting rates? Probably not, due to the complex and tangled influences of multiple historical, cultural and economic trends, which render bivariate analyses of relationships between media use and electoral participation ill advised. Schudson (1998) points out that US electoral participation rates were highest in the second half of the nineteenth century, when citizens were generally uninformed and uneducated, the media were limited and sensationalistic, and quality of public debate was largely undistinguished.

Bimber (2000) argues that political impact derives less from the character of the medium than from the character of information and the day-to-day culture of its use. The successful Jesse Ventura candidacy in Minnesota is widely cited as an example of grass-roots Internet populism; but in that case the Net was primarily used to organize the already engaged, not to mobilize disaffected or uninterested voters. Online financial contributions and voting online by the already politically active may prove more significant in the long run.

POLITICAL POLARIZATION

Perhaps the most central question for sociological analysis of changing technical structures of interpersonal and mass communication is the tension between forces of social integration and polarization. Many fear that the Internet will weaken the cultural center and "political commons" that network television and metropolitan newspapers provided. Negroponte, forexample, predicts that an artificially intelligent Web-based Daily Me will select news and information based on the predilections and prejudices of the individual cybercitizen and further displace the cultural commons.

Research on earlier media, however, indicates that individuals tend to be aware of the most popular cultural artifacts and to monitor the latest hot programs and motion pictures. Ideologically inclined individuals do choose to attend to media that reinforce their prejudices (e.g., conservatives listen to conservatively oriented radio talk shows), but expose themselves as well to opposing views. The Net's capacity for anonymous communication may heighten the level of extremist and hate speech in the early stages of diffusion. But institutions of self-regulation may emerge to constrain such expression in cyberspace, as they have in nonelectronic public forums.

DELIBERATIVE DEMOCRACY

Web proponents may concede that historically apolitical social strata are unlikely to be mobilized overnight by Internet political content, and agree that there are few signs thus far that the Internet has increased political fragmentation and polarization. But they insist that the Internet will enhance the quality of political discussion and the viability, meaningfulness, and diversity of the public sphere by lowering the access barrier to meaningful public speech.

No longer is it necessary to own a newspaper or television station to participate: The Web is a two-way medium, and every Internet receiver can be a publisher as well. Such claims provide critics of commercial (and especially American) dominance of the mass media and the international flow of news and culture with a new focal point for inquiry. Can the Web make a real difference? It is clear that the Internet significantly lowers entry barriers and other Downsian cost factors for participation in the electronic public sphere.

Bimber finds that many of the distortions of group discussion resulting from dominant personalities and group dynamics are reproduced in cyberspace, but he concludes that virtual political space (notably Usenet-style threaded discussion groups) has its place as a significant supplement to, if not replacement for, the face-to-face discussions of Habermas' idealized nineteenth century salon. Lowering the economic costs to initiate and sustain an accessible political voice-compare a teenager's bedroom-based Web site to the cost of sustaining a printed magazine or broadcasting facility-can lower access barriers for minority voices, as well.

Skeptics argue that the commercial incentives of advertising-based media may lead ultimately to an Internet culturally indistinguishable from modern commercial television. This debate is particularly interesting in the case of Web-based political campaigning in the United States, where by 2000; most candidates had their own Web sites, many with detailed issue and policy information unavailable through traditional media. Will such diverse sites attract sufficient traffic to sustain themselves? Or will dominant commercial portals like AOL or specialized startups dominate attention, paying for access to the public sphere through political advertising? As of this writing the jury is out, but researchers are actively studying elite and mass behaviour.

IMPACT ON ORGANIZATIONS: FLEXIBLE NETWORKS OR PANOPTICONS

Some management writers depict information technology as transforming organizations: replacing hierarchical bureaucracy with flat, networked structures in which local initiative supplants authoritative command; and replacing formal organizations themselves with "network organizations" in which agency is interstitial and strategy constantly renegotiated. Others suggest that digital telecommunications may increase management control by permitting unprecedented degrees of surveillance. In this section, we focus primarily on organizations' use of the public Internet, rather than on communications networks internal to the firm.

LIMITS ON INTERNET IMPACT

Little research bears directly on these claims, and what there is finds limited effects for three reasons. First, authors who make the strongest claims often conflate different types of digital technology, including workplace applications, local area networks, and the Internet. The Internet is less central to some notable organizational trends (e.g., the shrinkage of middle management) than computerization of internal functions.

Second, many structural changes associated with the "networked firm" predate the rise of information technologies alleged to have caused them. Although some argue that the Internet causes large firms to devolve into loosely integrated production networks by reducing information and transaction costs, the move toward network organizations was under way before the Internet became popular. (The Internet, though not determinant, is important. Although network forms emerged in response to competitive environments, new information technologies contributed to their rapid development.)

Third, technology's effects reflect not its inherent potential, as futurists assume, but active choices that are shaped by technology owners' perceived interests, existing organizational structures and routines, and by cultural norms. Many traditional firms heavily constrain use of email and the Internet, especially by clerical and service employees, and such firms often implement systems that facilitate surveillance rather than enabling flexible, decentralized interaction.

Telecommuting, once predicted to rise exponentially, is a good example. Of a national sample of 1050 workers interviewed in late 1999, 41% believed they could work effectively from home, but only 10% reported their employers provided that option (and 9% reported doing so at least once a week). Other evidence suggests that most employees use home Internet connections to supplement hours at the workplace, not to substitute for them.

WORK GROUP EFFECTS

Research on work groups (much of it in laboratory settings) suggests that electronic communications influence interaction style and work flow. Use of electronic mail compared to telephones, for example, enables workers to control the pace of their response and thus facilitates multitasking. Digital conferencing may make employees less risk-averse and render group decision-making less predictable, more time-consuming, and more egalitarian.

Whether such effects enhance organizational performance or will persist as the technologies evolve is uncertain, in part because they depend on details of system design and implementation. In vivo research suggests that formally egalitarian "network" structures may coexist with substantial hierarchy and centralization in patterns of communication.

FIRM STRUCTURE EFFECTS

There is little evidence that the Internet is reshaping organizational structures. O'Mahoney & Barley report that "whether information technologies further centralization or decentralization" varies depending on how managements use them. The few empirical studies of the relationships between digital technology and organizational size, buy-or-sell decisions, and organizational boundaries are anecdotal or inconclusive. The Internet may induce change, but we will not know until researchers undertake large-sample studies that specify changes precisely, treat separately different kinds of information technology, and distinguish effects on different kinds of workers and different business functions.

Take, for example, technology's impact on interfirm networks. Most electronic networks complement, rather than substitute for, more intimate media. For many "network organizations" propinquity is crucial in breeding trust and rapport among participants, for example enabling companies in small-firm networks to share information and exchange specialized assets. Spatial agglomeration is also central to the success of biotechnology firms (and to venture capitalists who sustain them).

The most thorough review of technology-transfer research emphasizes the role of "the mobility and activity of technically trained people" over that of impersonal networks.

Digital telecommunications seem most important for routine transactions (e.g., inventory systems in which multiple firms share a data base) and for communication among knowledge workers accustomed to scientific norms of exchange (e.g., R&D), and least sufficient when interactions entail risk and require interpersonal judgment.

INDUSTRY SPECIFIC EFFECTS

Studies of specific industries indicate that digital telecommunications can facilitate transformative change when market pressures require it and organizational resources and structures render it possible. For example, when fierce competition and deregulation provoked change and rising demand made it profitable, trucking firms used the Internet (with such other technologies as global positioning) to develop logistics capacity and reposition themselves as transportation-services companies.

Hospitals and medical practices have used the Internet to pool information across entities, enabling the emergence of the "integrated healthcare systems" that are transforming many regional healthcare markets. Other industries that have used Internet technology to effect significant changes are banking and financial services and, with distance learning, higher education. In each case, firms adapted the technology to specific strategies, rather than yielding to general technological imperatives.

Thus, the Internet is implicated in profound changes in organizational structures, practices, and strategies. But the extent and nature of these changes-which business functions they restructure, which employees they affect-vary markedly by industry. And rather than causing change, digital technologies are ordinarily pressed into the service of developments to which managers are already committed. The area is ripe for both organizational case studies that focus on the Internet's use in particular industries and organizational surveys that permit confident generalization.

The Internet is also implicated in organizational change in the public sector, where enthusiasts have hailed its potential for saving tax dollars, reducing red tape, and making government more responsive. In an empirically detailed and theoretically sophisticated study, Fountain has demonstrated both the potential and impediments to its realization. Implementing digital technology saves governments money, but how much depends on network externalities. It reduces some aspects of bureaucratic rigidity but strengthens others by embedding them in code. It enhances the flow of information to citizens and enables government workers to cut through red tape, but in expanding the latter's discretion, it risks imposing new forms of inequality among citizens in their relations with the state.

IMPACT ON CULTURE: BOUNTIFUL DIVERSITY, HYPERSEGMENTATION, OR MASSIFICATION

Many sociologists feared that the original mass media (general-interest magazines, radio, and television) would inexorably "massify" taste, as profit-seeking firms produced only those homogeneous and banal programs or texts with the greatest audience appeal. Since 1980, changes in consumer demand have combined with new media technologies to segment markets and differentiate cultural goods, enabling individuals and groups to individualize their media habits. As an "interconnected network of audio, video, and electronic text communication that will blur the distinction between interpersonal and mass communications and between public and private communications", the Internet seems designed to take these trends to their logical conclusion.

Not surprisingly, early observers viewed the new technology as profoundly liberating, opening up outlets for the creative energies of people of every taste and persuasion. Because posting information on the Web is so inexpensive, the technology's enthusiasts believed it would virtually eliminate barriers to entry in fields like music recording, book publishing, and even filmmaking. In this view, the Internet would democratize the flow of information, supplanting top-down dependence on traditional news and media organizations with bottom-up sharing among consumers themselves.

Such optimistic scenarios assume that the Internet's only impact is a direct one on costs (of cultural goods to consumers and of publication to producers). But a second, perhaps more important, effect of the Internet may be to induce the restructuring of the culture industries themselves. When goods are distributed on the Internet, they can be repackaged in many ways: newspapers, for example, can be disassembled, their parts distributed separately; recorded music can come with more textual documentation than will fit in a CD jewel box. New distribution systems may also alter the size distribution of firms within industries, the relative power of gatekeepers and artists, and the nature of competitive strategies.

The Web's earliest cultural impact has been in the music industry, where it has reinforced existing trends toward deconcentration, product differentiation, and the multiplication of market channels. Some observers suggest that economic imperatives will keep the Internet from realizing its technical potential as a font of cultural abundance. True, barriers to entry are formally lower; but savage competition for users' limited attention may erect new barriers based on investments in marketing and production. The major media producers are developing the Internet commercially after the model of earlier media (albeit with more interactivity), with the expectation that Internet content, broadcast entertainment, and news will soon enter homes through a single system.

A third position holds that corporate power will overwhelm the Web's liberating potential by radically accelerating long-term trends toward narrower market segmentation and more fine-grained product customization. In this view, Web sites' ability to use "cookies" to track users' browsing habits provides an unprecedented opportunity for targeting appeals. Marketers will divide the public into countless market segments and bombard them with messages that reinforce dispositions and tastes their previous browsing-and-buying patterns have revealed, engendering isolation and myopia.

We have little purchase on which perspective is right for two reasons. First, aside from industry reports that many users have robust appetites for free music and sexual images, we know little about cultural practice on the Web. To be sure, the Web offers a remarkable smorgasbord of free cultural products and services. But we know little about who uses them, due to the lack of scholarly research on the extent to which, and ways in which, Internet users listen to music, visit museum sites, or read literature online. Nor do social scientists know to what extent culture consumers use the Web to cultivate existing tastes or, instead, to explore unfamiliar genres.

Second, we cannot yet tell to what extent (and how) media firms will be able to wring profits from Web-based entertainment. They will develop the Web as mass medium only if consumer demand for entertainment suffices to justify large investments. Tendencies toward cultural fragmentation may be repelled by cultural omnivores: well-educated consumers with eclectic tastes for many (finely differentiated) genres. Government will influence the outcome through legislation and court rulings (e.g., the Napster injuncion) that define intellectual property rights.

The Internet's cultural effects may vary among user groups. Because marketers are most interested in reaching people who consume the most, their "fragmenting" efforts may focus on the well-to-do; but such users, especially when they are highly schooled, are the ones most likely to use sophisticated search strategies, so their online behaviour may be less easily affected. Castells predicts a Web "populated by two essentially distinct populations, the interacting and the interacted," the first using the medium's full capacity, the latter limited to a "restricted number of prepackaged choices."

THE EVOLVING INTERNET

Research on technological change teaches us that the relationship between technology and society is never unidirectional. Rather technologies are often developed in response to the agendas of powerful social actors. Initially, they shape themselves to the contours of custom; ultimately, they follow paths selected through struggles among groups seeking to turn technologies to their own interests. We see this malleability in the history of the telephone, which was created as a business tool (and even a broadcasting device), but which became an instrument of sociable interaction.

We see it especially in the history of radio, which emerged as an interactive medium tailored to the needs of military communication, grew into a point-to-point communications device linking amateur enthusiasts, developed into a commercial broadcast system beaming a standardized mass culture across national societies, and finally, under the impact of television's competition, transformed itself into a finely differentiated medium specializing in broadcasting musical genres to narrowly defined subcultural market segments.

If anything, the Internet is even more pliant because it combines point-to-point and broadcast capability within a single network. It can be a telephone: literally, or through email, chat rooms, and other forms of real-time communication between individuals. It can serve as a library: specialized Web sites "narrowcast" information to users interested enough to use search engines to find them. It can act as a soapbox for individuals expressing themselves to e-lists and discussion forums.

Or it can operate as a conventional mass medium: Internet Service Providers like AOL and services like RealMedia let providers broadcast information to huge user publics simultaneously. Precisely because it can be all of these things at once-because it affords users choices among multiple modes of appropriation that coexist at any given time-the Internet is unprecedentedly malleable. This malleability raises the stakes for actors who wish to shape its evolution.

The findings of individual-level research on Internet use reflect the technology as it has emerged, not patterns intrinsic to the medium itself. Economic competition and public policies will shape the extent to which the Internet develops as point-to-point communicator, library, or mass medium; and this, in turn, will alter the incentives and opportunities for different kinds of individuals to use it. Thus, the social impact of the Internet depends on the impact of society on what the Internet becomes. It follows that sociologists should be studying carefully the organization of the Internet field, as well as the manner in which different ways of organizing content shape patterns of use, because such research holds the key to anticipating and understanding the Internet's effects.

Sociologists have been largely remiss in meeting this challenge. A useful exception is Aldrich's analysis of the Web from the standpoint of community, in which he distinguishes among governance structures (regulators and informal consortia), commercial users, service providers to those users, browser developers, and other "infrastructural populations" (hardware and software firms, ISPs, search engines, and portal sites) that occupy niches in the Web's ecology.

Owen presents a useful overview of the Internet industry from an economics perspective, with a particularly thorough treatment of the underlying technology and of the firms that maintain the network and offer connection services. A small but interesting literature explores the Internet's emergent structure through analysis of the network created by the hyperlinks that Web sites send to one another. Early studies using huge data sets were able to map sites onto coherent topical clusters and also reported high levels of integration, with most sites reachable from most others at a path distance of four or less.

The Internet's future, and thus its social impact, will be influenced by the resolution of three crucial policy issues. The first, establishing equality in Internet access, is necessary to ensure that less well-to-do or technically sophisticated citizens are not excluded from the political, economic, and social opportunities that the Internet increasingly provides. As our discussion of empirical work on this issue demonstrates, a sociological perspective calls attention to the need to go beyond the conventional focus on access per se to explore inequality in the combination of technical and social resources required for effective participation.

The second, establishing meaningful and enforceable norms of privacy for Internet users, involves the quest for balance between the functionality that people and businesses seek from the Internet and the sacrifice of access to personal information that the technology currently requires people to offer in exchange. Sociological research on the beliefs and practices of Internet users, online vendors, and service providers is necessary to inform policy deliberations in this area.

The third, defining rules governing intellectual property for a world in which copying and transmitting cultural works is essentially costless, entails the search for a balance between incentives necessary to motivate creative workers and the interest of society in maximizing access to works of the mind.

Currently the pendulum has swung far in the direction of the companies that control rights to intellectual property, with implications not just for music-loving teenagers but for social scientists eager to access formerly public data bases as well. Sociologists can contribute to this debate by testing behavioural assumptions about motivations of creative workers and the requirements of markets sufficient to sustain production of intellectual goods.

Lessig makes a valuable distinction among three ways that states and private interests can regulate communications media: law, norms, and code. The Internet, he argues, is distinctive in that code-the details of the programs that facilitate the exchange of messages and information-is a particularly powerful source of social control, with direct regulation relatively less effective. His work calls attention to the importance of studying aspects of the technology that remain invisible to most observers (and of the need for sociologists studying the Web to acquire sufficient technical expertise to address these questions.).

Sociology has been slow to take advantage of the unique opportunity to study the emergence of a potentially transformative technology in situ. Too much of the basic research has been undertaken by nonacademic survey organizations, yielding theoretically unmotivated description at best, and technically flawed and/or proprietarily-held data at worst. The relatively few sociologists who study the Internet have focused disproportionately on virtual communities, a worthy topic, but not the only one.

And in that area, as well as in research on the Internet's impact on inequality, politics, organizations, and culture, we need to develop explanatory models that distinguish between different modes of Internet use and that tie behaviour directly to soc ial and institutional context. Research has suffered, as well, from a disproportionate emphasis on individuals, implicitly treating the nature of the Internet itself as fixed.

This is regrettable because this protean technology's character and effects will reflect the outcome of ongoing struggles among powerful economic and political actors. Yet few sociologists have examined the Internet's institutional structure, industrial organization, or political economy. Some sociologists are doing important work; but unless their numbers grow, a magnificent opportunity to build and test theories of social and technical change may go unexploited.

If sociology needs the Internet as a laboratory, policy makers need sociology to illuminate the collective choices that will shape the Internet's future. As Philip Agre has written, discussions of the Internet are often informed less by positive knowledge than by "the cultural system of myths and ideas that our society projects onto the technology." Social science remains the best hope for substituting knowledge for myth and informing public discourse about current conditions and policy alternatives.

6

Indian Transnationalism on the Internet

Feminist geographers have called for a re-evaluation of geography, incorporating studies of women's lives and activities in relation to various scales from the global to the local. The research agenda they envision is one that pays particular attention to differences in the construction of gender across political boundary lines and in the midst of cultural contact. This chapter endorses this project and uses original survey data to demonstrate ways that gender shapes the use of the Internet by Asian Indians (including both first-and second generation individuals).

The study contributes to the growing literatures on the geographies of women, geographies of globalization and transnationalism and geographies of socio-technical relations, as well as combinations of the above. At the intersection of these topics is a question regarding how Internet users of Asian Indian origin or ethnicity use the Internet as part of an overall communication strategy to coordinate global and local scalings of gender identity. The Internet consequently becomes a vital tool for the construction of transnational identities.

The results also suggest that Asian Indian women differ from men with regard to their total time online, the types of websites they visit and their overall pattern of mediated communication, and that these differences have an age-based component. So this study brings attention to embodied difference in transnational networks and particularly the spaces of gendered transnationalism.

GEOGRAPHIES OF WOMEN, GLOBALIZATION AND TRANSNATIONALISM

This chapter will focus in particular on the dialogue between feminist geography and theories about globalization, communication and transnationalism. Citing writings on globalization, McDowell argues that:

> Thse emphasis on interconnections means, I believe, that we have to rethink some of our traditional loci and emphases as geographers, turning to new ways of studying people who are in transit, whose identities are unfixed, destabilized and in the process of changing.

This argument provides an excellent springboard to the study of globalization through the lens of individual communication routines where increasing interaction through space affects gender relations, and vice versa. This project responds to discussions about the transformation of men and women's roles through the process of migration. A new twist on the feminization of the domestic sphere may be the construction of women as the defenders of national identity, despite various globalizing tendencies, with the nation and its associated symbols becoming a kind of home writ large. Yeoh and Willis apply this idea in the Asian context:

> While men are associated with mobility and agility to grapple with newly fluid and somewhat erratic forms of transnational capital, women are often positioned in official state discourse as stabilizing forces of the 'home' the cultural carriers of 'Asian values,' the antidote to westoxification and the preservers and reproducers of the family, the next generation, and ultimately, the nation, in an increasingly fluid and uncertain world.

These guardians of ethnic identity are often subject to either exclusions enforced by the 'host' society (such as in the United States where spouses of H-1B visa holders receive

H-4 visas that prohibit paid work), or to being over-represented in poorly paid service or labour-intensive manufacturing industries. They are also subject to oppression by husbands who are often the key (or sole) breadwinners and consequently hold a monopoly on power within the household, as well as to isolation from informal social support networks such as extended family that are often present in the sending-community context.

At the same time, the loosening of norms and expectations through the exposure to multiple norms and expectations, a kind of fluidity of social regulation produced by cultural contact, can be liberating for women. Thus, migration has differential implications for immigrant men and women with respect to the symbolism of national identity, the impact of their labour force participation, and the 'social reproduction' of their families and communities.

All forms of communication are drawn into this dynamic. Therefore, this study brings attention to the importance of women's use of the Internet within the larger process producing new transnational spaces that lie simultaneously between geographical realms and geographical conditions. This betweenness places the space of networking between North America and South Asia, between public and private realms, and between men's worlds and women's worlds.

The study follows Adams and Ghose in characterizing this betweenness as 'bridgespace'-a virtual space between two cultures and two places, that is sustained by the use of various media and that supports the negotiation of cultural difference during the process of relocation. This concept provides a foundational idea for understanding the specificity of the Internet as it is employed in transnational lifestyles. Asian Indian immigrant women in their daily lives are cast in traditional roles and encouraged (or forced) to become the 'cultural torchbearers,' emblems of what constitutes authentic 'Indian-ness' in diaspora.

As Dasgupta and Dasgupta suggest: "It is the icon of the perfect Indian woman, preserving culture in the form of religion, language, dress, food, and childrearing, which upholds community integrity." The question becomes whether these women, the primary transmitters of religious and cultural traditions within the household and local associations (Skop forthcoming), also assume this role in the techno-social network constituting the Asian Indian-American transnational actor-network, known henceforth as the 'Indo-American bridgespace.'

While the role of women in shaping and guiding global migration processes has increased recently due to structural changes in the economies of certain receiving countries, research indicates that among skilled immigrant populations women often sacrifice both professional and personal support networks for the sake of their husbands' careers, and this sacrifice often accompanies incomplete prior knowledge of the consequences of moving abroad.

Compounding this sacrifice is the fact that even after women acquire paid employment, cultural ideologies about the doctrine of separate spheres define the household as women's primary responsibility and govern most family structures and community relationships, especially with regard to the division of household and community responsibilities. Thus, Asian Indian women become an embodiment of traditional power relations surviving the force of a new set of 'host society' power relations.

However, as Latour argues: "what sociologists mean by the 'power of society' is not society itself-that would be magical indeed-but some sort of summary for all the entities already mobilized to render asymmetries longer lasting" and the entities involved are those that permit the formation of networks that act, actor-networks. To understand social relations including inequality or 'asymmetry' one must "follow the actors in their weaving through things they have added to social skills so as to render more durable the constantly shifting interactions."

On this account the Internet is not an object but rather a realm of agency in which people become certain types of actors operating at certain scales and in certain ways. People's ability to act through the Internet, or rather through a range of different computer network applications (e-mail, chat rooms, blogs, ordinary websites, sites supporting shopping and money transfer, sites supporting the search for a marriage partner, etc.) helps define who and what they are, and therefore becomes part of their 'personal' identities.

Such identities cannot be determined in a sweeping way. Some are liberating and enabling while others are confining and constraining. For example, Samavedam, the wife of an H-1B visa holder from India, was hopeful about her prospects in the United States, but:

Instead, she discovered a world initially confined to their Stamford, Conn., apartment. As [her husband] Donepudi left at 7 a.m., Samavedam tried to stay asleep so she wouldn't have to face a day 'sitting idle,' as she describes it. She rattled off how she kept busy: CNN, an afternoon nap, elaborate homemade meals, several immigration websites.

However, Pessar suggests that through migration women are able to achieve a certain degree of power and autonomy within their households, and Waters (2002) finds a similar situation among the trailing 'astronaut wives' from Asia, who over time acknowledge new freedoms gained through the anonymity they experience in their new setting. These examples reveal the complexity of the 'power geometry' of transnational communications shaped by sex-based differences in power, as well as gendered differences in both the experience of migration and the construction of cultural meanings.

Likewise, Parrado and Flippen argue that gender status changes among migrants in the United States are varied across different elements of gender relations (power, labour and cathexis) and that this variation is due to destabilizing forces arising from residence in a foreign environment. Bridgespaces are the actor networks supporting transnationalism and permitting steady interaction over and above the swirling currents of international economic, cultural and political change.

As such, there may be many parallels among different bridgespaces associated with the different diasporas existing in the world today (Arab, African, Indian, Latin American, etc.) since they all exemplify what Latour calls "localizing the global." The language of "space" in bridgespace and the language of the "actor-network" arise from the same impulse to ask "where are the structural effects actually being produced" and to understand what permits various sites to be interrelated:

Viewed in this way, every academic office the anthropologist's den, the physiologist's lab, the lawyer's library, the social theorist's study, the architect's studio, the consultant's office begins to take, in the observer's account, a star-like shape with a center surrounded by many radiating lines with all sorts of tiny conduits leading to and fro.

Every website is obviously such a point of convergence-a node within a network-but the lead of actor-network theory must be followed in recognizing the network qualities not just of the websites and the Internet (obviously digitally encoded and built into infrastructure) but also the networked 'social relations' they support (defined by who knows and affects whom). In other words, transnationalism is all about techno-social networks, and this study simply attempts to extricate one type of transnationality-the Indo-American bridgespace from the rest.

During the last decade, scholars have contributed to rethinking transnational flows that do not conform to the classic pattern of international migration. Rejecting the prevailing view of immigrants as persons who had uprooted themselves from their old society to settle in a new land, Glick-Schiller (1999) called attention to the fact that a significant number of migrants who settled in a new destination maintained strong ties with their place of origin. She proposed transnationalism as the new paradigm for the study of migration across the borders of nation-states.

According to this theory, even though migrants invest "socially, economically, and politically in their new society, they may continue to participate in the daily life of the society from which they emigrated but did not abandon". Thus the study of international migration becomes an investigation of migration as a 'transnational process'-a pattern in which people, although they move across international borders and settle in a new state, maintain social connections with their country of origin. People literally live their lives across international borders, straddling two worlds.

Doing so requires the assembly of networks of human and non-human elements: airlines, pilots, passengers and mechanics, banks and money transfer businesses, immigration lawyers and INS employees, but also programmers, websites, webmasters and web browsers. As Featherstone suggests: "the flows of information, knowledge, money, commodities, people and images" erode the spatial distances that formerly separated and insulated immigrants from one another. Goldring (1996) calls this a postmodern project of 'blurring borders' and Rouse suggests that "We have all moved irrevocably into a new kind of social space."

The process by which "immigrants forge and sustain multi-stranded social relations that link together their societies of origin and settlement", challenges the classic definition of migration as a single and permanent change of residence, occurring only once. It also blends and dissolves simplistic definitions of the global and the local. Those who migrate and form social, professional and commercial relationships in a new state while simultaneously maintaining or establishing familial, economic, religious, political or social relations in the state from which they moved can be defined as 'transmigrants'.

These transmigrants are hybrid entities dependent on socio-technical connections not only to act but in order to be who they tentatively and provisionally are. As Latour argues: "Subjectivity is not a property of human souls but of the gathering itself-provided it lasts of course" and since the self does not map simply onto the local: "We are cognitively, morally, and philosophically in place, and we are simultaneously spread out through space". To understand the different types of connections that transmigrants maintain in the place(s) that they left behind, many scholars of transnational migration have begun to use the concept of 'transnational community', suggesting cultural bifocality, the capacity to see the world through different types of lenses.

While transnationalism theory frames the scope of various contemporary studies, there is considerable confusion in the new vocabulary. In fact it has been tempting to employ 'transnationalism' and 'transmigrant' as catch-all terms: if "travelling home occasionally qualifies a person as a "transmigrant" the entire field is subject to the charge of banality". Portes suggests that three features must be met for transnationalism to occur: (1) the number of people involved must be significant; (2) nearly instantaneous communication across space must be available; and (3) the cumulative character of the process must facilitate rapid displacement across long distances and make participation in communication and information technologies 'normative.'

With regard to the third element, like other normative relations, the norms vary among participants. There are multiple standards within an 'immigrant group' as it is internally fragmented according to religion, (sub)ethnicity, age, sex, sexual preference, disability, and so on. For the purposes of this chapter, it is most important to note that norms emerge for female online transnationals that are different from those of male online transnationals, as well as varying among transnational populations, and the norms in turn help networked agents to determine who and what they 'are' as gendered transnationals.

In the worst cases, legal and social constraints caused by the movement from one place to another can lead to a loss of status for women immigrants from actual or potential skilled work, with some becoming 'trailing wives' and jobless dependents of H-1B skilled workers, as the example of Samavedam from above demonstrates. Techno-social connectedness here simply repairs a rift created by other means. But in other cases the means of establishing mobility and communication permit women to control their situations and gratify desires for inward and outward discovery.

The meaning and value of online communication, in particular, remains unknown. Therefore, by way of a preliminary foray, this chapter focuses on the sex-based variations of one diasporic group in its engagement with a technologically supported transnational space. The implications of previous research on Internet usage patterns call for more subtle measures of difference, such as those that can be illuminated by studies of specific cultural groups and their particular gendered uses of the Internet as well as studies of the ways that particular cultural and gendered values and attitudes intersect with Internet use.

The subject of transnational feminine identity and the Internet is one such focus. Thus, in asking questions about the cultural attitudes and use of the Internet of Asian Indians we expect to find that the process of migration influences the roles that men and women take on in bridgespace. Indeed, the research presented in this chapter confirms aspects of the broad narrative of Internet usage differences between men and women, and argues for a more dynamic view of the role of national origin in virtual space.

The analysis links usage and access data to demographic, cultural and social conditions to assess the composition and behavioural patterns of Internet users among a sampled group. A web survey was employed which was designed to identify persons of Indian origin (both first- and second-generation) and their patterns of Internet use. Despite the limitations of a small study (just under 150 surveys) and a non-random sampling procedure the study appears to confirm that gender plays an important role in the construction of transnational identities.

The study employed a web survey form with 27 questions, including single choice, multiple choices, and rating scale-type questions, administered online between July 2004 and July 2005. A total of 164 surveys were collected, and of these 147 surveys (89.6%) were usable for all forms of statistical analysis while 17 surveys were unusable or of only limited utility. Virtually a perfect balance between male and female respondents was obtained, which facilitated the investigation of gender-based differences in use of the Internet.

Respondents were recruited through various e-mail lists that were identified by visiting the websites of Asian Indian community organizations and members were invited to assist the study by forwarding the invitation to other members. Subjects were contacted by e-mail through published lists of officers and/or members of organizations such as the Gujarati Samaj of Houston, the Maharashtra Mandal of Los Angeles, the Tri-State Telugu Association, the Malayalee Association of Northern California, and so on.

These local/regional sub-ethnic group organizations are quite numerous in the United States, and they serve as an excellent means of identifying Indian immigrants and their children. Such organizations can be expected to attract persons with a strong sense of (sub)ethnic identity, so the survey results are not entirely representative of the entire cross-section of Indian-Americans.

However, they provide a basis for comparison within the universe of persons associated with local/regional sub-ethnic group organizations and those who are sufficiently comfortable with the Internet to fill out an online survey. In other words, it is not possible to make claims about the precise percentage of the Indian population in the United States that is online, but we are comfortable making claims about the character of the environment-the bridgespace-that online activities of Indians are helping to construct, and how gender differences within the community of 'online Indians' correlate with variations in the construction of transnational identities. The subjects are those who are relatively more involved in building, maintaining and stabilizing transnational networks between the United States and India, which is appropriate for a study of participation in such a network.

The questions on the survey were designed to obtain information regarding the demographic characteristics of each subject including age, sex, ethnicity, occupation and education; communication and transportation activities including frequency of travel to India; time spent using the Internet; the range of websites regularly used; views on cultural change, cultural preservation and key traditions; and use levels associated with various media constitutive of the Asian Indian-American bridgespace-music, films and language. Based on these questions, it was possible to discern several distinct differences between men and women, and to assert that Asian Indian women employ the Internet in a way that is distinct from that of Asian Indian men.

GENDER AND THE INTERNET

While the study incorporated all equal number of men and women, this fact does not make it possible to conclude that Asian Indian men and women access the Internet in equal numbers. Nonetheless, the balance is suggestive because no special effort was made to maintain this kind of balance. Equality in access is typical of the American population as a whole, where women are just as likely as men to have access to the Internet.

This differs from the patterns seen in Asian settings such as China, Japan and India or among other racial/ethnic groups in the US such as African-Americans. However, it does not appear as though Asian Indian men and women access the Internet in the same places. While 65% of male subjects reported using the Internet at both work and home, fewer than 35% of women reported accessing the Internet both at work and at home. Instead, most women (46%) used the Internet at home.

This is despite the fact that few of the women in the survey are stay-at-home parents (10%) many are employed as technical workers (13%), professionals (11%), healthcare providers (6%), and academics (4%). What appears to be the case is that there are some gendered dynamics that compel women to avoid accessing the Internet at work. As another way to understand whether Asian Indian men and women have different access the Internet, survey respondents were asked: "What are your main sources of information about the world?" (They could choose up to three sources from the following list: newspaper, television, radio, magazine, Internet, discussions with friends and co-workers, discussions with family.)

Nearly 97% of all respondents chose the Internet as their main source of information. Television (72%) and newspapers (56%) were also selected as major sources of information, but the Internet was overwhelmingly the favored point for access. At the same time, both men and women were less likely to use friends (37%), magazines (24%), radio (22%), and family (20%) as one of their three main sources for information. So, the Internet is clearly a significant space in which Asian Indians engage with the world around them, and it appears as though both men and women in the sample do so without constraint, although they go online in different places.

ONLINE TIME USE

At the aggregate-level, men and women in the sample are spending similar amounts of time on the Internet, with more than 65% of sampled individuals online between one and three hours daily. A small number (13% of women and 16% of men) utilize the Internet for six or more hours a day. But there is no significant difference between them to suggest that gender plays a role in this 'quantity' aspect of Internet use. However, the picture is complicated when the sample is stratified by age so that women and men are each grouped into a '25 and above' category and an 'under 25' category.

In this case, a marked age-based division is found in Asian Indian women's access to the Internet, with women under 25 accessing the Internet on average 3.8 hours per day and those 25 and above accessing the Internet significantly less, on average 2.5 hours per day. This divide was identified through exploratory data analysis, and although women in their late-twenties hardly qualify as 'old' by subjective or intersubjective standards, the terms 'older' and 'younger' will be applied here simply to indicate this data-driven cut-off. In techno-social interactions the mid-twenties may well be an important divide because they mark the watershed between the pre- and post-Internet generations.

Removing US-born women from the sample does not significantly alter this ratio: 3.8 hours again for the younger women versus 2.4 hours for the older women. Therefore, the younger women use the Internet a striking 58 to 59% more than the older women, based on a cut-off around 25 years of age.

Between the younger and older men there is a less striking but similar difference, with the younger men averaging 3.7 hours online and the older men averaging 3.5 hours online. Therefore, the gender gap in quantity of online time takes opposite forms depending on the age groups under consideration: for younger Asian Indians in the United States it is the women who are the primary users of the Internet and for the older Asian Indians in the United States it is the men who are the primary Internet users. Such subtleties are lost when use data are aggregated across all age groups because the high and low values cancel out.

INTERNET APPLICATIONS

Men and women subjects do not use the services provided by the Internet in the same ways when the sample is divided into age/sex cohorts. Survey participants were asked a series of questions about the online services or 'applications' they use. Services listed were email, translation services, chat rooms, discussion forums, web logs (blogs), Indymedia, email-to-phone text messaging and online games; the frequencies they could choose were daily, weekly, monthly, semi-annually or never. Some interesting disparities emerged, as well as some similarities between men and women.

Perhaps most revealing is that, in general, the women use email less frequently, if at all, while the men are much more likely to send and receive email on a daily basis. Indeed, only 51% of female subjects utilized this online service daily. This compares with male subjects, the vast majority of whom (73%) utilize email on a daily basis. Many women check their email on a weekly (26%) or monthly basis (7%) instead, and some never use email (11%). In this case, there is little dissimilarity between age cohorts.

A contrasting result appears with regard to chat rooms. This interactive online service is utilized by a large number of both men (51%) and women (40%) on a daily basis, and indicates the ease with which this service has become available on the Internet. Yet when the sample is disaggregated so that women and men are each grouped into a '25 and above' category and an 'under 25' category, a marked dissimilarity of chat room use becomes clear as the results reveal a significant difference between younger and older cohorts.

Both younger women (63%) and younger men (80%) are frequent, daily users of chat rooms. Fewer older men (33%) use this online service on a daily basis, but they are nearly twice as likely as the older women (18%) to do so. Although the gender gap in quantity of online 'chat' time favors younger men, this is a service that younger women are using quite frequently as well, at the same time that many older women avoid chatting at all. When considering other online services, the men and women in the survey were not significantly different either in terms of access and frequency of use; indeed, the vast majority never used online text messaging, translation services or weblogs (blogs).

Fewer than 16% of survey participants utilized online services that convert e-mail messages into phone messages (although of course this is high compared to many other populations who have no need for this service); less than 25% of Asian Indians use online translation services (e.g. English to Hindi, English to Tamil, Tamil to English, etc.); and no more than 33% participate in blogs.

While both men and women post comments and replies to discussion forums, as well as play online games, they do not do so frequently. The vast majority participate in these online services on a monthly or semi-annual basis. In all cases, though, women are less likely to use any of these services than men (measured simply as use/don't use). How these numbers compare to other groups in the United States is unknown, but some studies suggest that men are generally more likely to use online services because their familiarity with the medium develops more rapidly, in part through on-the-job learning.

Finally, although a majority of Asian Indian men and women (60%) do not ever utilize independent online news sources such as indymedia.org, there are some who access this type of service, and gender plays a role in explaining the variation. According to the survey results, men (especially young men), are more likely to use independent news sources (31%) at least once a month, if not more frequently, than women (21%). This suggests not only a difference in the amount of time spent utilizing various Internet services, but also a difference in the types of services used and the ways in which individuals engage with this virtual space. Websites constitute a particular type of service that is diverse and well known, so the next section breaks down websites by type.

WEBSITE TYPE

Because of the interest here in the role of the Internet in creating an electronic community across time and space, a series of questions were asked related to (1) the number of websites users regularly visit that are intended mainly for people living in India, born in India, or of Indian ancestry ('bridgespace' sites): and (2) the types of websites the respondent regularly visits within this broader category. Gendered patterns of usage are apparent in this segment of the study and one of the most striking results is the significant difference between the frequency with which Asian Indian men and women self-identify as users of 'bridgespace' sites.

A total of 77% of men do so as opposed to only 51% of women. Women (especially older women) are considerably less likely than men to identify themselves as users of these websites. This difference is born out by the data on use of specific types of sites. What types of Asian Indian-related websites are men and women visiting and how often are they visiting them? A series of frequency questions were employed (daily, weekly, monthly, semi-yearly and never) about particular types of Asian Indian-related websites the subjects had visited (including those geared towards Asian Indian immigrants, news, sports, popular culture, literature, politics, history, matrimonial services, shopping, students, religion and other).

The purpose of these questions was to gain a sense of the various ways in which Asian Indian Internet users are engaging the Internet to keep connected and create new ties across bridgespace and indirectly to assess their contribution to forming this virtual space as networked actors. Various gendered patterns are evident at the level of site-type usage. A significant majority of men (75%) visit websites with news from India on a daily basis. This compares with a much smaller number of women (36%) who frequent these Indian news sites everyday.

The men connect to both national and regional news sites, and utilize the Internet to keep up with daily events and even the weather in India. As a result, the bridgespace created by this particular kind of activity pattern is highly gendered, which in turn suggests that it either excludes women or else women do not receive the same gratifications from entering what is equated with the 'public' world covered by the news-a world from which they have previously been excluded. Keeping up with sports is also associated with male gratifications and this resonates in men's use of the Internet.

A total of 42% of male respondents checked out sports-related websites from India every day. Another 40% visited Indian sports websites on a weekly, monthly or semi-annual basis for a total of 82%. However, women hardly ever used these websites, with only 40% visiting sports-related websites at any point during the year and a modest 6% visiting such sites on a daily basis. Such divergences reify gender roles that are prevalent in society at large. Another male-dominated segment of bridgespace is associated with politics in India.

Some 52% of male respondents visited sites supporting various Indian political parties at some point during the year compared with only 28% of the women. This involvement of half of the male population and a quarter of the female population at least as spectators of Indian politics suggests that claims the Internet does not serve a political purpose for immigrant populations may need to be reconsidered. Frequent visitors to such sites may be seen as politicized even if they do not build or frequent websites designed for minority political mobilization in the United States.

Websites are clearly an important medium whereby men, including both old and young men, maintain their active connections to Indian news, sports and politics. Consequently they indicate a virtual, bridging space in which gendered transnational competences and knowledges are constructed. Survey results suggest two other areas of Asian-Indian bridgespace dominated by men. The first are sites supporting the transfer of money to India. Of male respondents, 42% used these types of websites on a regular basis throughout the year while only 26% of female respondents transferred money abroad in this way.

It is unclear from the survey where these monies are going (whether to individual investments or remittances to family members), but it is clear that men (especially older men) are significantly more likely to engage in online money-transfer activity than women. The second are matrimonial websites. Men appropriate Internet technology to attempt to craft new family ties in bridgespace; marriages are arranged across great distances in physical space with the aid of matrimonial websites that cater to Asian Indians abroad.

Although Asian Indian matrimonial websites are not as frequently used as many other types of Asian Indian websites, 34% of male survey respondents reported visiting such sites at some point during the year. Only than 16% of female survey respondents visit matrimonial websites at any time-a puzzling difference given that the matrimonial sites would seem to require an equal number of male and female users in order to function. The paradox is resolved by considering the Indian men's more active role in seeking wives whether as a prospective groom or as a brother or father of a prospective bride.

A woman does not have to use the Internet to be advertised on the Internet since her male relatives may take on this task for her (or from a different perspective, take the task from her). Furthermore, the preponderance of men using such sites suggests a pattern of marriage-based immigration where single men in the United States establish a foothold then obtain wives from India so that at this end of the matrimonial chain in fact there are more men involved. However, men did not dominate all areas of bridgespace. Women led in the use of sites selling specialty items (saris, spices, books, food, videos, songs, etc.) with 59% as opposed to 49% of men using such sites at least yearly.

More strikingly, five times as many women as men use these sites on a weekly basis. Women are also more likely to use sites relating to traditional Indian culture (festivals, carnatic music, and so on). This difference is slight, with 83% of the women visiting these sites as opposed to 76% of the men, but at the monthly frequency, women are much more likely to use such sites (28% as opposed to 17% of the men).

Combining these observations, a pattern can be envisioned in which women in the household shop online about once a week and enrich their personal or familial ties to traditional cultural resources (narrowly defined as traditional Indian goods and commodities, traditional music and information about festivals) while men maintain a sense of current events and private affairs in India through news, information, sports, politics, monetary transfer and marriage planning.

This pattern suggests that both women and men in diasporic and transnational communities play the role of 'cultural torchbearer,' but what is meant or implied by 'culture' differs on the basis of gender. The research indicates that Asian Indians in the United States (first and second generation) maintain a gendered social space of online interaction. This space is further differentiated by age. In the most abstract sense, it appears that the male and female sides of bridgespace have a different relation to time or rather temporality-the social construction of time.

Men are involved with aspects of Indian culture that change or go through episodes such sports competitions and elections while women are involved more in backward looking, past-sustaining cultural preservation activities. However, it should be noted that the younger women (under 25) spend the most time online of any of the respondents but do not appear to spend much of that online time actually engaging with what we are calling bridgespace. Rather, it appears they are more interested in Internet activities that lack an ethnic or nationalist dimension. They are perhaps less anxious than others to maintain their family's or their own Indianness.

For this reason, the women's 'cultural torchbearer' role indicated by previous research and by the women's small lead in accessing traditional cultural and commodities online is not a role they seem to take on with great alacrity. Cyberspace may even permit young women in their late teens and early twenties to avoid bearing the torches of Indian culture since their extra hours spent online are not dominated by the use of Indian-oriented websites.

In contrast, female subjects 25 years of age and older are noticeably inhibited in their use of the Internet. These women may be excluded from the Internet by technical inability or a spatially-restricted and 'privatized' self-image. But it is more likely that older women are too busy in 'real' space, acting out their role as cultural torchbearers in everyday interactions within the home and community rather than using the Internet to engage in Indian-related websites, replace lost social ties and/or to create new social support networks.

As social reproducers who must manage a household and a career, as well as keep track of and/or contribute to the everyday affairs of the immigrant community, older women may simply not have enough time or desire to engage in Indo-American bridgespace. Thus, it would appear that gender roles and national identity construction are manifested differently by the under 25 group of women and the 25 and above group. Setting aside these differences, the involvement of bridgespace in the lives of all of the study participants can be seen.

These, it should be recalled, were selected (on a non-random basis) not through their frequent use of the Internet but rather through their involvement in local/regional sub-ethnic group organizations. This is an in-place form of social organization that was used to obtain the contact information for an initial sample that was subsequently expanded through a snowball technique.

Therefore, an unusually high level of involvement in ethnic activities through physical gathering is the primary way in which the subjects are non-representative of first and second generation immigrants from India. Nonetheless, it was found that about 90% used the Internet to follow news from

India; roughly 85% visited websites relating to popular Indian music, movies or television shows; and more than half visited sites relating to Indian traditional culture, history, music and literature. In these capacities bridgespace appears to be fundamental to Indo-American transnational networks.

It has been argued that bridgespace sites are not isolated 'things' or 'texts'; rather, they are nodes in a network of websites, webmasters, programmers, computers, data transmission links, codes, protocols, merchants, activists, journalists and 'ordinary' web surfers sustaining a transnational, gendered sense of identity. That the network reaches between continents is not, perhaps, as surprising as the fact that it is bound up in identity formation in a way analogous to a physical place where men and women enter and occupy the place differently.

It appears as though Indo-American bridgespace has a male-dominated character at this point in time. But also important is the observation that men and women using this bridgespace are interacting in it and that such interaction supports self-definition on multiple axes of identity including gender, age and nationality. The study provides only a snapshot of the uses and users of Indo-American bridgespace. Gender construction among migrant populations is not simple and linear but rather a complex form of cultural accommodation that interacts with multiple physical, virtual and social contexts.

Techno-social contexts like the one studied here reflect not only the structural environment that immigrants face in the United States but also the cultural standards imposed by diasporic or transnational communities. They are facets of the nearly instantaneous and persistent communications across transnational space and accordingly evoke the term 'globalization', but as such should not be read as a simple technological assemblage reaching through space, lifeless mechanisms simply connecting places, or worse yet technological apparatuses that cause things to happen in the 'social sphere.'

Bridgespaces are diverse and heterogeneous; the opposite of naive models of technology-driven globalization that presume that homogenization must arise from participation in large-scale flows. Instead, they show how technology becomes social and vice versa as people incorporate heterogeneous elements into their constructions of individual and collective identities. It suggests ways that mediated interactions are bound into the bundle of ties that hold people to places (however far apart) and to each other (however divided they may be by various asymmetries of power and knowledge). Accordingly, a few emerging dimensions of social space have been charted.

7

The Ethics of Women on the Net

E-mail is the story behind the story in the age of global autobiography. It is a story that is less easy to tell, partly because it is simply so much bulkier. For the ten pages in which Bray-Crawford explains her visions for preserving indigenous Pacific culture, there were pages more of e-mails about "where the discussion or people themselves are coming from." For the book as a whole, there were over 2,000 messages on a busy listserve. This pattern must be repeated for so many of the published auto/biographies, or even legal, educational, and medical testimonies of today.

Ruth Picardie's confessional columns in The Observer magazine about getting breast cancer were paralleled with daily e-mails to friends in a style just as grumpy and witty. The Women's Court at the Permanent Arab Court to Resist Violence Against Women solicits testimonies through e-mail on its website. At the International Auto/Biography Association conference in Vancouver in 2000, Helen Buss, Suzanne Bunkers, and Brenda Daly read aloud their e-mail exchanges as theorists as well as writers of autobiography.

Autobiography may break many of the rules of art, but it is a positively obedient child compared to the id-like spread of writerly desire and demand in electronic letters. Yet e-mail is also the genre that can most literally force us to rethink the very adult questions of the politics of life writing in a time of globalization. The essential argument I wish to make is that e-mail is a symptomatic form of life writing in the context of a network society. It is a symptom of a new kind of everyday mediation, in both regressive and progressive forms.

You probably know this yourself, as an academic reader called constantly into written relationships, sometimes swamped by them, and often tempted into them as a means to write for a more present and satisfying audience than the general public of a one-day-to-be-finished book. Yet it is perhaps because e-mail is so symptomatic, so omnipresent and half-articulate, that it has not been analyzed in literary circles as much as autobiography and biography, which have received so much attention as genres of our age. But as my opening story shows, e-mails often form the white of the egg within which the autobiographical yolk is suspended: networks of writerly and political relations nurturing the newborn voice of an individual or group. They are the distracting babble of multiple internal monologues, but they are also the group of friends in the night preparing the court case.

But unlike testimony, e-mail itself is not designed for the court. The second part of my argument is that e-mail, like all letters, is best understood in terms of an ethics of care, not an ethics of justice. The point of this is not to say that there is anything inherently nice, cuddly, virtuous, or politically correct about the form: a second's reflection on your own experience will confirm that letter writing is of all forms most colored by its context-a "protogenre," as Charles Bazerman has astutely described it.

What the framework of an ethics of care does allow, however, is a refreshing approach to the essential themes that an analysis of life writing must consider: truth and art, identity and relationship, witnessing and healing, recovery and revenge. It does this by beginning from the premise of interdependence rather than autonomy. This extends the usual thinking about the ethics of life writing as a matter of justice. It lets us struggle directly with the relational dimension of life writing. This is why I have chosen to think about e-mail through the case of a feminist group's members talking to each other, where the politics of relationship were always in view.

GLOBALIZING RELATIONSHIPS

Women on the Net (WoN) was a group of over one hundred women and men activists, academics, information technology people, and Non Governmental Organization employees brought together by the Society for International Development in 1997. They were funded by the United Nations Educational, Scientific and Cultural Organization to meet, establish a listserve, and then reunite physically a year later at a conference on Gender and Globalization at the University of California at Berkeley. Wendy Harcourt, Director of Programs for the Society for International Development and the group's coordinator, explains the aims of the discussion:

- First, to encourage women, particularly in the South and in marginal groups in the North (and Central and East Europe), to use the Internet more easily as their space, thereby empowering women to use technology as a political tool.
- Second, to open up and contribute to the new culture that was being set up on the Internet from a gender perspective at once local and global.
- Third, to bring together individual women and men working from different institutional bases to explore a transnational women's movement agenda in response to and shaping evolving telecommunication policies.
- And fourth, to create a resource base which could be tapped into by different women's groups in navigating the Internet ("Cyborg" 1).

This group interests me as a bunch of academics and activists, northerners and southerners, easterners and westerners trying to relate to each other-historic divisions whose electronic reconciliation was implicitly hoped for in the aim of creating a "transnational women's movement agenda." If only I had the space to introduce all of them! The people mentioned here are chosen due to their contribution to the book. There was Alice Mastrangelo Gittler, with the New York International Women's Tribune Center that broke communications history in reporting from the Beijing UN women's conference in 1995, until she chose to work at home with her small son "and test the limits of global telecommuting." Wendy Harcourt, an Australian in Rome, and committed personal e-mailer. Lourdes Arizpe, cultural anthropologist from Mexico and a maverick intellectual in UNESCO's cultural program at the time.

There was Arturo Escobar, Professor of Anthropology at the University of Massachusetts, who works on Latin American ecoactivism; Gillian Youngs, at the Centre for Mass Communication in Leicester; and Fatma Alloo, founder of the Tanzania Media Women's Association and now webbing up community organizations who do everything from sex education to swapping traditional Zanzibari women's cloth designs. Laura Agustin, a popular educator, student of migration, and researcher, works with women sex workers.

There was Marisa Belausteguigoitia Rius, doing her Phd at Berkeley in Ethnic Studies and anticipating welcoming the whole bunch there at the conference, although worrying whether the academics would be friendly to all these people who work in the real world. And Kekula Bray-Crawford, who I have already quoted, dreaming of an archipelago of indigenous cyberculture in the liquid continent of cyberspace. This was not then a group of friends, or even of close colleagues, but professionals brought together by social policy makers with public money and a political agenda.

They were not writing privately to each other, but taking part in the cloister of a listserve. Yet there are two aspects that I find particularly interesting about this group from the point of view of e-mail as a form of life writing. The first is that although in no sense literary, the project was explicitly conceived of as "an experiment in the politics of communication". And the second is that they brought with them feminist perspectives that suggested that the individual pursuit of right relationship could be, indeed should be, and intimately related to social movements for global development. The opening e-mail, sent by Marisa Belausteguigoitia Rius, suggests both concerns in her acutely deconstructive style:

I am thinking of concentrating on: place-consciousness, the socialized conception of place and overall the political use of global/local, space/place con-fusions, parallel to a careful, microscopic analysis of the demands for going 'back into place'. I think that focusing this from a complex academic angle and also from our activist and institutional experience we will 're-conciliate' the visions of academia, activism and government institutions in the necessity of grounding our analysis and projects 'from below'.

This may lead us to frame the analysis 'creating transformative spaces for alternative futures'. And through this, also help us to locate a hyphen, a mark (scar?) in this alternative (alter-native) and figure out what is 'other' (alter) and what is native (place-bound).

Challenging the way that globalization has undermined local cultures, Rius's pun on "alter-native" figures the hope that it can be made to accommodate "native" interests. This establishes the group's political stance towards the internet. Rather than an escape into a utopian cyberspace where all difference will be erased along with bodies, nations, wars, and arguably, political resistance, networking must be "grounded" in the material contexts of people's use and abuse of information technology.

The interesting thing here is that "place-consciousness" is also proposed as a theme that can "re-conciliate" academic, activist, and institutional visions. It is the common difference that will allow the "experiment in communication." But Rius's location of a hyphen in an "alter-native" globalization was ironically too linguistic and not place bound enough. Although the academics were quite at ease with using electronic communication to problematize communication, the activists pushed for a more literal "situating" of perspectives.

As Harcourt describes, "there seemed to be a danger of spinning off into abstractions that did not root the group's work clearly enough in the stated aim to empower women working in the South. There was considerable anxiety about discussing issues as activists and women of color in an academic setting". Pi Villuvea, a technician working in Isis International-Manila, a feminist resource center with a new Information Technology base, pointed out:

'Mediating Borders' is a good metaphor for the work we are doing. But 'we' are also different from one another. 'We' have different points of reference. The members and collaborators of WoN are women working in women's resource and information centres ... in international agencies ... in academia, in Internet Service Providers (ISPs). Then there are also the men whose role in an initiative called 'Women on the Net' is presumed but not necessarily clear to everyone. (I don't mean the individual men who are already part of WoN, but men as a group. I raise this query in part because it is not clear to me how WoN will and should respond if other men would like to join the network.)

We are also mediating borders inside WoN. Take, for example, some of the words used to frame the proposed Berkeley discussion:

Ventriloquism, patriarchal cyberdiscourses. Even the word cyborg, the name of our mailing list.... These are words not normally used by individual women and women's groups I work with. (Harcourt, "Cyborg" 6)

And not necessarily the words that everyone in the group worked with. Bray-Crawford forwarded an e-mail of Arturo Escobar's to her partner asking for "translation," and Laura Agustin asked "I hope we are not dreaming about a utopian 'unity'", while Lis Brown, working for the United Nations said:

I agree very much with [Pi] about how to focus the discussion. We work at different levels, and while being interested in theoretical debates, my main concern is now to make the link with the practical day to day lives and realities of women, some of whom don't even know yet that the Internet exists ... how to make the Internet useful (and accessible of course) for women in remote urban or rural areas of developing countries, and how they can make optimal use of the medium in support of their process of (economic) empowerment.

The familiar question of identity now challenged the abilities of "place" to function as mediator. But it was here in these old debates between academia and activism, the privileged and the less privileged, that e-mail proved both focus of conflict and potential resource. Promising intimacy, it facilitated the admission of alienation. But to the same degree, it broke the alienation of academic and public statement. Harcourt intercepted Bray-Crawford's request for translation by suggesting that:

> Your warmth and energy comes across the cyberwaves and opens out ... the struggle you and other indigenous people are going through in quite another way from me reading about it in books and journals. I feel I can support and be with you in some way. For me this is about another way of being or here and now that is for me very politically feminist as I reach out to you as a woman doing this and we are finding ways to support each other. The references Gillian and Arturo make to feminist literature, ecologist thinking and philosophy in fact celebrate much of what you are doing, and that for me is what is so important in terms of connecting and making the effort to understand how we can work together in our different places.

Harcourt's e-mail began to "place" the discussion emotionally as well as materially, and Bray-Crawford wrote back enthusiastically. Laura Agustin followed this by pointing out that the debate over "abstract thinking" in the group reflected educational histories, and "that's where we have to tolerate and accept differences". As one of the academics, Gillian Youngs responded that she "would feel very sad if anyone thought that my comments identify me as someone locked in a world of academic non-communication." The "confession" that followed, however, was of being emotional about ideas:

> The incredible exchanges about language in the last few days moved me intellectually as well as emotionally and I suppose that's a confession I can make here. I find it hard to separate my practical desires and imaginings from my intellectual and emotional ones, I have all my life and that's why academic life and its different dimensions including teaching and educational teamwork as well as thinking, sharing ideas and writing, is comfortable for me. There are important ways that I feel at home in it. It is not an abstract realm to me, it is very practical in so many ways.

In these e-mails, the question of academic abstraction intriguingly displaces that of electronic virtuality, in which it is merely the physical body that is obscured. The extraordinarily large "socio-emotional" element that so many have remarked in e-mail, the product of its interactive immediacy, here allows the experience of academic life to become visible.

In the context of a group that was attempting to mediate global differences in an academic setting, this kind of life writing was a key to creating the trust that could genuinely mediate borders as the meeting in Berkeley drew near. Analysts like Sherry Turkle have suggested that textual virtuality is so popular precisely because people can conceal their physical status. It is true that for the activists, e-mail appeared to hold off "the symbolism of power embedded in face-to-face communication," which may be a reason for e-mail's popularity with "women, and other oppressed groups of society" and "lower-status workers in company-based networks".

But Women on the Net were equally concerned to establish new forms of authenticity and responsibility online. Marisa Rius, for example, suggested that the "circulation in cyberspace of information without a body" could be "the same old story of kidnapping others' voices or reproducing others' concerns, disregarding politics of place-based experiences". Wendy Harcourt suggested that e-mail's "personal and even poetic" language is an attempt "to help people gain a sense of who 'I am really' beyond the typing on the screen". These concerns with trust and reliability are apparently far more typical of net-users than many postmodern celebrations of virtuality would suggest.

The group's development politics however made "situating" oneself a response to globalization. Standpoint theory has been influential in encouraging "personal narrative" in academia, as well as the validation of testimony in human rights activism. In e-mail's less public version of these personal turns, the emotional risks are raised, for individual relationships are more obviously at stake. At the same time, in a group like this one, emotional exchange is acknowledged as a crucial aspect of "place-consciousness."

IDENTITY, DIFFERENCE, AND FEMINIST LETTERS

What can we learn from this "experiment in the politics of communication" for the question of "auto/biography in a global age"? First, just how central communication is in a "network" society. The economic as well as political price of being "switched off" from the network is constantly in the minds of the development workers. E-mail has proven to be the most popular form of computer use, and significantly, the form that has most excited activists in non-western countries.

On one level, this is simply because it is the cheapest, easiest form of internet communication (cheaper than listserves in fact), and thus a public relations tool fast becoming as important as radio, television, or print. But it also registers subtler claims for access to the new public spheres of virtual community. E-mail, like our "multi-faceted, virtual culture is not a fantasy, it is a material force because it informs, and enforces, powerful economic decisions at every moment in the life of the network".

This interdependence of political representation on and offline is signaled directly by the fact that the success of Women on the Net's listserve, conference presentation, and book secured further funding for IT training in the Southern women's projects, as well as a Rockefeller grant to continue a research group on "place-consciousness." In 1999 members of the group met in Zanzibar to discuss the potential of "the virtual world" to communicate across traditional divides of gender, class, culture and nation. Women who had never seen a computer before are now meeting virtually and face to face to tackle themes such as domestic violence, social justice, and sex education (Harcourt, "World Wide Women").

More symbolic is that the group nurtured the kind of "auto/biography" that so much of this conference celebrates. Alice Mastrangelo Gittler helped disseminate the extraordinary testimonies of women at the Beijing Women's conference in 1995. Arturo Escobar writes of Amazon indigenous activist testimonio and petitions on the web. Wendy Harcourt writes online of her reaction to the heightened Israeli-Palestinian conflict, as someone of Jewish heritage ("SID-WID"). Fatma Alloo networked with women organizing a conference in Mumbai in 2003 on Empowering Women through Information and Knowledge: From Oral Traditions to ICT.

Several spoke at the Berkeley conference with a personal appeal, and it is apt that this chapter itself has come out of generous e-mails from Wendy Harcourt. Life writing and life story appear here as a continuum of relational forms responding to global networks, going from private e-mail to listserves to personally presented testimonies to published memoirs. In this light, we can appreciate further the significance of Women on the Net as a writing as well as political experiment.

The group's coherence as a community was facilitated by e-mail's distinctive combination of abstraction and affect, undermining old binaries of emotion and thought that were institutionalized (at least in fantasy) as professional divisions between academics and activists, westerners and southerners. Less overt, but also important to e-mail's mediating function, was its role as outlet for everyone in the group as professional writers. The computer's muddling of professional and personal spaces facilitates e-mail as an "off-duty" writing, replacing not so much the letter as the phone call.

Although e-mail's deceptive intimacy often causes professional lapses and relationship blow-ups, "soft dialogue" was nurtured as part of a discourse about communication. In this respect, Women on the Net join a long history of feminists using letters to explore women's-and feminist-identity (Jolly). This springs from the genre's "feminine" association. Readdressing love letters and family missives to other women in novels like the Three Marias' rewrite of The Portuguese Letters, Alice Walker's The Color Purple, or academic editions of women's letters, the epistolary has asserted women's headily romantic identification as confidantes.

But as the women's movement diversified throughout the 1980s, the letter motif repeatedly flips into the discovery of internal differences. Love letters turn into "open letters," such as Audre Lorde's confrontation with Mary Daly over her representation of black women in Gynecology. Anxious epistolary essays proliferate, women's letters pages debate furiously. It is for this reason that Mary Jacobus in 1986 mooted the metaphor of "correspondence" as focusing the movement's problem: we have to find a way to recognize difference and sameness simultaneously.

Letter writing, Jacobus felt, was the best genre for improving "the structure of feminist exchange" itself, because it is premised on a reader's right to reply, the unfinished nature of representation, and most of all, on the "shifting and composite differences which at once make up and discompose readerly identity". Women on the Net reflects the more sophisticated thinking about identity as coalition that characterizes the women's movement today; for example, in the differentiating term of "place" and the topic of "mediating borders" as the group's conference presentation. Gillian Youngs suggests there are interesting parallels "between the concrete connective qualities of the Net and the present open and self-conscious goals of feminist politics".

Fatma Alloo, writing from "the steaming island of Zanzibar," affirmed that "my most innovative and stimulating work have been as a result of my interaction with academicians on the one hand and the grounded community on the other hand. When I say academicians I mean intellectuals who have NOT remained in ivory towers of theories that never play a part in mobilizing communities or impacting change." She concludes with a metaphorical appeal to alliance across these differences:

> Now my dears I have spoken of my country and analysed it as I see it. I am on the cyborg. What does this make me? A journalist, an IT freak? An intellectual? a feminist?-you got it! We have to move out of compartmentalization and incorporate a movement with a pulse and feel the ripples and if we are to be the delicatessen so be it!

CARE ETHICS, E-MAIL, AND CITIZENSHIP

Many have celebrated the virtual communities of the internet as a realization of Jurgen Habermas's vision of democracy regenerated through egalitarian dialogue, a return to the conditions of an emerging civil society in the eighteenth century Enlightenment (Rheingold). Certainly Women on the Net answers to "the Republic of Letters" at the time, described by Annie Barnes as grounded on a "conscious notion of international intellectual cooperation" resulting not in "the creation of a commission or an institute, but in the founding of an ideal state".

Although it is tempting to interpret today's mass cultivation of personal correspondences as a new Enlightenment, I propose that such theories depend too much on fantasies of reason and equality. E-mail is ambiguous, volatile, and deceptive even in such carefully managed groups as this one. But Women on the Net instruct us in its self-consciousness about these dimensions of dialogue. Although much of the discussion sprang from the problem of access, it was the emotional exchange that proved most interesting and important in creating community.

Here an ethic of care supplies the missing term. Care begins from the premise of interdependence; some philosophers even say inequality-where one is more dependent than the other, like parents and children. The idea is that right relationship is defined by a particular response to another's need, not by conformity to a generalized and universal law of justice; not to treat everyone fairly (even if it hurts them), but to make sure that no one is hurt. This ethic dreams of and reasons about liberation through rather than despite emotional relationship. Feminist philosophers have identified this as a typical source of women's moral reasoning (Held).

In lots of ways autobiography has been produced and consumed under the sign of equality and autonomy, no matter how relational its origin and content. Auto/biographical studies is full of such examples: Sidonie Smith's eloquent plenary at the "Life Writing and the Generations" conference at La Trobe University in 2002, for example, on the personal narratives of Korean comfort women told for the cause of "women's rights as human rights." But even these collective forms of testimony, or the more subtle forms of relational autobiography like J. M.

Coetzee's memoir celebrated by David Parker, for instance, do not quite enact the "global age" in the way that the more directly dialogic form of the letter does.

E-mail can remind us that life writing may "repair the social fabric" best by preserving, transforming, and nurturing individual relationships. The unfinished, inchoate nature of e-mail, the particularity of its inspiration, even its domestication of professional or authorial identity, here may be the point. And the endless question of access, however tedious, represents the everyday philosophical work of confronting and mediating otherness. Here we see debates over impersonation on the net in quite a different light. The issue is not a general truth but the truth of the relationship, not a question of matching real to virtual, but the integrity of response in either medium.

Marisa Rius's worry over "ventriloquism," for example, was not about disguise per se, but whether e-mail would take the form of "active circulation of our voice through others' cyberspace" or "passive impersonation of others' concerns". In displacing the question "is it true" with "does it nurture?" we can perhaps begin to solve the conundrum posed by Paul John Eakin in his discussion of the ethics of life writing. Eakin sets out the problem as a clash of interests between the right to privacy, not only of information but of the more intangible "personality," and the right to free speech.

An ethics of care shows this contradiction to be founded on a conception of individuality as a property in competition with other properties, although, as Eakin shows so well, identity itself is inherently relational. Rather than adjudicating whose life belongs to whom within a law premised on the assumption of violent competition, an ethics of care proposes the everyday weighing up of potentially compatible needs. An example comes again from Kekula Bray-Crawford. She suggests that the solution to indigenous Pacific culture's lack of intellectual property rights is "indigenal mapping"-the creation of internet communities by Pacific islanders.

This of course is the heroic version. How does the community of dialogue deal with conflict and disappointment?

Just as relationships of care are intensified in letters, so they can amplify the special painfulness of care's failure, as many feminists would attest. And how does an ethic of care measure up to the much more typical ethos (it is hardly an ethic) of the network society: "a culture of the ephemeral, a culture of each strategic decision, a patchwork of experiences and interests, rather than a charter of rights and obligations"? We may rightly fear the "privatisation of sociability" that probably describes most e-mail exchanges, buzzed out through the working day in blips of "I'm bored, entertain me."

The answer can only be modest. Sociologists such as Manuel Castells, and Michael Hardt and Antonio Negri view today's social movements as progressive responses to global networks. Mimicking the flows and decentered organization of financial politics, they refuse the temptations of postmodern fundamentalism. Women on the Net exemplify this embryonic civil society talking back. E-mail is then not simply the nurturing white around the yolk of a more public form of testimony, but the semi-private, semi-public genre of an age of multiple and constantly shifting privates and publics.

For gender activists this holds obvious opportunities in dislodging the traditional masculine color of the public. More generally it lets us think about expanding private principles of care into realms traditionally reserved for the public law of justice. This is a huge political challenge, even in the blessed imaginaries of activist listserves. But I want to end by considering one sign of political recognition: the current lobby for the "Right to Communicate," spearheaded by UNESCO.

This is recognized by many governments as a fundamental human right, though it has yet to be ratified internationally. Fascinatingly, it goes beyond traditional "freedoms" of opinion, expression, information, and the press, to include "the notion of universal access to information and communication technologies ... as both a technical and a social infrastructure; the right to public access; and public participation in both the means of communication and towards policymaking".

Potential criteria for care ethics are also visible in its recognition of linguistic rights and the sustenance of indigenous languages and culture. Groups like Communication Rights for the Information Society, and the Global Community Network, who are currently lobbying for gender awareness, could be even more promising for attention to care as well as justice.

E-mail has none of the ethical clarity of testimony as a form of "auto/biography" in a global age. But by making relationships with others far away or in very different situations from ourselves apparently so easy, it raises equally immediate ethical questions. These are questions we no doubt all experience personally, as we re-enter the neon twilight of academic e-mail life.

AGE AND GENDER IN SOAP OPERA CYBERFANDOM

"Virtual" ethnographic investigation of soap opera "cyberfan" discussion groups refutes claims of resistive public space, finding that industry infiltration, "netiquette," and other factors construct these Internet forums as sites of "escape" rather than politics. Moreover, "polyvalent" readings tend to reproduce the demographics strategy of advertisers-a strategy which flatters young female audiences at the expense of their older counterparts.

Critical/cultural media scholars debate the extent to which audiences interpret and use hegemonic texts in resistive ways. Political economists examine the issue macroscopically, arguing that the structures, processes, and commercial imperatives of capitalist media institutions determine a range of available content, restrict access and ownership and, inevitably, reproduce hegemonies that help to maintain unequal power relations.

Many cultural studies scholars shift the focus to the microscopic, localized consumption of media audiences, with some contending that a repertoire of appropriative strategies regularly confounds these forces of domination, particularly in the hands of those whose marginal status cultivates interpretive ingenuity. Some scrutinize fan subcultures, arguing that collective audience engagement facilitates resistive activity. Such claims emanate from ethnographic audience study, generally via focus groups, interviews, and observation.

In an effort to spearhead a unifying direction for critical/cultural media studies, a "multiperspectival" approach blending analyses of production, text, and consumption has been recommended. While it is difficult to thoroughly dissect all three levels in a single, small-scale effort, attempts have been made to intertwine two levels in one analysis or multiple levels in succeeding investigations. Gender-related work has been in the forefront of this effort.

Examples include O'Brien's (1996) exploration of the texts and historical and institutional contexts of Disney animated features and Livingstone and Liebes' textual consideration of motherhood on American soaps as informed by their earlier audience inquiries. As Livingstone and Liebes note, "audience research is in danger of replacing textual analysis by studies of audience response without asking what viewers are responding to." Condit concurs and adds that ignoring the "presumed intents of sources" can exacerbate this blind spot.

This chapter examines soap opera "cyberfandom"-computer-mediated communication (CMC) and culture in cyberspace discussion groups devoted to television serials-to assess the ways in which these forums welcome and/or inhibit the voices of traditionally marginalized viewers. The study was conducted through "virtual" ethnography entailing participant observation by this researcher over a four year period in discussion groups on Usenet and information services such as CompuServe and America Online (AOL).

This chapter will endeavor to inter-relate analyses of the contextual/institutional imperatives of soap opera production with the interactions and interpretations of cyberfans and the conditions and structures under which these interactions occur. Ultimately, the investigation refutes claims of resistive public space, finding that industry infiltration, "netiquette," and other factors construct these thrums as sites of "escape" rather than "politics." Moreover, matters significant to older women and minorities are slighted, reproducing the "divide and flatter" demographics strategy of the advertisers and their media cohorts.

CYBERSPACE AND EMPOWERMENT

"There is no race. There are no genders. There is no age. There are no infirmities. There are only minds. Is it Utopia? No, it's the Internet." So posits a 1996 commercial for MCI. In fact, the information superhighway, with its numerous web sites, online services, and discussion groups, has been characterized by some as a panacea providing for potentially empowering and open exchanges of information and opinion and by others as another communication technology to be commodified by "the powers that be" and used to protect and extend their vested interests. Interrogate the Internet, an interdisciplinary group examining the implications of cyberspace, hesitates to automatically equate information with emancipation.

They argue that beyond the "structural barriers that keep many voices from being heard," there is a tendency for Usenet newsgroups and similar forums to "reproduce and reinforce" existing hegemonies through a "pastiche in which new media refer to old, and vice versa". They also maintain that while cyberspace travelers are not "collections of cultural dopes," resistance should not be merely assumed but, rather, "understood as a function of reflexivity and communication".

In spite of these reasonable warnings, many scholars studying CMC in discussion groups do equate power with free speech and free speech with lack of government regulation, ignoring the likely reproduction of hegemonic values imported from the larger culture. For example, MacKinnon (1995) content analyzes newsgroup postings for indicators of deference to a single power such as a newsgroup moderator or author of "netiquette" guidelines as evidence of a governmental "Leviathan" encroaching upon Usenet as if such entities were the only sort of barrier to potentially subversive discourse.

While these researchers gloss over finer issues of cultural hegemony and opposition, those who have studied the collective activities of soap opera fans have not. The social, collaborative contexts of soap opera reception and interpretation have been theorized for more than a decade, since a trend toward public viewing was observed. More recently, Brown studied soap opera fan "friendship networks" in which oral "gossip" allows women to "negotiate their positions in society" and derive pleasure through the construction of collective meanings and insights which acknowledge their subordinated role.

The importance of such "collectivized" appreciation is stressed by Condit in arguing that private pleasures are fleeting and largely inconsequential in their potential for social impact. With the advent of the soap opera cyberfan, the opportunities for collaborative negotiation have proliferated. Discussion groups are merely one type of outlet, allowing fans to publicly post instantaneous and/or reflective negotiations with the primary text(s) as well as meta-textual material, such as magazines. They can also respond to initial posts or simply "lurk," perusing the sentiments of others and, perhaps, considering those views in light of their own negotiations.

Baym's study of the soap opera newsgroup on Usenet identifies it as a site populated primarily by women, whereas more than seventy percent of Internet users overall are male. Baym sees within this "primarily female subculture" opportunities and strategies for critical resistance and appropriation. Moreover, she argues that a certain egalitarianism prevails because "gender, race, rank and other features of cultural identity are not immediately evident".

So, the sentiments of the MCI commercial are being re-articulated in much of the research. Similarly, Harrison & Bielby contend that an assumption of equality and relative anonymity results in freer participation, and they valorize cyberspace as a place where fans' "mattering maps converge" in a way that both "celebrates and validates their knowledge". Still, they observe that some voices emerge as more authoritative than others, just as Baym acknowledges the potential for cliquishness and tension between established participants and newcomers.

Thus far, the use of cyberspace to investigate audience readings of particular, contested popular texts has been limited. Unpublished studies related to soap opera and online fandoms do exist, and include Griffin's effort to gauge gay male interpretations. Additionally, Blumenthal collected online conversations among the fans of two soap operas for less than a month's time in her recent study reaffirming the genre's privileging of the feminine.

Still, despite the absence of large-scale efforts to explore audience readings against specific content, studies of soaps and cyberfandom would appear to affirm the existence and, in fact, the extension of a "critical gaze" within soap opera fan collectives. However, Baym warns that "the voicing of multiple interpretations" can degenerate into "flame wars" in which fans battle over their individualized meanings of stories and characters. Condit's distinction between "polysemous" and "polyvalent" texts also has relevance.

According to Condit, what is frequently mistaken for contradictory interpretation arising from textual openness may actually be contradictory evaluation of a common reading? So, when flame wars erupt, the panacea of collective pleasure and empowerment may be doubly confounded. These quandaries raise a number of issues. Are online meanings complicit with hegemonies in operation beyond the cyberspace playground? If so, which meanings gain acceptance and which are explicitly or implicitly discouraged?

Can disharmony on the Net diminish the potential for pleasure and resistance among marginalized audience groups? Does anonymity in cyberspace increase the likelihood of political debate or make it seem unwelcome, unnecessary and/ or irrelevant? And, if some voices emerge as more authoritative than others, whose are they? In what ways do "the powers that be" have a direct or indirect effect on the range of meanings circulated?

While this investigation, and the larger project front which it comes, concur that kibitzing on Net bulletin boards can be an empowering pleasure in and of it, these analyses go beyond the above-mentioned audience studies to address these neglected issues and to examine cyberspace deliberations in conjunction with the ideologies inherent in the producers' commercial imperatives.

SOAP OPERA, FEMINISM, AND "THE POWERS THAT BE"

That "the personal is political," soap opera researcher Charlotte Brundson reminds us is "the most resonant and evocative claim of 1970s Western feminism." This belief that "the oppression of women as women is most consensually secured" within the private realm has been, according to Brundson, a primary impetus for feminist study of media culture generally and of soap opera particularly.

Indeed, Mumford (1996) theorizes the genre's focus on the "private sphere of intimate relations", arguing this sphere's predominance even when such relations are exposed, as they often are, within public settings. She reasons that since personal matters are made public in the soap opera narrative, one is tempted to celebrate this "destruction of the private realm" as a generic feature that is implicitly, if not explicitly, feminist. Still, she recognizes that this very destruction tends to de-politicize personal issues, much as patriarchal ideology instructs us to relegate politics to the public arena.

The peculiar tendency of popular culture is, as Mumford echoes other scholars, to display politics in terms of its private, emotional impact while denying that the private sphere can, itself, be a site of political struggle. Thus, she accedes: "There are no politics-and there is therefore no feminism-in the soap opera community". So, the question arises, is this also true of the soap opera cyberfan community? Scholars have variously considered cyberspace in terms of conventional notions of space, with most acknowledging the novelty of accessing and interacting within a public forum from the privacy of the bedroom or study.

Clearly, then, it has been the potential for individuals (as opposed to commercial organizations) to address large numbers of people through CMC that has been most praised as an egalitarian and empowering potential of the technology. Accordingly, it is all the more crucial to determine the extent to which the de-politicization of the soap opera text-its insinuation that the personal transcends the political-is reproduced in discussion groups devoted to the genre.

Toward that end, the economic imperatives of soap opera production and their attendant political meanings require illumination. Since women hold the "power of the purse" when it comes to foodstuffs, clothing, cleaning products, health and hygiene products, and cosmetics, soap operas were designed and are still intended to sell commodity audiences of women to those who advertise such items. And, since women spend more on these products when they are first establishing their households, forming brand loyalties, and having and raising children, the most lucrative target audience has been women between the ages of 18 and 49.

This tendency is further complicated by the fact that most fans begin watching soaps in their teens and gradually become "hooked," allowing producers to take them for granted (up to a point) and to continue skewing content and representation in favour of the younger audience they hope to entice and secure for the future. As Baby Boomers have begun to creep past that "magic 49," the soaps have attempted to lure viewers at increasingly younger ages.

A relatively new daytime drama, Aaron Spelling's Sunset Beach (NBC), was expressly created to feature Generation Xers largely unrelated by blood, eschewing the traditional soap opera focus on multi-generational families. Just as patriarchy perpetuates a double standard of aging, valuing women primarily for their youthful appearance and reproductivity rather than for qualities honed by age and experience, the imperatives of commercial television favour women whose life stage and cultural understandings determine or foster the need for disposable diapers and tampons as well as, according to the advertisers' market research, more generous quantities of cold remedies and mascara.

Conveniently, though not coincidentally, capitalism and boardroom politics facilitate patriarchy and bedroom politics-and vice versa. As we have seen, research on the interactions of soap opera viewers, both on and offline, applauds the feminine subculture created out of the primary text. However, there is little attention paid to what vested interests connected to soap opera consider to be the most crucial marker of identity in addition to gender-age. If women may find solace as women within a "community" of soap opera enthusiasts, it should not be assumed that these women are not at cross purposes, both within and beyond this subculture, in terms of age and other aspects of identity.

In fact, it is more than conventional wisdom that an advertising strategy for seducing the young adult market is to compliment it at the expense of older, less-desirable consumers. This "divide and flatter" tactic can have even more efficacy for women, since the double standard of aging is an entrenched but, often, invisible hegemony. There are no watchdog groups who consistently monitor and/or lobby the media on this sole or primary basis.

Age, gender, class, and race are considered separately in analyses of representation on the Net. But, while the prevalence of women in soap opera discussion groups might mitigate against their under representation elsewhere in cyberspace and in the larger culture, this is not likely to be the case with respect to class, race, or age. The cyberspace generation gap persists within soap opera discussion groups, as Baym recently observed.

Moreover, it is not the mere fact that negotiations in such groups often float behind the text to the motivations of "TPTB" (the powers that be) or, in more indignant critiques, "TIIC" (the idiots in charge), which evidences resistance to hegemony, but whether or not the consensus remains one of resignation to and acceptance of these motives and/or the content they generate as natural and immutable. So, when young Matt Cory sweetly reassured his older fiancee that "it doesn't matter how old you are, it matters how much you love" and counseled her to "trust in the universe" just before their two-year long romance unraveled irretrievably on the NBC soap Another World, the de-politicization of the private realm and of soap opera generally was evident and acquiesced to by most cyberfans.

Even for many who embraced the story, if an older woman/younger man romance couldn't survive into marriage it was merely a function of destiny and the strength of their love. It had little to do with the soap's well-publicized ultimatum to get "demographics up" or be canceled, the fact that a minority of fans thought that this kind of couple was "nauseating," or even that the writers had stated that they were concerned about snubbing young female viewers by keeping this "hunk" with an older woman.

The relative acceptance of this narrative turn as an artistic decision made in the service of "true love" rather than one expressly designed to flatter some fans and marginalize others in the service of profit, reveals a key impediment to meaningful empowerment. With this example in mind, let us now turn to a broader consideration of soap opera discussion groups and their possibilities for inclusion, politics, and resistance.

In assessing the amenability of Internet forums to resistive fan activities, three crucial areas will be considered-the effects of "netiquette" guidelines upon open discussion, the related issues of "polyvalence" and discord in cyberspace and their impact on potentially empowering pleasures, and the encroachment of commercial interests and their priorities.

Network etiquette, or "netiquette," evolved out of early cyberculture, ostensibly to compensate for the lack of nonverbal cues and to preserve open and respectful communication. Yet, rules of netiquette have the potential to reproduce the larger culture's hegemonic inhibitions. They can be particularized within a given newsgroup and according to individualized notions of proper social behaviour.

While policies prohibiting explicit advertising and the posting of private e-mail correspondence are de rigueur on Usenet, sanctions against "flaming" have received the greatest scholarly attention. Thompsen lists more than a dozen publicized meanings of this term, all dancing around the notion of intentionally heated, incessant, or rude communication. Still, he observes distinctions based on whether one is sending or responding and/or being hostile or merely emotional.

Since we are considering soap opera forums, it is useful to localize our notions of flaming to the Usenet soap opera newsgroup(s), where Baym noted that the activity is strongly discouraged. Curiously, the "Frequently Asked Questions" advisory on "Inappropriate Posts" periodically disseminated on these newsgroups does not explicitly define or prohibit flaming. Instead, participants are warned against responding to "trolls" whose only purpose is to "start trouble even if the troll him/herself gets immolated in flames." Trolling, then, can be understood as a hostile, provocative post that is intended to invite flames-thereby conceived as belligerent replies-and to "challenge the long-standing traditions of the group." A poster who declares that "soap operas suck" is clearly a troll, the advisory explains, before admonishing participants to resist the bait.

Such interpretations are liquid, however, and this can be appreciated when posts dealing with representational issues are scrutinized. For instance, a poster who blatantly announced his/her "Asian-American rage" in the subject heading went on to lambaste soaps for their treatment of Asians. Those who responded did so primarily to designate the poster as a troll, thereby short-circuiting any serious discussion of minority inclusion. But, was this poster only trying to make trouble and invite flames?

Similarly, on AOL bulletin boards, an African-American fan that repeatedly censured Another World for its under-representation of blacks was automatically castigated and labeled a racist herself. While her language was uncompromising, she appeared to be sincere in her opinions and not merely "baiting." But, even the most courteous responses warned her that unless an overtly discriminatory message was purveyed on the show, racism was an unfair charge.

And, because this viewer posted on no other topic, she was considered a traitor among true fans and told to cease and desist. Occasional, carefully worded posts of this ilk are tolerated, as long as the poster is clearly interested in, if not favorable towards, other facets of the soap. Even so, they are few and rarely generate extensive deliberation compared to those tackling "lighter" topics.

In terms of age and similar issues, this loose interpretation of trolling can be even more problematic. On the Usenet soap opera newsgroup, Days of Our Lives fans were serious when implying, in one case, that a forty-something character was too old to "play the young couple in love" and, in another case, that the sight of two midlifers in bed was "gross," and some did politely challenge their assumptions. Yet, when an Another World fan on AOL proclaimed that she was "going to be sick" just thinking about how "adorable young Matt" once preferred a woman "old enough to be his mother" when he is "cute enough to be with any woman he wanted," only one or two very gentle, self-effacing reproaches followed.

The result is that hegemony-reinforcing messages are aired without sufficient rebuttal and their underlying politics remain unexplored. The assumption that such viewpoints are aberrations and not taken to heart can play right into the hands of those who reproduce them in the culture. Clearly, in the case of the intergenerational love story, the attitude expressed by this fan was taken seriously by the powers that be, who catered to it by ending the story, disgracing and back-burnering the older woman, and placing the young man in a featured romance with an unsullied heroine considerably younger than he.

And, gradually, many of the names and Internet "handles" of those who had been vocal devotees of the unconventional couple became less visible on several of the bulletin boards. Some retreated to e-mailing groups and conversed primarily with one another while their viewpoints faded from public display. Age and related matters emerge in other ways.

Many Another Worm cyberfans rallied after discovering, late in 1995, that the network was threatening to cancel the show if it didn't boost demographics by emulating its highly rated, youth- and fantasy-oriented companion soap, Days of Our Lives. Days of Our Lives was immediately disparaged for preferring models to actors, victimizing women, and for storylines involving demon possession and premature burial. However, the fact that Days of Our Lives also tends to relegate its older cast to its most bizarre plots and/or to pigeonhole them as over-the-top villains or sanitized, storyless "listening posts" was not discussed in this context.

An unhappy Another World fan on Usenet directed her ire at Days of Our Lives fans and their postings, saying that she feels "insulted and ashamed" to weed through subject headings such as "Sami is a big fat whore...." She was ignored, and the text's role in setting its audience's conversational agenda was not examined. Later, when a troll labeled an actress who returned to Another World after her maternity leave a "planetoid," those who seized the opportunity to begin a dialogue on the politics of appearance and gender were scolded for taking the bait. "This newsgroup is about Another World," a poster responded vehemently. "It is not about weight, it is not about gender, it is not about race...."

On AOL, the assumption that politics and soap opera are mutually exclusive was echoed when some posters began discussing feminism in connection to an Another World couple. "If you want to post something political go to a political folder," they were warned. "Soaps have offered an escape from everyday life and when these issues are raised I want to scream." Although a few begged to differ, the topic was soon dropped and the use of words such as "politics" or "feminism" continued to be regarded with suspicion.

This poster's use of the term "everyday life" is intriguing in light of its significance in the empirical analysis of lived experience advocated by the project of cultural studies. Its characterization as something which necessitates escape also is pertinent to key debates concerning the implications of women's uses and interpretations of romantic, fictional texts such as soap operas and romance novels.

For example, Ang takes Radway's germinal study of romance novel production, text, and audience to task for its theorization of the pleasure derived from reading as merely compensatory for personal satisfactions women seek but are unable to achieve in "real life" under patriarchy. She counters with the argument that the fantasies provided by such texts might be, in and of themselves, empowering.

One could, therefore, interpret the poster seeking refuge from "politics" to be buttressing Radway's claim that engagement with romantic fiction is an escape from the drudgery of everyday life or use it to illustrate Ang's contention that the fantasy play it offers is key to envisioning a better world. Either way, the apparent need to contain debate in order to accommodate the gratifications of some fans at the expense of others is noteworthy.

Although Baym argues that sensitive personal issues are addressed on the Usenet soap opera newsgroups, this study observes pressure to avoid linking these issues to larger political contexts. This pressure mimics that which is exerted upon soap opera creators who are often sanctioned against dealing with "socially conscious topics" to avoid offending segments of viewers.

This brings us to a consideration of the apparent effect of discord and the polyvalent readings it reflects. The ignominious end to the intergenerational love story on Another World left little room to read this relationship as authentic or viable and, therefore, differing attitudes toward the story's resolution reflect polyvalence rather than polysemy. Although the creators did allow (if not privilege) an interpretation of viability at points before the story's decline, the realization of opposing interpretations and evaluations in cyberspace stood to diminish whatever limited and inconsequential pleasures individual readings might have bequeathed.

Moreover, the pleasure of younger fans in seeing their "hunk" say "good riddance" to the older woman is in conflict with that of more marginal viewers who reveled in the subversive quality of the original story. Either way, the emphasis is on defending one's interpretation or evaluation rather than relishing it. And the defense cannot become too "political," for that, too, is discouraged. Accordingly, the celebratory postures of soap opera scholars who have studied face-to-face fan groups as well as those who have assessed fans' online conversations of brief duration and/or without corresponding examination of specific content or institutional practices may be called into question.

In addition to the noticeable "silencing" of fans of the controversial romance, there was in the course of this researcher's observation a turnover in online participation which, despite the uncertainty of cyberspace identity, appears to reflect a shift from an older to a younger population. This could be detected in the cyberfan reactions to a story on Another World in February of 1998 in which two characters met their untimely ends in a vehicular collision.

One, a relative short-termer, was portrayed by an actor popular with primarily younger fans who considered him a "hunk" of unimpeachable credentials. His resignation from the show was reason enough for many of them to declare: "I'm outta here." The second victim was a long term character-the father of the program's premiere young heroine-whose demise was occasioned by the actor's dismissal as the latest in a spate of firings of veteran performers.

On one website bulletin board there were no less than five subject headings and 25 posts bemoaning the death of the younger hero while only two subject headings and six posts expressed regret over the exit of the veteran. These latter posts were exceedingly intense, but their "whistling in the wind" quality was palatable. "They just don't care about us," a "32-year viewer" observed. The paucity of likeminded responses indicates that "they" includes the younger generation of fans who, by omission if not by outright antagonism, appear to devalue the pleasures of their older counterparts.

Antagonism is a more conspicuous manifestation of age-related biases transferred from the balance sheets of the networks and advertisers into cyberspace. With the demise of the older hero in the spring of 1998, Another Worm had effectively reduced its number of baby boom characters to three and only one middle-aged woman remained as part of an ongoing romance.

This fiftysomething duo, Carl and Rachel, had its share of enthusiasts-one of whom had been attracted to the show for what she described as the "passionate love between two people in my age group." Others took exception, however. "Personally it disgusts me to watch them," stated one of several outspoken dissenters. "Carl reminds me of the dirty old man down the street." "Nauseous is the word that comes to mind," echoed a second. The wishes of these naysayers were soon granted when the actor who portrayed Carl was fired, leaving the program potentially bereft of love stories featuring older women.

Age-discriminatory sentiments are not limited to this couple or to Another World. "I have absolutely no interest in watching John or Marlena get passionate," remarked a poster about the sole midlife romance on Days of Our Lives. "[It] reminds me too much of my parents." Of diva Erica Kane on All My Children, one fan bristled: "She makes me want to puke; she has to be almost 50." Another chimed in: "I'm sick of all the stories and men revolving around her dried up behind." Middle-aged mavens Stephanie and Sally from The Bold and the Beautiful fared even worse, being dismissed by one discriminating viewer as "flaccid, shriveled monsters."

Additional signs of this generational divide can be seen in responses to the Matt and Vanessa romance on Guiding Light. Although similar to the scuttled older woman/younger man love story on Another World, this relationship had endured into marriage, perhaps owing to the vigilance of its mostly older fans. Still, there were persistent protests from primarily younger viewers who found the idea of such a marriage "ridiculous" and who hoped for Vanessa's scheming daughter, Dinah, to steal the heart of her stepfather.

When Vanessa underwent a near death experience after the birth of her child, one detractor began a bulletin board subject heading entitled, "Vanessa, go toward the light." Added a likeminded fan: "I agree, send Vanessa into the light. Then let Dinah and Matt raise the baby." These remarks were in direct conflict with the delighted reactions of Matt/Vanessa followers happy to see some attention paid their favorite couple after a long dry spell.

Their marginal pleasures were, in this instance and at this juncture, consecrated by creators but not by the derisive judgments of other fans. In smaller, face-to-face fan groups such as those studied by Brown; affirmation of these pleasures might be possible. But, amidst the larger, more diverse collective inhabiting cyberspace, cohesion and validation are constantly threatened. If the pressures of netiquette and the gradual silencing of marginalized audiences can neutralize or discourage political debate and foster the goals of the powers that be, so, too, can the interventions of those very powers.

Obviously, "official" network websites constitute one type of forum for these interests, but their visibility elsewhere has also escalated. Soap Opera Digest, for instance, instituted its own forum on AOL which includes message boards that soon exceeded the unsponsored AOL boards in traffic and gradually led to an integrated Internet website. The forum and website also provide interviews, polls, and tidbits linked with its current issue, the cover of which is prominently displayed.

Accordingly, the agenda of the magazine helps to set that of the message boards. And, as Fiske observes, the magazines are not independent of the larger soap opera enterprise since they "rely on studio press releases and cooperation for their material and access to their players for interviews." The networks' sites on AOL and Microsoft Network also house soap opera bulletin boards subject to the same spillover. So, the soaps' desire to promote younger stars and their stories registers on these sites and filters into the content of the message boards.

One article in Soap Opera Digest fueled a scant, shortlived, but angry outcry on the magazine's AOL site and illustrates how soap opera publications embrace the imperatives of the industry upon which they depend. In a critique of One Life to Live, the magazine argued that the program was "wasting" too much story on its aging cast members when the younger audience would not be enticed:

> What were they thinking by showcasing so many graphic scenes of, shall we say, "mature" people having sex? ... fans are "treated" to Carlotta's fantasies of Hank, which has us thinking 9 1/2 Eeks.... As for Dorian, it's nice that post-menopausal women can still rip up the sheets with the best of them.

If the previously recounted slights against older women and couples on the soaps are any indication, the sentiments of this piece concur with the preferences of the favored audience and may contribute to the marginalization of older viewers and their identifications. Additionally, media sponsored forums provide an expanded means by which diverse groups of viewers can, however fleetingly, experience an illusion of empowerment, when any actual audience influence proceeds primarily from market research keyed to the producers' demographic goals.

As Intintoli concluded from the comments of an insider in his exhaustive, backstage analysis of Guiding Light: "... whereas the degree to which the story could be changed by mail was limited, suppliers liked the audience to feel it can affect the show." Despite the privileging of youthful stories, characters, and sentiments, soap opera cyberfan sites still offer equal access and participants may over-estimate their impact accordingly.

But, what about industry encroachment on the presumably independent Usenet soap opera newsgroups? The evolutionary structure of these newsgroups is relevant. When a single soap opera newsgroup became too unwieldy, the solution was to divide it into three separate newsgroups according to network. So, like many of the commercial bulletin boards, these newsgroups now reproduce and assist the networks' efforts to create a "flow" which carries the same audience from one of their soaps to another. It becomes necessary for someone who watches soaps on two or more networks to subscribe to and manage more than one newsgroup-a disincentive to channel surfing.

Other examples of indirect influences emerged when Another World was under the axe. Those who protested content changes linked to the push for demographics were consistently chastised by other fans and accused of endangering the soap's status. Fans who had endeavored to keep the show on the air through letter-writing campaigns, etc., had taken a leadership role and determined that such negative commentary was counterproductive to the goal of keeping the show afloat at all costs, even if it was becoming Another World in name only.

Though well-intended, these leaders were instructing fans to do exactly what the powers that be hoped-that is, to continue watching even if the "new Another World" didn't suit them and thereby allow them to be taken for granted while other audience segments were courted. Those in the industry have also exerted some influence through their participation in discussion groups. During Another World's cancellation hubbub on Usenet, an insider began providing insightful information on decision-making behind the scenes. While he didn't reveal his official position, his input was highly valued, with much of it eventually confirmed in magazine articles and interviews.

Quick to toe the party line, he defended a controversial executive producer who had improved the show's demographics and scolded fans who did not appreciate the changes that preceded this: "Why the sniping at Another World? If bottom line-motivated NBC sees reason to give the show a chance and continued support based on the numbers, why can't the people here?" And, amazingly, nobody (except this researcher) contested the notion that NBC's profit motivated criteria should also be their own. The act of (politely) challenging this insider's recommendation seemed to border on heresy and was dismissed by some as flaming.

Despite some rankling over demographics, fans do seem to accept the system that determines what they will see. For instance, they will argue that the advertisers are incorrect in their preference for teens and twenty-somethings when Baby Bloomers possess equal or greater numbers and disposable income. Said one 45-year-old: "I have two children, ages 16 and 7, and I buy plenty of laundry detergent and every other thing that `younger' women who have school-age children buy."

Or, younger viewers will question the assumption that they are only intrigued by youthful characters and storylines. But, the issue of whether gender, age, race, or class should make an audience a more valuable commodity in the first place is seldom raised. The mechanisms by which commercial television operates are a given. Based on this look at the impact of netiquette rules, conflicting interpretations and evaluations of soap opera characters and stories, and the direct and indirect influences of the industry upon soap opera discussion groups, it is plain that the vision of a public cyberspace where all are represented and the assumptions of cultural producers can be effectively redressed is, perhaps, too optimistic.

The feminist dictum that "the personal is political" seems not to be significantly advanced by the soap opera text's reception and negotiation in these forums. After feminist scholars initiated a justifiable defense of female audiences who had been summarily dismissed for their devotion to soap opera and other "feminine" texts, many of them neglected to adequately deliberate the limits of the pleasure and resistance they chronicled. This researcher acknowledges that many soap opera fans are able to intuit the reasons their enjoyment is belittled by the larger culture.

Although a haven from such external disapproval, soap opera discussion groups on the Net provide new spaces for the disparagement of marginal women's pleasures more so than for the "collectivized" celebration of such pleasures. As Interrogate the Internet contends, "the structure of the technology and the content" are intimately entwined with the "broader cultural context" and commercial imperatives of media filter into these groups and privilege the pleasures of the producers' "preferred" segment of the audience.

This occurs when the more marginal segments-nonwhite and, especially, older women-are compelled to incessantly defend their interests amidst the diminishing options and returns offered by soap opera creators or else fall silent. As Condit argues, there is a "greater work load imposed on oppositionally situated audience groups," and the effect of such burdensome labour may be to muffle their voices.

This occurs when "escape" from the politics of everyday life sought by some viewers and catered to by creators mitigates against the satisfaction other fans derive from situating their interpretive pleasures within a more explicit political framework-such contextualization being a prerequisite for social action. Netiquette rules, such as those against flaming, appear in practice to sanction the first gratification and constrain the latter.

Industry infiltration on the Net and the deference of some vocal fans to the imperatives of the industry also work to inhibit meaningful politicization. I am not claiming, however, that hegemonic values reproduced in cyberspace discussion groups' axe not political, but that the cultures of soap opera and cyberspace mitigate against fans recognizing them as such. As a result, efforts to steer debate in any explicitly political direction seem to halt prematurely.

The myth that personal issues and opinions, including those pertaining to soap opera characters and stories, somehow remain outside the purview of "true" politics, is perpetuated. My purpose here is not to advocate a reductionistic, political-economic view of these processes, but to caution against over-simplification on the other side of the equation. Just because many soap opera fans are savvy, critical consumers of the text and, in certain instances, the economic imperatives behind it, does not mean that their views are typical or part of some large-scale, resistive impulse.

And, just because the Internet has been touted as a place where marginal voices can be heard does not mean that existing cultural and economic arrangements have no bearing on the disposition of these voices and perspectives. Additional study must continue to focus on the push-pull of hegemony vs. resistance on the Internet as elsewhere.

As this research indicates, however, the advertisers' strategy of "divide and flatter" subjects the "feminine subculture" of soap opera fandom to rupture along other lines of identity. Minorities and their concerns are under represented, older characters, viewers, and themes are slighted, the private is divorced from the public, and cultural hegemonies-such as the double standard of aging-persist and even flourish.

Just because the age, race, gender, or class of cybersurfers might not be immediately obvious, it does not follow that there is equality of participation or that such traits are not central to the commercial goals of the powers that be or to politics generally. Pretending otherwise does not change this; it can, in fact, play into the hands of those who help to reproduce hegemony while insisting, as Another Worldly writers did, that "it doesn't matter how old [or what color, or what gender, or how wealthy, etc.] you are." At this juncture, Mumford's judgment lingers: "... there are no politics-and there is therefore no feminism-in the soap opera community." And, the cyberfan community appears to be no exception.

8

Transforming Communication Pedagogy

How do we "do" emancipatory feminist teaching when we have not observed it or experienced it ourselves? The author argues here that service-learning is a useful strategy for feminist communication educators to begin challenging the power relationships of traditional pedagogy. Pioneered in the 1960s and '70s, this pairing of traditional course work with community service is now used as a learning model in schools around the nation. Because service-learning allows educators to forge relational links between ourselves, our students, our neighbors, and the communities in which we live, it deserves careful consideration from feminist educators.

In recent years, communication scholars have become more aware of the transformative, affiliative potential of their research. Groundbreaking work by feminist and activist scholars has led us to acknowledge and value the interdependence of researchers and subjects. Increasingly, we can envision a world comprised of relationships rather than rules, a world built on human connection, as discussed in the work of Carol Gilligan, bell hooks, Patti Lather, Miriam Belenky, and many others. We find growing merit in the idea of research as a participatory exchange or collaborative dialogue with other people in which domination is replaced by cooperation, and we strive to incorporate such dialogic practices into our own scholarship.

It may be harder to incorporate these approaches into our teaching, especially in hierarchical environments. We may see ourselves as scholars struggling to understand and transform social relations, particularly those which play out inequalities constructed around gender, race and class, but feel caught up in authoritarian practices in our classrooms. We may conduct research to illuminate and challenge the hidden social processes of daily life, but be hesitant to dismantle our existing power relationships with our students. We may also suffer from the lack of practical examples: how do we model emancipatory feminist teaching if we have not observed or experienced it ourselves?

Though not usually identified as a feminist approach per se, service-learning is a useful strategy for challenging the power relationships of traditional pedagogy. Service-learning is defined by T.K. Stanton (1990) of Stanford University's Public Service Center as a teaching method which combines "structured, intentional learning with public and community service". Derived from the experiential education theories of John Dewey and pioneered in the 1960s and '70s as a learning model, the method is now used in elementary and secondary schools as well as institutions of higher learning around the nation.

Educators who apply this experiential model bring their students into direct contact with various types of contemporary social problems and efforts to solve them. In typical forms of service-learning, students may work with people in charitable organizations, health care facilities, youth groups, nursing homes, public interest groups and so on, performing environmental research, tutoring, nutritional analysis, oral history, voter education, community journalism, and many other forms of outreach.

Such direct experiences, grounded in the curriculum of particular courses and disciplines, give students opportunities to field-test theories and insights they have been exposed to in class while at the same time working cooperatively for the greater good. C. K. Della-Piana (1996) described her students' experience of "learning to work with others who did not have the same values, beliefs, and concerns, yet had a commitment to community service and the passion to make a difference.... It was providing enlightened and humane service and committing oneself to the common good". Proponents say that service-learning may be the first time their students have ever recognized the need for their skills and engagement in the world around them.

In bringing service-learning to the classroom, educators also reach out, and learn by doing so. To create successful service-learning projects or programs, teachers must engage in ongoing dialogue with public groups and agencies, their students, and each other. Becoming part of a community which consensually constructs and shares knowledge, we are guided and informed by our fellow residents, by the parents of our students, our leaders, organizers, activists, and critics. As we develop this consciousness and share it with our students, Parker Palmer (1990) asserts, we talk more about those ways of knowing that form an inward capacity for relatedness.

SERVICE-LEARNING AS FEMINIST STRATEGY

Feminist and activist scholars have increasingly come to value research which unpacks the various meanings of community. Early definitionsgenerally included the concepts of social connectedness, territorial organization and physical location. When most social relationships occurred in geographic proximity, M. Janowitz (1967) notes, communities were characterized by local elite with local institutionalized patterns for controlling social change. Scholars of social change continue to see the geographic community as a critical site for political mobilization because it is where problems of daily living conditions can be discussed, and where groups with common interests may form and act together.

Today, scholars of the late 20th century lament the erosion of community participation in civic, professional and volunteer associations and note the rise of affinity groups based on shared electronic "experiences". Popular new technologies have been credited with establishing "virtual communities," far-flung groups of people linked by common interests. These understandings of community refer to collections of values shared by diverse individuals and disseminated via electronic media such as talk radio, global satellite television, and the Internet. Members of these communities are "bound by a sense of identity, shared values and interaction" or linked by "a common interest or shared circumstance", not by physical space.

There is a real danger in thinking that virtual community supercedes or addresses the needs of physical, geographical community. Out on the streets, in our physical communities, on our campuses and in our neighborhoods, people still suffer the shared predicaments of oppression, isolation, and need. The widespread electronic sharing of values has not resulted in a blossoming of relationships of care in the physical world. Feminist researchers and teachers still need to pay attention to the community of the body-creating and sustaining embodied relationships in the contexts of gender, ethnicity, age, and geographic location.

Since the 1970s, communication scholars have sought to understand how some groups of people evolve into functioning communities possessing a sense of collective identity and interdependence. Jurgen Habermas uses the term "communicative action" to denote the collective efforts of people who share consensual interpretations of situations and events. By sharing meanings, people "harmonize their plans of action on the basis of common situation definitions" and may form an interdependent "community of interest" in which members act for the common good.

Feminist scholars are also interested in the transformative potential of relationships of community and connectedness. Feminist theories of care have helped us to envision a world "comprised of relationships rather than of people standing alone, a world that coheres through human connection rather than through systems of rules". In this view, individuals link to one another in a fundamental attitude of protectiveness or caring, acting not out of competitive self-interest, but toward the good of a more equitable society. Individual identity develops in the context of relationships and is shaped by our responsibility to and connection with others.

If we agree with P. Palmer that community is "a capacity for relatedness within individuals", how do we model it with our students? Too often we disregard the physical community and its relationships in the classroom. Traditional hierarchical educational strategies do not encourage children, adolescents or young adults to take part in problem-solving dialogues or action within their own communities. Indeed, Ernest Boyer (1990) observes, "it is possible for American teenagers to finish high school without ever being asked to participate in life in or out of the school-never encouraged to spend time with lonely older people, help a child who has not learned to read, clean up litter on the street, or even do something meaningful at the school itself".

Many students leave school behind without learning how to affiliate with others or how to take collective action for systemic change. This is a relational gap which service-learning proposes to fill. According to R. L. Sigmon (1990), the learning objectives of this approach "are formed in the context of what needs to be done to serve others". Ideally, the approach is structured on the premises that those being served control the service(s) provided; that those being served become better able to serve others and themselves by their own actions; and that those who serve are also learners and have significant control over what is to be learned.

At its best, C. Bachen (1994) observes, "community service may foster in students and the people in their communities a deeper understanding of the human condition, including the structural factors that reinforce poverty and prejudice ... (and) a lifelong commitment to working for equality and justice". Service-learning also acknowledges students' agency in their own lives. Behind classroom walls, the teacher might be tempted or pressured to cast herself as the holder of wisdom, but out in the community, students often have more "street knowledge" or local survival skills than their teachers.

The service-learning educator abandons the sage on the stage position to act as a guide from the side, helping students make connections between the theoretical concepts they learn in school and their own experienced realities. Service-learning instructors and students forsake their traditional roles, K. Krupar (1994) notes, to develop a collegial sharing of power, accountability and tasks: "This pedagogy requires that students become profoundly and actively involved in their own learning, that they discover for themselves rather than accept verbal and written pronouncements, that they learn to map uncharted territories and that they find themselves through the processes of trial and error".

Rather than telling students what to think and do, service-learning educators generate discussion about how to think and do, encouraging students to reflect upon the complexities of their social worlds. The most widely made claim, and the one most promising to feminist educators, is also perhaps the most controversial: that service-learning creates a foundation for a personal commitment to social responsibility. Harkavy & Puckett (1994) say that academically based community service supports "the promotion of civic consciousness, value-oriented thinking and a moral approach to issues of public concern among undergraduates".

Stanton (1990) argues that community service deepens the experience of students, "potentially stimulating in them passionate reactions to social injustice and a commitment to work for change". And Ernest Boyer (1990) posits that service can lead students to see that they are "not only autonomous individuals but also members of a larger community to which they are accountable".

Obviously, this possibility harmonizes well with feminist goals of liberatory research and praxis, which envision new forms of socio-political relationships linking individuals to one another in bonds of caring and commitment. The experience of service-learning might help our students comprehend feminist perspectives such as Carol Gilligan's "ethic of care" or Sara Ruddick's vision of "holding", which she describes as social relationships based on a fundamental attitude of protectiveness.

Involved community contact might help students understand why Julia Wood calls for the full integration of models of caring into public life: "Appreciating the profound interconnections among humans enables all individuals, regardless of age, sex, race, or class, to understand and participate in life in ways forever closed to those whose rigid autonomy diminishes their capacity to form intimate relationships and to appreciate differences". For its emphasis on leading students to committed social relationships with their communities, service-learning seems a perfect pedagogy for feminist educators.

LIMITATIONS OF LEARNING THROUGH SERVICE

Service-learning also has its constraints, and feminist practitioners can strengthen it where it is most vulnerable-in the area of critical consciousness. Although the goals of service-learning are worthy and designed with liberatory intent, critics question whether merely "exposing" students to social problems is a useful or ethical way to stimulate dedication to social justice and commitment to action. They raise the possibility that such learning programs have little to do with genuine community service and instead involve a form of paternalistic, "feel-good" benevolence. Edward Zlotkowski asserts that service-learning may lead some students and educators to disregard the traditions and objectives of specific learning disciplines in favour of the pre-determined "discovery" of a sentimental, ideologically fixed view of the service experience.

In a critique of outreach efforts by U.S. students in Mexico, Ivan Illich, attacks "the belief that every American has something to give, and at all times may, can and should give it". He argues that well-meaning middle-class American students are ill-equipped to help poor people in developing nations, or their own. Instead, he asserts, they are often filled with a self-involved missionary zeal which is insulting at best, and might also be dangerous to the people they are allegedly trying to "help."

He cautions students, "It is profoundly damaging to yourselves when you define something that you want to do as `good,' a `sacrifice,' and 'help' ". Similarly, R. L. Sigmon

(1990) points to the "self-deception" of those who claim to be aiding others when they are actually serving their own interests. He notes that learning goals may be superimposed by educators rather than derived from the service task: "We spread around our talents and knowledge because we have it to use and enjoy sharing. We do research in communities to justify our positions or test a promising methodology. We do group-oriented work because we are trained in group process ... We advocate for the poor, young, elderly, and minorities because we want to serve without realizing that they may not be impressed". Instead, he argues, educators should be asking if the proferred service makes sense to those expected to benefit from it.

Even at its most self-reflexive, the service-learning approach cannot resolve all of the ethical or practical dilemmas faced by educators who are interested in adopting more egalitarian or liberatory pedagogies. The social intervention inherent in service-learning is criticized both for activism and for paternalism. S. Shapiro notes that approaches to education for citizenship historically have been associated with the collective effacement of minority and immigrant cultures.

In some contexts, Wood notes, caring may be seen as the responsibility of those deemed culturally subordinate. Thus, the service aspects of service-learning may seem problematically linked to the "traditionally female" characteristics of nurturing and care, an association critiqued by some feminists as disempowering. Ethical dilemmas in research and pedagogy cannot be avoided, Della-Piana (1996) asserts, but is "continuously confronted, tenuously resolved, and inherently wrought with self-interest and power". This is an area where feminist research perspectives may interact with service-learning pedagogy to good effect.

Feminist scholars have often visited the politics of class and privilege in the study of the "other," questioning the hidden social processes of daily life and pointing out contradictions in the relationships between researchers and the groups of people with whom they study. Feminist inquiry often seeks to illuminate disparities between liberatory theory and the physical conditions of its praxis. Because feminist scholars are dedicated to the exploration of liberatory theories and methods in research and teaching, and because we are willing to open our efforts to examination by other participants in a knowledge-constructing dialogue, we may be able to introduce our students to community service from a more egalitarian perspective.

Feminists who teach human communication or media skills at the high school or university level are especially well-positioned to integrate service-learning into the curriculum. For example, high school students in Philadelphia have conducted an oral history project of their neighborhoods, while college students have compared and applied different approaches to relieving intergroup ethnic and cultural tensions. Students in writing classes at a Maryland university have performed community service and reflected on the personal implications of these experiences in journals, while a women's studies class in Washington, DC, has involved college students in semester-long internships with groups like the Children's Defense Fund, the Institute for Women's Policy Research, and the D.C. Rape Crisis Center.

Though it is not usually described as a feminist approach, service-learning offers a model for a more egalitarian and socially proactive pedagogy. The pairing of traditional course work with community service brings our students into direct contact with contemporary social concerns and allows them to take part in efforts to respond, opening the classroom to the feminist ideal of social relations based on caring or interdependence. Service-learning also gives us a framework for placing more emphasis on students' agency. Community experiences allow students to test theories they have considered in class against insights gained in the field.

They foreground the value of community building and the importance of each individual's contribution to the common good. And they encourage us-students and teachers alike-to open our own efforts and results to examination by others. Of course, we must guard against sentimentalizing the service experience, and we must be critical and careful in its use. Some of the significant drawbacks to service-learning, pointed out by supporters and detractors alike, are easily recognizable in its practice.

On the other hand, service-learning encourages educators to broaden the relevance of their material and pedagogy. It allows us to build "real-world" concerns and connections into a wide variety of academic subjects and encourages us to develop ongoing working partnerships with community organizations and groups. In this way it brings new immediacy to communication education and forges relational links between ourselves, our students, our neighbors, and the communities in which we live. Therefore, it is an approach that deserves careful consideration from feminist educators. In our search to find promising models of social interaction for ourselves and our students, we may do worse than to consider the potential of service-learning.

DIGNITY VERSUS LIBERTY

In every corner of the Western world, writers proclaim "privacy" as a supremely important human good, as a value somehow at the core of what makes life worth living. Without our privacy, we lose "our very integrity as persons," Charles Fried declared over thirty-five years ago. Many others have since agreed that privacy is somehow fundamental to our "personhood." It is a commonplace, moreover, that our privacy is peculiarly menaced by the evolution of modern society, with its burgeoning technologies of surveillance and inquiry.

Commentators paint this menace in very dark colors: Invasions of our privacy are said to portend a society of "horror," to "injure [us] in [our] very humanity," or even to threaten "totalitarianism," and the establishment of law protecting privacy is accordingly declared to be a matter of fundamental rights. It is the rare privacy advocate who resists citing Orwell when describing these dangers. At the same time, honest advocates of privacy protections are forced to admit that the concept of privacy is embarrassingly difficult to define.

"[N]obody," writes Judith Jarvis Thomson dryly, "seems to have any very clear idea what [it] is." Not every author is as skeptical as Thomson, but many of them feel obliged to concede that privacy, fundamentally important though it may be, is an unusually slippery concept. In particular, the sense of what must be kept "private," of what must be hidden before the eyes of others, seems to differ strangely from society to society. This is a point that is frequently made by citing the literature of ethnography, which tells us that there are some societies in which people cheerfully defecate in full view of others, and at least a few in which the same is true of having sex.

But the same point can be made by citing a large historical literature, which shows how remarkably ideas of privacy have shifted and mutated over time. Anyone who wants a vivid example can visit the ruins of Ephesus, where the modern tourist can set himself down on one of numerous ancient toilet seats in a public hall where well-to-do Ephesians gathered to commune, two thousand years ago, as they collectively emptied their bowels. If privacy is a universal human need that gives rise to a fundamental human right, why does it take such disconcertingly diverse forms?

This is a hard problem for privacy advocates who want to talk about the values of "personhood," harder than they typically acknowledge. It is a hard problem because of the way they usually try to make their case: Overwhelmingly, privacy advocates rely on what moral philosophers call "intuitionist" arguments. In their crude form, these sorts of arguments suppose that human beings have a direct, intuitive grasp of right and wrong-an intuitive grasp that can guide us in our ordinary ethical decisionmaking.

Privacy advocates evidently suppose the same thing. Thus, the typical privacy article rests its case precisely on an appeal to its reader's intuitions and anxieties about the evils of privacy violations. Imagine invasions of your privacy, the argument runs. Do they not seem like violations of your very personhood? Since violations of privacy seem intuitively horrible to everybody, the argument continues, safeguarding privacy must be a legal imperative, just as safeguarding property or contract is a legal imperative. Indeed, privacy matters so much to us that laws protecting it must be a basic element of human rights.

This kind of argument can certainly make a powerful impression on first reading, since it is true that we can all imagine some violation of our privacy that seems very horrible. This is especially so when the writings in question are composed by scholars with a real literary gift, like Fried. Nevertheless, no matter how anxiety-inducing it may be to read these authors, their arguments only carry real weight if it is true that the intuitions they evoke are shared by all human beings. Yet all the evidence seems to suggest that human intuitions and anxieties about privacy differ.

We do not need to refer to the practices of exotic ancient or modern cultures to demonstrate as much: It is true even as between the familiar societies of the modern West. In fact, we are in the midst of significant privacy conflicts between the United States and the countries of Western Europe-conflicts that reflect unmistakable differences in sensibilities about what ought to be kept "private."

To the Europeans, indeed, it often seems obvious that Americans do not understand the imperative demands of privacy at all. The Monica Lewinsky investigation, in particular, with its numerous and lewd disclosures, led many Europeans to that conclusion. But the Lewinsky business is not the only example: There are plenty of other aspects of American life that seem to Europeans to prove the same thing. Let me offer a variety of examples from France and Germany, two countries that have been my focus in recent research, and that are my focus in this Chapter as well.

Some of the things that bother French and German observers involve what Americans will think of as trivialities of everyday behaviour. For example, visitors from both countries are taken aback by the ill-bred way in which Americans talk about themselves. As a French article warns visitors to the United States, America is a place where strangers suddenly share information with you about their "private activities" in a way that is "difficult to imagine" for northern Europeans or Asians. Americans have a particularly embarrassing habit, continental Europeans believe, of talking about salaries.

It is "normal in America," an Internet site informs German tourists, for your host at dinner to ask "not just how much you earn, but even what your net worth is" -topics ordinarily quite off-limits under the rules of European etiquette. Talking about salaries is not quite like defecating in public, but it can seem very off-putting to many Europeans nevertheless. But it is not just a matter of the boorish American lack of privacy etiquette. It is also a matter of American law.

Continental law is avidly protective of many kinds of "privacy" in many realms of life, whether the issue is consumer data, credit reporting, workplace privacy, discovery in civil litigation, the dissemination of nude images on the Internet, or shielding criminal offenders from public exposure. To people accustomed to the continental way of doing things, American law seems to tolerate relentless and brutal violations of privacy in all these areas of law. I have seen Europeans grow visibly angry, for example, when they learn about routine American practices like credit reporting.

How, they ask, can merchants be permitted access to the entire credit history of customers who have never defaulted on their debts? Is it not obvious that this is a violation of privacy and personhood, which must be prohibited by law? These are clashes in attitude that go well beyond the occasional social misunderstanding. In fact, they have provoked some tense and costly transatlantic legal and trade battles over the last decade and a half. Thus, the European Union and the United States slid into a major trade conflict over the protection of consumer data in the 1990s, only problematically resolved by a 2000 "safe harbor" agreement.

Europeans still constantly complain that Americans do not accept the importance of protecting consumer privacy. Those tensions have only grown in the aftermath of September 11. Something similar has happened with regard to discovery in civil procedure: American law allows parties to rummage around in each other's records in a way that seems obnoxious and manifestly unacceptable to Europeans. The result, in recent decades, has been a seething little war over discovery. The circulation of the nude photos of celebrities on the Internet has produced another such conflict, with Europeans acting alone to penalize Internet service providers.

For sensitive Europeans, indeed, a tour through American law may be an experience something like a visit to the latrines of Ephesus. Correspondingly, it has become common for Europeans to maintain that they respect a "fundamental right to privacy" that is either weak or wholly absent in the "cultural context" of the United States. Here, Europeans point with pride to Article 8 of the European Convention on Human Rights, which protects "the right to respect for private and family life," and to the European Union's new Charter of Fundamental Rights, which demonstratively features articles on both "Respect for Private and Family Life" and "Protection of Personal Data."

By the standards of those great documents, American privacy law seems, from the European point of view, simply to have "failed." But it is not just that Europeans resent and distrust the American approach to privacy: The reverse is also true. Anyone who has lived in the United States knows that Americans can be just as obsessively attached to their "privacy" as Europeans, sometimes defending it by resort to firearms. As for American law, it too is obsessed with privacy. Indeed, some of the most violently controversial American social issues are conceived of as privacy matters. This has been true of abortion for thirty years. With the Supreme Court's decision in Lawrence v. Texas, it is now true of homosexuality as well. It is simply false to say that privacy doesn't matter to Americans.

In fact, let us make no mistake about it: When it comes to privacy, there are plenty of European practices that seem intuitively objectionable to Americans. Some of these have to do with seemingly minor aspects of the anthropology of everyday life, most especially involving nudity. If the Europeans are puzzled by the ill-bred way in which Americans casually talk about themselves, Americans are puzzled by the ill-bred way in which Europeans casually take off their clothes. Phenomena like public nudity in the parks of German cities are particularly baffling to Americans, but so are phenomena like the presence of female attendants in men's washrooms.

It is genital nudity that Americans find most bizarre: One's genitalia are "privates" in the full sense of the word in America, and one does not ordinarily expose them in public, and certainly not before the opposite sex. Even breasts are supposed to be kept covered in the United States-as the occasional female European tourist has discovered, when arrested (or even jailed!) for sunbathing topless on an American beach. ("Those Americans are Out of their Minds!" howls a headline from a Swiss tabloid reporting one such incident from Florida.) Even American advertising, which doesn't stop at much, doesn't show bare breasts.

Public nudity may seem little more than a curiosity (though we shall see that it raises revealing problems in the European law of privacy). But here again, it is not just a matter of norms of everyday behaviour; it is a matter of law. There are numerous aspects of European law that can seem not only ridiculous, but somewhat shocking to Americans. For example, continental governments assert the authority to decide what names parents will be permitted to give their children-a practice affirmed by the European Court of Human Rights as recently as 1996.

This is an application of state power that Americans will view with complete astonishment, as a manifest violation of proper norms of the protection of privacy and personhood. How can the state tell you what you are allowed to call your baby? Nor does it end there: In Germany, everybody must be formally registered with the police at all times. In both Germany and France, inspectors have the power to arrive at your door to investigate whether you have an unlicensed television.

Evidence that Americans would regard as illegally seized is routinely considered in continental adjudication. In France and Germany, according to a recent study, telephones are tapped at ten to thirty times the rate they are tapped in the United States-and in the Netherlands and Italy, at 130 to 150 times the rate. All of this will make many an American snigger at the claim that Europeans have a superior grasp of privacy. What kind of "privacy" is there, Americans will ask, in countries where people prance around naked out of doors while allowing the state to keep tabs on their whereabouts, convict them on the basis of unfair police investigations, peer into their living rooms, tap their phones, and even dictate what names they can give to their babies?

Evidently, Americans and continental Europeans perceive privacy differently. Privacy advocates sometimes try to downplay these differences. The felt need for privacy, they insist, is in fact universal, and the only real difference is that American protections are the product of piecemeal legislation, less systematically developed than European protections as yet, but nevertheless evolving in a European direction. There is certainly some truth in this: There are indeed important resemblances between the systems on either side of the Atlantic. Any proper account of comparative privacy law will have to explain many similarities as well as many differences.

Nevertheless, when all is said and done, it is impossible to ignore the fact that Americans and Europeans are, as the Americans would put it, coming from different places. At least as far as the law goes; we do not seem to possess general "human" intuitions about the "horror" of privacy violations. We possess something more complicated than that: We possess American intuitions or, as the case may be, Dutch, Italian, French, or German intuitions.

We must make some effort to explain this fact before we start proclaiming universal norms of privacy protection. In particular, we will not do justice to our transatlantic conflicts if we begin by declaring that American privacy law has "failed" while European privacy law has "succeeded." That is hogwash. What we must acknowledge, instead, is that there are, on the two sides of the Atlantic, two different cultures of privacy, which are home to different intuitive sensibilities, and which have produced two significantly different laws of privacy.

So why do these sensibilities differ? Why is it that French people won't talk about their salaries, but will take off their bikini tops? Why is it that Americans comply with court discovery orders that open essentially all of their documents for inspection, but refuse to carry identity cards? Why is it that Europeans tolerate state meddling in their choice of baby names? Why is it that Americans submit to extensive credit reporting without rebelling?

These are not questions we can answer by assuming that all human beings share the same raw intuitions about privacy. We do not have the same intuitions, as anybody who has lived in more than one country ought to know. What we typically have is something else: We have intuitions that are shaped by the prevailing legal and social values of the societies in which we live. In particular, we have, if I may use a clumsy phrase, juridified intuitions-intuitions that reflect our knowledge of, and commitment to, the basic legal values of our culture.

Indeed, to get a handle on our transatlantic privacy conflicts, we must begin by recognizing that continental European and American sensibilities about privacy grow out of much larger and much older differences over basic legal values, rooted in much larger and much older differences in social and political traditions. The fundamental contrast, in my view, is not difficult to identify. In one form or another, it is a contrast that has been noticed by observers of the transatlantic scene for a century. It is the contrast between two conceptions of privacy most recently distinguished by Robert Post: between privacy as an aspect of dignity and privacy as an aspect of liberty.

Continental privacy protections are, at their core, a form of protection of a right to respect and personal dignity. The core continental privacy rights are rights to one's image, name, and reputation, and what Germans call the right to informational self-determination-the right to control the sorts of information disclosed about one. These are closely linked forms of the same basic right: They are all rights to control your public image-rights to guarantee that people see you the way you want to be seen. They are, as it were, rights to be shielded against unwanted public exposure-to be spared embarrassment or humiliation.

The prime enemy of our privacy, according to this continental conception, is the media, which always threatens to broadcast unsavory information about us in ways that endanger our public dignity. But of course, this concern does not end with media exposure. Any other agent that gathers and disseminates information can also pose such dangers. In its focus on shielding us from public indignity, the continental conception is typical of the continental legal world much more broadly: On the Continent, the protection of personal dignity has been a consuming concern for many generations.

By contrast, America, in this as in so many things, is much more oriented toward values of liberty, and especially liberty against the state. At its conceptual core, the American rights to privacy still take much the form that it took in the eighteenth century: It is the right to freedom from intrusions by the state, especially in one's own home. The prime danger, from the American point of view, is that "the sanctity of [our] home[s]," in the words of a leading nineteenth-century Supreme Court opinion on privacy, will be breached by government actors. American anxieties thus focus comparatively little on the media. Instead, they tend to be anxieties about maintaining a kind of private sovereignty within our own walls.

Such is the contrast that lies at the base of our divergent sensibilities about what counts as a "privacy" violation. On the one hand, we have an Old World in which it seems fundamentally important not to lose public face; on the other, a New World in which it seems fundamentally important to preserve the home as a citadel of individual sovereignty. What Europeans miss in Americans is a sense of the demands of public face; indeed, Europeans have been denouncing American law on that ground since at least 1903.

When Americans seem to continental Europeans to violate norms of privacy, it is because they seem to display an embarrassing lack of concern for public dignity-whether the issue is the public indignity inflicted upon Monica Lewinsky by the media, or the self-inflicted indignity of an American who boasts about his salary. Conversely, when continental Europeans seem to Americans to violate norms of privacy, it is because they seem to show a supine lack of resistance to invasions of the realm of private sovereignty whose main citadel is the home-whether the issue is wiretapping or baby names. The question of public nudity presents the contrast in piquant form.

To the continental way of seeing things, what matters is the right to control your public image-and that right may include the right to present yourself proudly nude, if you so choose. To the American mind, by contrast, what matters is sovereignty within one's own home; and people who have shucked the protection of clothing are like people who have shucked the protection of the walls of their homes, only more so. They are people who have surrendered any "reasonable expectation of privacy." Now, let me emphasize that this contrast is not absolute.

These are complex societies, which are home to a variety of sensibilities, concerns, traditions, and mutual influences. There are certainly some Americans who find the European idea of dignity appealing. This is notably true of Justice Kennedy, whose opinion for the Court in Lawrence v. Texas expresses admiration for European approaches, and who tries energetically to found his opinion on ideals of both liberty and dignity.

For that matter, there are no doubt Europeans who find the characteristic American approach appealing. Moreover, it is certainly the case that both forms of the protection of privacy are in force to some extent on both sides of the Atlantic: There are some protections against the media and the like in the United States, and there are certainly some American tort cases protecting people's public image. As for Europe: There are certainly some quite far-reaching protections against the state there, and there is certainly law protecting people within the bounds of the home.

So it would be wrong to say that there is some absolute difference between American and continental European law. But the issue is not whether there is an absolute difference. Comparative law is the study of relative differences. Indeed, it is the great methodological advantage of comparative law that it can explore relative differences. No absolute generalization about any legal system is ever true. It would be false, for example, to say that American law is hostile to the social welfare state: It is easy to think of exceptions to that generalization.

But what is true is that American law is more hostile to the social welfare state than continental law-and that is a statement that is not only true, but highly important to understanding the world in which we live. In comparative privacy law, too, it is the relative differences that matter. Americans and Europeans certainly do sometimes arrive at the same conclusions. Nevertheless, they have different starting points and different ultimate understandings of what counts as a just society.

There are certainly times when the two bodies of law approach each other more or less nearly. Yet they are consistently pulled in different directions, and the consequence is that these two legal orders really do meaningfully differ: Continental Europeans are consistently more drawn to problems touching on public dignity, while Americans are consistently more drawn to problems touching on the depredations of the state. Indeed, as our many transatlantic conflicts suggest, the distances between us can often stretch into the unbridgeable.

It should be obvious enough that this is not a contrast that we can understand by reflecting on the supposed universal intuitive imperatives of "personhood," or of "the integrity of the person." One's sense of personhood can be grounded just as much in an attachment to liberty as in an attachment to dignity. Maybe Europeans feel that their personhood is confirmed by the fact that their bosses are obliged to respect their privacy in the workplace, or by the fact that they can freely strip and sun themselves in central Berlin. That does not prevent Americans from feeling that their personhood is confirmed when they sit at home, a shotgun across their knees, determined to resist taxation.

No, the issue is not that one side of the Atlantic has discovered true "personhood," while the other lags behind. Something else is going on. The only way to think straight about these differences is to reflect on the core social values of dignity or liberty. The comparative law of privacy is not about the intuitive preconditions of personhood, but about contrasting political and social ideals. In the United States those political and social ideals revolve, as they have for generations, primarily around our suspicions of the police and other officials, while on the Continent they revolve unmistakably around one's position in society, one's "dignity" and "honor."

The political and social values of "dignity" and "honor" are indeed what is at stake in the continental concept of privacy, in ways that we can only understand if we dig deeply into continental traditions. That is what I propose to do in the next few Parts of this Chapter, focusing, as I have done in a series of related publications, on Germany and France, the two dominant legal traditions of the Continent. Here I must begin by summarizing work I have published on a variety of aspects of European "dignity."

Where do the peculiar continental anxieties about "privacy" come from? To understand the continental law of privacy, we must start by recognizing how deeply "dignity" and "honor" matter in continental law more broadly. Privacy is not the only area in which continental law aims to protect people from shame and humiliation, from loss of public dignity. The law of privacy, in these continental countries, is only one member of a much wider class of legal protections for interpersonal respect.

The importance of the value of respect in continental law is most familiar to Americans from one body of law in particular: the continental law of bate speech, which protects minorities against disrespectful epithets. But the continental attachment to norms of respect goes well beyond hate speech. Minorities are not the only ones protected against disrespectful epithets on the Continent. Everybody is protected against disrespect, through the continental law of "insult," a very old body of law that protects the individual right to "personal honor."

Nor does it end there. Continental law protects the right of workers to respectful treatment by their bosses and coworkers, through what is called the law of "mobbing" or "moral harassment." This is law that protects employees against being addressed disrespectfully, shunned, or even assigned humiliating tasks like xeroxing. Continental law also protects the right of women to respectful treatment through its version of the law of sexual harassment. It even tries to protect the right of prison inmates to respectful treatment, to a degree almost unimaginable for Americans.

Why does continental law work so hard to guarantee norms of "respect," "dignity," and "personal honor" in so many walks of life? This is a question to which I believe we must give a different answer from the one Europeans themselves commonly give. Europeans generally give a dramatic explanation for why dignity figures so prominently in their law: They assert that contemporary continental dignity is the product of a reaction against fascism, and especially against Nazism.

Having experienced the horrific indignities of the 1930s and 1940s, continental societies, Europeans say, have mended their ways. Europe has dignity today because Europe was traumatized seventy years ago. This is an answer that is often embraced by Americans, too-most notably Robert Kagan, in his recent bestseller Of Paradise and Power. And indeed, it is hard to resist a story with so much natural drama. But I have tried to demonstrate that the real story is different, and much more complicated. The European culture of dignity is not well-understood as any kind of simple reaction against fascism; even the place of fascism in the making of European dignity is more ambiguous than one might suppose.

In fact, the history of the continental law of dignity begins long before the postwar period. It begins in the eighteenth, and even the seventeenth, centuries. The continental societies that we see today are the descendants of the sharply hierarchical societies that existed two or two-and-a-half centuries ago-of the aristocratic and monarchical societies of which the France of Louis XIV was the model. In point of fact, continental law has enforced norms of respect and dignity for a very long time. In earlier centuries, though, only persons of high social status could expect their right to respect to be protected in court. Indeed, well into the twentieth century, only high-status persons could expect to be treated respectfully in the daily life of Germany or France, and only high-status persons could expect their "personal honor" to be protected in continental courts.

Members of the lower orders-the vast majority of the population-certainly had no meaningful right to respect. Quite the contrary. What we see in continental law today is the result of a centuries-long, slow-maturing revolt against that style of status privilege. Over time, it has come to seem unacceptable that only certain persons should enjoy legal protections for their "dignity." Indeed, the rise of norms of respect for everybody-even minorities, even prison inmates-represents a great social transformation on the Continent.

Everybody is now supposed to be treated in ways that only highly placed and wealthy people were treated a couple of centuries ago. Germany and France have been the theater of a leveling up, of an extension of historically high-status norms throughout the population. As the French sociologist Philippe d'Iribarne has elegantly put it, the promise of modern continental society is the promise that, where there were once masters and slaves, now "you shall all be masters!"

The uncomfortable paradox, as I have tried to show, is that much of this leveling up took place during the fascist period, for fascist politics involved precisely the promise that all members of the nation-state would be equal in "honor" that all racial Germans, for example, would be "masters."

For that very reason, some of the fundamental institutions of the continental law of dignity experienced significant development under the star of fascism. In fact, the fascist period, seen in proper sociological perspective, was one stage in a continuous history of the extension of honor throughout all echelons of continental society. This long-term secular leveling-up tendency has shaped continental law in a very fundamental way. Contemporary continental hate speech protections, for example, can be traced back to dueling law: In the nineteenth century, continental courts protected the right to respect only of the dueling classes.

Today they protect everybody's right to respect; indeed, the rules of dueling have had a striking influence in the Continent, sometimes being imported bodily into the law. Contemporary protections for prison inmates have a very similar history: In the eighteenth century, continental law maintained sharp distinctions between high- and low-status punishments. If executed, high-status offenders were beheaded, while low status offenders were hanged; if spared, high-status offenders were housed in comfortable apartments, while low-status offenders were subjected to degrading penal slavery. In the two centuries since the French Revolution, the old high-status forms of punishment have gradually been generalized to all: All inmates are now treated according to a regime of imprisonment that was once reserved to figures like Voltaire.

When continental lawyers speak of "privacy" as a set of rights over the control of one's image, name, and reputation, and over the public disclosure of information about oneself, they are speaking to these selfsame continental sensibilities. To be sure, they are talking about privacy in a way that many Americans also talk about it. The idea that privacy is really about the control of one's public image has long appealed to the most philosophically sophisticated American commentators, from Alan Westin, to Charles Fried, to Jeffrey Rosen, to Thomas Nagel.

In its most compelling form, the claim has come from Robert Post: For Post, privacy law protects norms of dignity that are "civility rules," just like the norms of etiquette; and without the protection of such norms, he argues, no society can maintain any form of community. Moreover, similar ideas can already be found in the most famous of American articles, Samuel Warren and Louis Brandeis's 1890 The Right to Privacy.

All of these American writers have viewed the danger in the violation of our "privacy" as the danger that we will lose the capacity to control what Erving Goffman famously called our "presentation of self"-our image before the eyes of others in society. All of them have thought of our right to privacy, perhaps a shade paradoxically, as our right to a public image of our own making, as the right to control our public face.

Indeed, it is precisely for that reason that they have insisted on the connection between privacy and personhood.

So the prevailing continental conception is also the one that most thoughtful American commentators on privacy and "personhood" have found the wisest and most sophisticated. But if this conception has triumphed in continental law, it is not because European lawyers possess any unique measure of wisdom or sophistication. Nor is it because they alone recognize the norms that are necessary for the maintenance of community.

Human communities can be founded on the widest variety of norms. As for law: It is not about the worldly realization of wisdom or sophistication as such. Law is about what works, what seems appealing and appropriate in a given society, and the conception of privacy as control of one's "image" has succeeded because it fits into continental social traditions, and into a quotidian continental culture of respect. Continental privacy is "continental" in much the way that continental hate speech law is "continental," and in much the way that continental prison law is "continental." For that matter, it is "continental" in much the way that continental etiquette is "continental"-for, pace Professor Post, the norms of "civility," far from being universal, vary dramatically from community to community.

Indeed, etiquette makes, as so often, a striking example of the social roots of European dignitary law. It is not an accident that both etiquette and privacy law show the same anxious preoccupation with "public image." Thus, it is common for continental etiquette guides to open with a section called "how we present ourselves before the world"; or "the politesse of appearances"; or more broadly a section on how to maintain the correct external look and manners. Rules about how to dress and how to wear makeup are part of continental etiquette just as are rules about how to comport oneself on the street, at the table, or in the workplace.

Continental etiquette is indeed overwhelmingly about "the presentation of self in everyday life," just like continental privacy law. In fact, continental authors sometimes consciously present etiquette and privacy law as related subjects: For example, you can buy a book for German journalists, published by the leading German newspaper, called Kleiner Knigge des Presserechts-a little etiquette book of press law-which treats all of the standard questions of privacy as questions of good manners.

But it is not just that the conception of privacy as control over one's image fits into the traditions of continental etiquette. It fits into the continental traditions of dignity, respect, and personal honor more broadly. As we shall see shortly, continental privacy law, like most continental law of respect, developed largely from the law of insult. It even has connections with dueling. It has a Nazi history. Most generally, it fits within the tradition of status revolution that has shaped so much of continental law-the revolution of leveling up.

Indeed, continental privacy protections offer perhaps the paradigmatic example of high-status norms that have been generalized to the wider population. For as we can all instantly recognize, the conception of privacy as control over one's public image is a conception originally and primarily concerned with the doings of very high-status persons.

Indeed, critics have always insisted that a notion of privacy as a right to control one's "image" is a notion primarily of interest to people of very high status-to personages like the Warrens of Boston, or for that matter like Princess Caroline of Monaco, whose affairs still provide constant grist for the continental privacy mill. The conception of privacy as control of one's image rests, at base, on the idea that one ought to be able to keep one's name and picture out of the newspapers. This is obviously a conception that matters primarily to members of "society" as the term is used in the phrase "society pages."

And that is just what we see in continental privacy law: a high-status conception of privacy, a "society" conception of privacy. In fact, it is almost comical to read off the names in the captions of the leading postwar continental cases. Open a book on comparative privacy law, and here are the names you will see: Princess Soraya of Iran, Princess Caroline of Monaco, Prince Ernst August of Hanover. There is a remarkable disproportion of royalty in continental privacy thinking. Down to this day, in fact, German texts list royalty first among the classes of "public figures" who require special treatment in the law of privacy, while French texts, the product of a deeper democratic tradition, only list royalty second, after politicians. "Members of the aristocracy" too are presented as classes that had to be specially treated.

These are textbooks written in worlds that remain very different from ours. Even the nonroyals and nonaristocrats involved in the leading European privacy cases are often very prominent persons indeed: Hjalmar Schacht, former Nazi finance minister, Robert Barcia, longtime eminence grise of the French Trotskyite party. Indeed, an American cynic who wants to mock the vaunted continental commitment to privacy will point gleefully at these names.

At core, the American will sneer, the continental protection for privacy grants everyone alike the right to be safe from paparazzi. Does this really have anything to do with the values of a true democracy? At best, continental privacy law is not a form of protection for universal human "personhood," but a means of regulating the relations between celebrities and the rest of us.

Nevertheless, as I want to insist, to take that mocking attitude would be to underestimate the moral claims of European leveling up, as it expresses itself in privacy law. There is more to the law than its practical impact. The law also aims to express social values-the continental law of privacy as much as or more than any other body of law. What the continental law of privacy expresses is the fundamental social importance of a commitment to extend royal treatment to everyone. Indeed, we cannot understand our transatlantic conflicts if we do not recognize the authentically wide social application of "society" privacy in continental law.

Over the past several generations, the basic commitment to control of one's public image has been extended well beyond its origins in the problems of the Princess Carolines of the world, in ways that do indeed affect the lives of ordinary people. This is most especially true of the areas where the conflicts between continental and American norms are most heated-areas like consumer data, credit reporting, public nudity, and the dignity of criminal offenders.

These are all realms of life in which continental law has forcefully extended privacy protections to noncelebrities and nonroyals. Control of one's "image," in the continental mind, now includes more than everybody's right to keep one's names out of the newspapers. It also includes everybody's right to control the use of one's consumer data and the like, everybody's right to privacy in the workplace, everybody's right (if one should need it) to respectful imprisonment, and more. Continental privacy law is, as it were, "society" privacy for everybody.

One recent German popular guide to the law proudly puts it in this way, in language that deserves to be underlined. Privacy rights, the book explains, are part of a larger law of the "defense of personal honor," and nowadays it's not just the "royal houses" whose image is threatened; "everybody is in danger." Silly enough-but also truly appealing in its way. Of course it matters to insist that everybody counts the same way royalty does, from racial minorities and prison inmates on up through the ranks of society.

THE RISE OF FRENCH PRIVACY LAW

There is no better way to grasp this continental social ideal than to trace its historical development, from its origins in the nineteenth-century world of dueling, through the Nazi period, and on into its modern forms. Continental jurists have always tried to understand "privacy" as a species of personal honor. In particular, going back to the nineteenth century, continental thinking has always treated privacy as a value primarily threatened by two forces: the excesses of the free press and the excesses of the free market.

From the point of view of the nineteenth-century continental tradition, there were two things that peculiarly menaced a respectable person's "honor": loose talk, and the grubbiness of the world of buying and selling. Continental privacy law has been shaped by a longstanding battle waged against both. Indeed, the history of continental privacy law has been, in essence, the history of the resistance, in the name of "honor," to two of the fundamental values of American liberty: the value of free speech and the value of private property as distributed through the market.

French law developed mostly over the period of 1790 to 1900, while German law developed later, from about 1880 to 1960. The two traditions have peculiar emphases. French law has had to struggle in a distinctive way with France's recurrent periods of sexual license, and German law was peculiarly formed by the events of the Nazi period and after. Nevertheless, both remain recognizably continental, and recognizably different from American law. In particular, in both countries, the law of privacy protection was built using the doctrinal resources of the classic continental law of personal honor-the law of insult-in tandem with the law of artistic and intellectual property.

Let us begin with France. French ideas about the protection of "private life" date at least to the early modern period. High-status families have always sought to protect their privacy in France, and they have sometimes succeeded. For example, for several centuries the French nobility successfully fought off efforts to require public registration of the mortgages on their real property, which would have exposed their finances for inspection. There were other ways, too, in which high-status ancien regime Frenchmen sought to protect their privacy.

But the modern history of French privacy protection, which has been sadly neglected, begins with the Revolution, and most particularly with the introduction of freedom of the press. Freedom of the press has always made leading French observers nervous, even ones with very liberal beliefs. Thus, the first French effort to create constitutional protections for freedom of the press was already accompanied by a proviso intended to guarantee that "private life," as an integral part of personal "honor," would not be subject to press depredations.

The Constitution of 1791, the first detailed revolutionary blueprint for a new kind of European liberal society, included extensive protections for freedom of the press. But at the same time, it added protections against "calumnies and insults relative to private life." One of the draftsmen of the Constitution, the Jacobin Jerome Petion, speaking during the flush of revolutionary excitement in August of 1791, explained the intent of the new document in this way: A vigorous free press was unconditionally necessary for the maintenance of liberal government.

Nevertheless, it was true that those very press liberties threatened the "private person." For that reason, it was important to confer upon persons whose private lives had been violated some legal recourse against "insults." To do so would not undermine the freedoms gained in the Revolution. On the contrary, it would achieve a revolutionary end. In fact, the "new doctrine," with its emphasis on the rights of ordinary private persons, directly "contradicted the ideas of the ancien regime." After all:

> In the ancient regime the least offense given to what would be called the honor of a man of position was a serious crime, which could not be punished severely enough, while an offense to a simple citizen hardly received any attention on the part of the law; but for that very reason, the new doctrine is all the more correct and in conformity with the principles of the new order of things.

The first manifestation of "privacy" in French law thus came in the form of a classic statement of the ambition to bring everybody up in status. The introduction of privacy protections was indeed akin to contemporary developments like the introduction of the guillotine. The guillotine arrived shortly after Petion gave this speech, as a means of extending the high-status privilege of beheading to all persons. It too belonged to a "new order of things" in which everybody's honor was to be protected.

These remained the characteristic ideas of French privacy law thereafter-notably in 1819, the year of the passage of the first post-Napoleonic law lifting press censorship. As the Restoration successfully established its authority, the government of Louis Philippe consented to tolerate a freer press. But the idea of press freedom continued to trouble even liberally minded Frenchmen, and the classic nineteenth-century statement of the importance of privacy emerged as soon as press censorship was even partially lifted.

In fact, it came once again from a leading advocate of press reform: Pierre-Paul Royer-Collard, a leading politician, professor of philosophy at the Sorbonne, and hero of French liberalism. Royer-Collard, even as he defended press liberalization, gave a famous speech warning that private life had to be "walled off" ("muree") against the danger of "calomnie," insult. The press, he said, had to be free, but the only proper realm for press freedom was the public sphere, and even true facts about private life could not be lawfully published. In the course of his speechifying, Royer-Collard produced a classic morsel of French metaphoric oratory"private life must be walled off!" that established itself as a standard continental slogan, repeated well into the twentieth century.

To be sure, what Royer-Collard produced was an oration, not a law, and for several decades thereafter there was little by way of protection for privacy in the letter of French law. For that reason, French legal historians treat the period of the 1820s through the 1840s as a time when there was simply no protection for private life. But it is a real mistake to conclude from the absence of law about privacy that no protection existed. In this period, one's private affairs remained a matter of one's honor, and one's honor remained a thing more precious, as French authors regularly declared, than life itself.

During the decades after 1819, the primary means of protecting one's honor was through the duel, and "private life" was defended, at least sometimes, in exactly that way. Thus, the dueling literature listed "the delicacy of private life" among the aspects of "honor" that demanded protection. And it was indeed so protected, as we can see from the example of one of the most famous dueling incidents in French history, the case of the Duchess of Berry. The Duchess was a leading royalist agitator and mother of the Comte de Chambord, the pretender to the throne.

While she was being held prisoner in a fortress in 1833, after an attempt to foment rebellion, it was publicly revealed that she was pregnant-even though she had been widowed for some years. As Louis Blanc described the resulting scandal, the Duchess's "intimate life" was "exposed to the insulting commentaries of the multitude"; "in vain," he added, "had she counted upon that solidarity of honor that reigns among relatives, even ones of obscure social condition, and that, protecting families, saves them from scandal by keeping secrets."

Her family did not defend her, but several royalists did: This famous violation of royal privacy caused more than one duel between royalists and republicans-including one in which several royalist journalists challenged several republican ones to a gigantic duello, and another in which the eminent General Bugeaud killed a member of the Chamber of Deputies. The honor of "private life" was not protected by the law in the 1830s, but it was defended.

By the mid-nineteenth century, though, this extravagant world of dueling honor began slowly to fade, and questions of private life began to migrate into the law. In part this reflected uneasiness about the traditions of dueling, as commentators demanded that questions of honor be settled in court. But it also reflected shifting patterns of both political and sexual liberation. In the middle of the nineteenth century, the claims of the free press became more insistent, and public morality became less strait-laced. Both developments created privacy problems for French law.

Already in the 1850s, some famous cases affirmed the core privacy right that would come to be known in French law as the "right to one's image." These first cases involved deathbed photographs-in two cases, deathbed photographs of celebrity beauties, and in one case the deathbed photograph of a kind of Mother-Teresa-type street missionary. But it was the following decades that saw the most striking developments-in particular, developments that involved the comparatively unbuttoned sexual atmosphere of later-nineteenth-century Paris.

Sexual license and the law of privacy have always gone hand in hand; and France had been famous for its relatively loose morals since at least the eighteenth century, the aristocratic age of Watteau, Boucher, and Fragonard. This tradition revived in the mid-nineteenth century, the age of the cancan, and it gave rise to numerous "privacy" issues, as cultures of sexual liberation tend to do. Especially beginning in the gay years of the 1860s, "right to one's image" cases began to multiply.

A particularly famous 1867 case involved Alexandre Dumas pere, the author of The Three Musketeers-itself an important document of nineteenth-century French dueling culture. Dumas pere, then well on in years, became involved in a love affair with Adah Isaacs Menken, a thirty-two-year-old Texas actress and horsewoman, famous for appearing on stage dressed only in a body stocking. Obviously reveling in their rejection of bourgeois values, the scandalous Menken and Dumas posed (together with Menken's mother!) for several more or less salacious photographs.

Some of them showed Menken in her underwear. Others showed her in amorous poses with Dumas, who was not wearing a jacket. Dumas, whether through inadvertence or sheer glorious indifference, did not enter into any express agreement with the photographer about the rights to publish the photos. Seizing his chance, the photographer tried to register his copyright in what were highly marketable images. In responding to the photographer's application, the copyright officials were not entirely without delicacy: They forbade him to display the photos showing Miss Menken in her underwear. With regard to the other photos, though, they gave the photographer free rein, and he marketed them widely, causing an international scandal.

Dumas, perhaps under pressure from his family, sued. But could any objection be raised in law? This was a difficult question in the 1860s. The photographer had a property right, the copyright in the photographs. Indeed, Dumas admitted in open court that he had sold the rights. This was the mid-nineteenth century, and property rights were generally regarded as something close to sacred in the legal cosmos of the day. Nevertheless, adventurous legal thinkers were beginning to challenge the sanctity of private property, and the Dumas court did the same.

If Dumas did not have the property right, was there any countervailing "right" that he could claim? In a seminal decision, the Paris appeals court answered that question by holding that he had a new kind of "right to privacy," which qualified the absolute claims of the law of property. The court adopted Royer-Collard's famous 1819 language about "private life": Even if a person had tacitly consented to the publication of embarrassing photos, that person must retain the right to withdraw his consent.

"The very publication" of such photos could put such a person on notice "that he had forgotten to take care for his dignity, and remind him that private life must be walled off in the interest of individuals, and often in the interest of good morals as well." The court accordingly rendered the photographer's property right effectively meaningless, ordering him to sell all rights in the photographs to Dumas. Privacy, the court had effectively held, must sometimes be allowed to trump property, at least where lascivious images were involved: One's privacy, like other aspects of one's honor, was not a market commodity that could simply be definitively sold.

Any sale by a person who had momentarily "forgotten his dignity" had to remain effectively voidable. In subsequent cases, involving some of the most famous artists of the day, this sort of thinking began to gel into a developing fight to one's image-an important part of the French law of privacy, understood as an aspect of the law of artistic and intellectual property. One memorable 1877 dispute, for example, involved Jean-Auguste-Dominique Ingres, the brilliant history painter and portraitist.

The cult of nude figure drawing was at its height in mid-nineteenth-century France, and Ingres frequently found it difficult to capture the ladies who sat for him unless he had first sketched them nude. Of course his society clients would not agree to sit nude themselves, so Ingres hired models with appropriate body types, and did nude sketches to which he added the recognizable heads of his clients. It was a consequence of this louche artistic practice that a nude sketch of one of his sitters, Madame Moitessier, appeared among his effects at his death in 1868.

When his executor tried to sell the drawing, Monsieur Moitessier sued. The court hearing the case, like the Dumas court, assigned the property right in the sketch to Ingres's successors. But, again like the Dumas court, the court held that Monsieur Moitessier had a privacy right, a right to his wife's "image," which served to limit the artist's property right. The court held that property itself recognizes limits established not only by positive law, but also by social norms [les convenances sociales]; that the first of these norms consists in the respect owed to the inviolability of the domestic hearth; that that inviolability would be offended if the image of the more de famille could be surrendered to the publicity of a banal public auction.

The court accordingly ordered the dealer in possession of the sketch to sell it to Monsieur Moitessier. The same basic analysis was confirmed in yet further high-profile cases over the following decades, which established the principle that we have a "sacred and inalienable right over ourselves, and consequently over the reproduction of our image." The most famous of these was the 1900 lawsuit between James Whistler and the Baronet Eden, which Whistler himself chronicled in his little screed The Baronet and the Butterfly. In part, French privacy law was thus the product of the culture of the Paris art world, with its nude models, defiant immoralism, and large artistic egos.

The cases that grew out of that world generally concluded that there was a right to one's "image" that was distinct from, and in tension with, rights of property. But that was only one of the strains in the making of French privacy law. The other had to do with the free press, and it reflected exactly the same anxieties that had accompanied press liberalization in 1791 and 1819. Indeed, it was in the tradition of uneasiness about the free press that privacy received its first formal statutory protection of the nineteenth century, in 1868, during the waning years of Napoleon III's imperial regime.

Over the course of the 1860s, the period of the so-called "Liberal Empire," Napoleon III granted increasing civil rights in France. This included the creation of a new press policy in 1868, which, with some limitations, allowed effective freedom of the press. The French press, meanwhile, had been experiencing a small renaissance of critical and satirical reportage, as well as a renaissance of French caricature in the work of artists like Honore Daumier.

Attitudes had not changed since 1819, though, and the new law aimed to guarantee that freedom of the press would not open the door to insulting intrusions into the lives of respectable people. Thus, it carefully provided that, though the press was in principle free, every publication in a periodical of "a fact of private life" was a criminal offense-a punishable contravention, just as other insults were contraventions. An interpretive circular of the Ministry of Justice added that while there was of course room for criticism of artists and other public figures, even the latter were (as they would continue to be) protected against "defamation and insult." Concerns about the care of one's dignity thus continued to shadow press liberalization, just as they had in 1791.

With the fall of Napoleon III, the climate certainly changed, and when the Third Republic turned to the regulation of the press, in 1881, its new statute said nothing about "privacy" as such. Nevertheless, courts continued to insist on the sacred character of "la vie privee"-for example, in forbidding a writer to base a novel on events revealed in the course of a criminal trial. All told, France was, by the 1870s and 1880s, the home of a very visible law of the protection of privacy. The reigning French view was captured by a characteristic account that appeared in 1888, two years before the publication of Warren and Brandeis's Right to Privacy.

In that year, Emile Beaussire, an eminent legal philosopher of the day, summarized several decades of French development in the following way: The right to privacy was to be ranked among the rights to honor more broadly. This of course raised doubts about its place in the law. For understandably, Beaussire wrote, people viewed their "honor" as something that should be preserved through dueling, not through law: "When my honor is attacked, I gain nothing by filing suit against my calumniators." Nevertheless, in the modern world, even persons of honor had to have recourse to the law, and the law had to occupy itself with persons of honor.

This was the right context for understanding the right to privacy, for violations of privacy involved nothing less than the revelation of "infamous secrets," which could destroy the honor of such persons as a respected "p6re de famille." And outside the most exceptional circumstances, the law could not allow such violations:

Private honor, whatever its value per se and whatever its source, must be protected from all offenses. People have certainly mocked the excesses of the maxim "private life must be walled off." ... [Nevertheless,] [t]he prying and insults of the world may be ... more or less innocent or more or less culpable: no matter what, they violate the law when they tend to destroy, through public revelation ... honor [consideration] justly or unjustly acquired....

Similar accounts of the right to privacy as a right to "honor" made their way into other textbook accounts by the end of the nineteenth century as well, and the importance of the protection of "honorable" privacy was something close to orthodoxy in France by the 1890s.

In Germany, similar developments were underway by the late nineteenth century. The world of the developing German law of privacy was not the overheated world of Paris high art, though, with its nude models and lascivious photos. Instead, it was the heady world of the German philosophy of free will. Moreover, German privacy law developed more slowly than French law, not really establishing itself before the middle of the twentieth century. And when German privacy law did establish itself, it was in connection with the painful experience of Nazism.

The German tradition of privacy protections is perhaps easiest to understand if we emphasize one point: German privacy law grew in large part out of an effort to create a richer German alternative to the ideas of liberty that grew up west of the Rhine, and especially to English ideas of liberty. The protection of privacy in the German tradition is regarded as an aspect of the protection of one of the most baffling of German juristic creations: "personality." Personality is a characteristically dense German concept, with roots in the philosophies of Kant, Humboldt, and Hegel.

Standard texts describe this concept in the daunting language of continental philosophy. As one recent author explains, the German law of personality is a law of freedom-the law of the Inner Space, "'in which ... [humans] develop freely and self-responsibly their personalities.'" Standard texts also lodge the concept in the drama of modern German history: This law of freedom, they tell us, has especially flourished since the 1950s, when Germans applied the lessons they had learned from the Nazi disaster. Clearly "personality" is somehow central to German legal culture. But the concept is likely to seem elusive to most readers. What is the "Inner Space"? How does guaranteeing the freedom of the "Inner Space" represent an antidote to Nazism?

To get a firmer handle on these difficult ideas, we must dig deeper into German intellectual history, and even into German theology. Personality is indeed a concept that Germans have often invoked where Americans would invoke liberty, and like liberty it does involve a kind of freedom. But from the beginning it was never quite the same as American freedom. Where Americans often think of "freedom" as opposed primarily to tyranny, nineteenth-century Germans often thought of "freedom" as opposed primarily to determinism. To be free was, in the first instance, not to be free from government control, nor to be free to engage in market transactions.

Instead, to be free was to exercise free will, and the defining characteristic of creatures with free will was that they were unpredictably individual, creatures whom no science of mechanics or biology could ever capture in their full richness. For Germans who thought of things in this way, the purpose of "freedom" was to allow each individual fully to realize his potential as an individual: to give full expression to his peculiar capacities and powers.

This idea of "free" self-realization is as old as Leibniz, or even Erasmus. Indeed, its sources lie unmistakably in Christian Humanism. But in its modern form, it is an idea that was especially championed by Wilhelm von Humboldt in the early nineteenth century. The early nineteenth century was a period when Germans were struggling with the economic liberalism of Adam Smith, trying to learn the lessons of Smith while preserving some role for a managed economy as well as for ideals of freedom that were not defined by the market.

For writers of the period like Humboldt, it seemed essential to insist that human flourishing required the pursuit of individual fulfillment in forms the market could not provide. The paradigmatic free actor, for such German philosophers, was commonly the artist more than the consumer. The German philosophical tradition on the subject of freedom was thus close in spirit to the German tradition of so-called "national" economics, a school critical of free trade and in many ways of the free market more broadly. That does not mean that German philosophers (or German economists) did not believe in the freedom to buy and sell, of course.

Nor does it mean that there have never been English or American writers who have found the German approach wise and beautiful. It means only that the German tradition always put less of an emphasis on consumer sovereignty, and more of an emphasis on unfettered creation, than the Anglo-American tradition did-and most especially on the unfettered creation of the self, on the fashioning of one's image and the realization of one's potentialities.

This approach to the problem of freedom formed a fundamental part of what Leonard Krieger, writing in the wake of the Nazi experience, famously called "The German Idea of Freedom": an idea different from Anglo-American ideas of liberty-an idea focused much more on inward self-realization, and consequently much more open to the exercise of state power and regulation of the market.

Now these are philosophical ideas that are both vague and grandiose, and they are not obviously easy to translate into law. Certainly, they do not seem as easy to translate into law as the ideas of an Adam Smith. Nevertheless, they were embraced by German jurists of the second half of the nineteenth century, and particularly of the 1880s. This was the period when German public policy began to turn away from Smithian laissez-faire ideas, endorsing social insurance, cartelization, and protectionist policies.

It was also the period when German philosophers turned strongly toward neo-Kantianism, a philosophical style fascinated with the tension between free will and determinism. It was during this same period that German lawyers began to turn away from seemingly crass Western ideas of personal liberty, endorsing the theory of personality as the true theory of freedom. Inspired by both Kant and Hegel, a number of leading legal thinkers set out to create a German law that would match the German philosophy of personality in depth and subtlety. In particular, they developed a German tradition that treated the protection of privacy simply as one aspect of the protection of personality more broadly: Privacy, for Germans, became one part of "free self-realization."

Like their French predecessors of several decades earlier, German jurists in and after the 1880s perceived their problem as a problem of honor, to be dealt with through the law of insult, in coordination with the law of artistic property. German society, like French society of the same period, was strongly attached to norms of respectability and honor, notably as asserted through dueling. It was also a society in which the law of insult played a correspondingly large role in legal thinking.

But the French way of talking about the problem was not very satisfactory to German scholars. When French authors like Royer-Collard or Beaussire spoke of "insults," they based their arguments on clumsily drafted modern statutes and vague "social norms." German scholars preferred a more solid juristic foundation, with citations to authoritative ancient texts and explorations of basic problems in legal philosophy.

Rather than talking about ill-defined social norms, German jurists accordingly embarked on an impressive reinterpretation of one of the most confusing bodies of traditional law: the ancient Roman law of insult, which they combined with the law of artistic property to create a new body of personality law. This German reinterpretation of the ancient law of insult is one of the finest examples of nineteenth-century juristic virtuosity, and one of the most famous. It deserves to be described, even if only briefly, not least because it exercised an important influence on American scholars like Warren and Brandeis.

Let us then follow nineteenth-century German reasoning. The ancient Roman law of insult was by no means easy to use as a basis for a modern law of personality. The ancient Roman texts were extremely muddy. In very early Roman law, which produced a cryptic statute on the matter, the law of insult-injuria-seemed to cover certain injuries to a person's possessions? In addition, there were early Roman sanctions against casting spells, engaging in certain now-mysterious forms of public insults, and inflicting bodily injury.

Very gradually, over the long course of Roman history, this early grabbag of legal prohibitions also came to cover various kinds of disrespectful and insulting speech and treatment. In particular, as the confusing texts of the Digest of Justinian seem to show, it came to protect respectable women against lewd comments, and to guarantee to a certain extent that low-status persons would show proper deference to their betters, as well as that high-status persons would not insult their inferiors.

A variety of other interferences with the rights of other persons also apparently came to be considered "injuria." Nowhere did the Roman jurists explain how they thought that physical "injuries" to persons and their possessions were related to verbal "injuries" directed at respectable women by mashers and the like, or give any account of what social purposes, if any, the Roman law of injuries was thought to serve. This was not easy stuff to work with, but German scholars went to work with a will. In particular, they worked in the Hegelian tradition.

Hegelian legal historians brought a characteristic approach to the understanding of legal evolution-an approach founded on Hegel's account of the history of punishment. According to the Hegelian view, the history of punishment was one in which the primitive talionic rule of "eye for an eye, tooth for a tooth," had gradually given way to more sophisticated concepts of proportionality. This was an evolution, as Hegelians saw it, in which a naive view of the world obsessed with things-eyes and teeth-had gradually evolved into a view of the world capable of grasping larger immaterial values.

The creators of the German law of "personality" interpreted the development of the ancient Roman law of insult in the same way-as an evolution of the "spirit" of Roman law, as Rudolf von Jhering, the most brilliant of German law professors, called it, from the material to the immaterial. The argument ran as follows: Honor had always been at stake in the law of insult, even in the earliest periods.

At first, the Romans, still obsessed with things, had thought that the law could only vindicate monetizable rights, mere material rights. But as sensibilities about honor grew richer and deeper, these early legal protections gradually ripened, until the law grew to cover all aspects of honor, protecting also against verbal insults and other shows of disrespect. The evolution of the law of honor, like the evolution of the law of punishment, was thus an evolution in the "spirit of the times"-one in which primitive protections for merely monetizable interests had gradually matured into sophisticated protections for "noneconomic" interests.

That slow evolution, from the material to the immaterial, was moreover continuing in the modern world: The modern world was now producing what Jhering called, in a famous 1885 article, the law of "insulting tortious injuries." In particular, modern protections were now evolving beyond protections against immaterial verbal insults, to include the protection of such immaterial goods as one's name and one's photographed image, one's control of one's correspondence, as well as access to modern amenities such as the telegraph and the tram.

Jhering was one of a number of German scholars to make this sort of argument, some relying on ancient Roman law, some drawing on Germanic sources. This Hegelianized law of insult was one main strand in the new German law of personality. The other was the law of Urheberrecht, creators' rights. The rights of an artistic or intellectual creator, in German law, were partly rights of copyright. But they also were beginning to extend beyond mere copyright to include a broader right to control the use of one's work, in the name of protecting one's reputation as an artist-what in continental law is today called "droit moral de l'auteur."

For German scholars who thought of "personality" as the right to free self-creation, the law of artistic and intellectual property was a natural source, to be exploited alongside the law of insult. After all, personality was precisely about self-creation. And of course, protection of the creative rights of the artist, a nineteenth-century innovation, was a classic example of the new modern sensitivity to immaterial interests. The law of insult, united with the law of artistic creation, thus made for what seemed to Germans a solid foundation for a law of personality.

The idea that personality was really about an amalgam of personal honor and artists' rights was popularized beginning in the late 1870s by an influential writer named Karl Gareis. Related approaches were developed in particular by the most deeply learned and intellectually adventurous of turn-of-the-century legal thinkers, Josef Kohler. Some important cases came into this German line of thinking as well: In particular, there was a case that prohibited the distribution of photographs of Otto von Bismarck on his deathbed. As always in the continental tradition, the hunger of the press for images of highly placed persons drove the law onward.

These were very influential ideas in the developing German social order of the late nineteenth century. By the early twentieth century, German law had incorporated a wide variety of personality rights into its statutory schemes. The scandal over Bismarck's deathbed photos led, in 1907, to the introduction of statutory protections for one's image, as part of a larger scheme regulating rights in works of art. Meanwhile, the German Civil Code, which went into force in 1900, included protections against the appropriation of one's name and the impairment of one's credit, alongside protections for life, body, health, and liberty.

The 1909 law on unfair competition included a characteristically German provision protecting enterprises against untrue statements that harmed their operations or their credit, and the Bismarck-era law on freedom of the press granted a right to respond. Perhaps most importantly, the Criminal Code included a prohibition on insults. All of this added up to protections that were hardly insignificant by the eve of World War I. The Weimar era saw a number of further important cases, particularly involving members of the formerly imperial Hohenzollern family and like personages.

In short, there were plenty of "personality" protections in German law by the early part of the twentieth century. Nevertheless, the Civil Code itself, which went into force in 1900, did not endorse an unbounded right of personality-much to the dismay of many legal scholars. Indeed, it is an important part of German legal lore that personality was neglected in the Civil Code.

This peculiarly German form of freedom, German lore tells us, was not embraced by the Code, which instead endorsed crassly market-oriented values. The German literature routinely declares that personality was only fully protected in the 1950s, as a consequence of the new commitment to freedom and dignity that took hold in the wake of Nazism. Indeed, the protection of personality is widely presented as the core institution of a German private law shaped by the reaction against Nazism-"one of the most essential achievements," as a standard textbook says, "of the post-war period."

This is not, however, correct. With this we come to a delicate point, which I have touched on before and now must touch on again. Here, as elsewhere, contemporary German institutions of dignity have a Nazi history. In point of fact, the

Nazis too were committed to the protection of personality. This German form of freedom was one that appealed to the Nazis just as it appealed to the later makers of the twentieth-century social welfare state. The story is entirely typical of the history I have recounted elsewhere.

The Nazi regime, like other fascist regimes, made great efforts to proclaim the importance of "honor"-and most especially the importance of the honor of low-status persons, as long as they were racially German. This led the regime to insist on norms of respect for workers in the workplace, and in everyday life as well. In just the same way, it led the regime to insist that all Germans, whatever their social station, had a right to the protection of their personality. Otto Palandt's standard commentary to the Civil Code explained it this way in the early 1940s:

> The "right of personality" did not receive any definitive regulation in the Civil Code. Life, body, health, and freedom are protected through [section] 823 I, and so is the right to one's name.... A general right of personality is alien to the Civil Code. However, there is nothing in the Code that excludes it.
>
> National Socialist legal feeling [National-sozialistisches Rechtsempfinden] regards the Volk-comrade as a member of the Volk community, who fulfills the demands of his legal position in the service of the Volk community, and who as such has a claim that the legal position that has been conferred upon him be safeguarded and protected against attacks of any kind. In this sense, it can be said that the Volk-comrade has a general right of personality that ought to be recognized, one whose content extends beyond the above-mentioned personality interests listed [in the Code], including in particular a right to join in the common labour of the community and a right to recognition, respect, and honor.

The draft Nazi Civil Code, never enacted, was even more assertive in its insistence on a universal German right to protection of personality. The Nazis presented themselves as protecting honor to its fullest extent, in return for the sacrifices demanded of the German Volk. Of course the insistence on honor for Germans was paired with an insistence on the dishonor of others-of persons who were "sick or foreign." Like all Nazi extensions of "honor" to the lower orders, this too belonged to the politics of the most vicious kind of exclusion. It is for that very reason that the rare historian who deigns even to talk about the Nazi period insists that there is no connection between Nazi ideas and the doctrines of the postwar period.

Nevertheless, it is much too simple to dismiss the Nazi experience as a rejection of the traditions of German personality law-whether we are talking about the history of legal doctrine, or about the social history of the law. As a matter of doctrine, the Nazis did endorse the general right of personality. As a matter of social history, the Nazis did guarantee, here as elsewhere, the claim to honor of low-status Germans. Ordinary Germans who would come to pride themselves on their "dignity" in the 1950s and 1960s were Germans who had been taught to pride themselves on their "honor" twenty years earlier. The consequence, painful as it is to acknowledge, is that Nazi law directly prefigured the law of postwar Germany.

By the 1950s and 1960s, to be sure, the standard commentary to the Civil Code was no longer grounding the "general right of personality" in "National Socialist legal feeling" and the requirement that the "Volk-comrade" work for and with the community, as it had done in the 1940s. Instead it was (rather reluctantly) grounding it in the constitutional right to "free self-realization." But in both eras, the commentary talked a lot about "honor," and the net result was that the German civil law acknowledged a "general personality right" in each.

In point of fact, the protection of personality is not a product of postwar reforms, as German scholars must have known perfectly well during the 1950s. It has grown in tandem with the German social welfare state, and the downward social extension of a claim to honor, throughout the twentieth century. Be that as it may, the protection of personality has especially flourished since the 1950s. The Basic Law of 1949 did embrace the German tradition of personality protection in its famous Article II, which guarantees that "[e]very person has the right to free development of his personality, insofar as he does not injure the rights of others."

This was a forceful restatement of the German idea of freedom. In subsequent years, Article II has indeed come to stand at the foundation of the extensive German protection of privacy, among other personality interests. A number of cases of the 1950s established the principle that the Civil Code had to be understood in light of this constitutional provision, as guaranteeing a right to the protection of personality. The postwar law of personality is now a central institution of German dignity in the (perhaps endangered) world of German market socialism.

9

Contemporary Continental Law

The old traditions described above have remained strong down to the present postwar day, in both Germany and France. Postwar developments were more tentative in France than in Germany. Protections for "privacy" were proclaimed by de Gaulle's government in exile shortly before D-Day, presumably in the effort to win over former collaborators. Nevertheless, lasting change had to wait until 1970, when the Civil Code was amended to introduce new protections. Still, today protections for privacy are a proud part of the law in both countries-and in both, they have retained much of their nineteenth-century coloration.

To be sure, the law of privacy in both countries is today regarded as distinct from the law of insult. Nevertheless, traditional nineteenth-century values, with their honor-oriented, suspicious attitude toward the free press and the free market, have continued to make them felt, even in a world in which the privacy of ordinary folks is vigorously protected.

The continental chariness about the free market shows, for example, in the treatment of consumer credit reporting and other consumer data. Credit reporting is an especially revealing example. Here the basic continental rules grow out of longstanding continental traditions. Historically, as a matter of etiquette, one's financial affairs were very much one's own affairs. One did not talk about money matters unless absolutely necessary: Indeed, money, as a standard etiquette guide will tell you, was simply "a taboo subject" among respectable people.

The only persons whose finances were routinely revealed to the public were insolvents and bankrupts. That attitude has had a marked influence on European privacy law-most notably in the traditional French rule that made it a per se violation of privacy rights to reveal another person's salary. (Indeed, a French text on the law of privacy will still casually list "health, love, sex and earnings" as the areas of life self-evidently in need of privacy protections.)

The same attitude has had an influence on the continental law of credit reporting. In France in particular, consumer credit reports are provided only by official sources, and they are provided only in the case of persons experiencing serious financial difficulty. They offer, as it were, only a watch list of persons who are proven credit risks. Anything else, to the French mind, would represent an intrusion into financial privacy. One's financial information is information "of a personal character," over which one must have control just as one must have control over one's image.

The German approach is less directly interventionist. Credit reporting is provided not by government agencies, but by industry collectives known as "Schufas." Even in Germany, though, there is significant regulation: Consumers must sign a contractual clause expressly permitting lenders to share data about them, and before any data is shared, the law requires a careful balancing of the privacy interest of consumers against the interests of financial entities, theoretically in every individual case. As in France, moreover, German reporting focuses on classic sorts of negative information associated with insolvency and default.

European credit reporting is thus the direct descendant of the old European law of bankruptcy: It is law that stigmatizes the dishonorable failure to pay one's debts, not law that allows merchants to pry into the buying habits of honorable, solvent persons. Certainly anything like the American practice of compiling an accessible record of any individual's credit history seems like a dangerous exposure of private life to most Europeans.

All very continental-but at what cost? As any American law professor will surmise, it inevitably means that consumer credit is less easily available in continental Europe than it is in the United States. Indeed, these privacy norms must contribute significantly to the making of a continental world in which credit cards have made much slower progress than they have in the United States-a world that in general is not founded on the system of consumer credit. It may be difficult for Americans to understand why continental Europeans should resist our well-developed credit-reporting practices. In the long run, good credit reporting ought to make life easier for everybody, and indeed make everybody richer. But, for the continental legal tradition, the basic issue is of course not just one of market efficiency.

Consumers need more than credit. They need dignity. The idea that any random merchant might have access to the "image" of your financial history is simply too intuitively distasteful to people brought up in the continental world. The protection of consumer data reflects in many ways the same clash of attitudes. Europeans have aggressively condemned traffic in consumer data: It is, European lawyers believe, a serious potential violation of the privacy rights of the consumer if marketers can purchase data about his or her preferences, and regulation is thus imperative.

The resulting protections are embodied in the European Commission's forceful Privacy Directive of 1995, under which Europeans claim the authority, as the Wall Street Journal puts it, to play "Privacy Cop to the World." Americans have of course been much slower and more hesitant to regulate, with the resulting battles that I have already described.

And indeed, the continental attitude is not easy for Americans to understand. After all, there is a benefit in the traffic in consumer data. If marketers can learn more easily what my preferences are, they can provide me more easily with the goods and services I seek. To put it in the language of

American law and economics, trafficking in consumer data lowers search costs: It makes it easier for buyers and sellers to find each other, creating sales that would otherwise not have been made, and thereby enhances the efficiency of the market.

Not all Americans would approve of the theories of law and economics, of course. Nevertheless, on some level, the relaxed attitude of law-and-economics scholars toward the market is clearly widely shared among American policymakers. This does not mean that Americans do not experience some anxiety about the traffic in their "private" information. But it does mean that American law has been far less categorical in its condemnations than European law.

Whereas European law allows the collection of consumer data only for limited purposes and limited times, upon explicit consent of the affected person, and under government supervision, Americans are much more willing to tolerate industry self-regulation. Most of all, when they do propose regulation, they tend, in a characteristically American way, to favour "market-based solutions to personal data protection," as Pamela Samuelson writes, "over the strict comprehensive regulatory regime adopted ... in Europe."

Indeed, Europeans have a harder time seeing the benefits of free-market solutions. As another leading scholar puts it, Europeans "trust government more than the private sector with personal information." Why is this? It is not hard to understand if we keep in mind the continental traditions I have described. Privacy is an aspect of personal dignity within the continental tradition, and personal dignity is never satisfactorily safeguarded by market mechanisms. Ever since the case of Dumas pere, continental law has resisted the notion that one can definitively alienate one's "dignity."

Dignity, to this way of thinking, simply must be treated differently from property. As one French scholar insists, contrasting the American attitude with the French, one can freely dispose of one's liberty, but one can never be permitted to freely dispose of one's dignity. If one accepts that premise, one should accept the proposition that any consumer's consent to the sale of his or her data should have only limited effect at best. After all, "the importance of one's image," as a recent French article puts it, is greater than ever "in the information society."

Here again, consumers need more than cheap goods and services, just as they need more than easy credit. They need dignity. If your consumer profile is floating around somewhere in cyberspace, you are not in control of your image. A just world, from this point of view, is a world in which everybody's respectability is carefully protected. This sort of thinking has far less resonance in America than it does in Germany and France. We will never quite share the intuitions that fuel the continental conviction that trading in consumer data must be prevented, or at least sharply limited by law.

As these examples suggest, continental privacy is not just for Princess Caroline, Princess Soraya, or Prince Ernst August. It is for the ordinary person as well, in his or her guise as consumer. It is also for the ordinary person in his or her guise as worker. Continental law has made considerable efforts to guarantee the privacy of workers in the workplace, at least within the limits of the possible. Worker e-mails, for example, are vigorously protected in a way that is not the case in America.

There are protections for workers' other private documents, guarantees against video surveillance, and rights to use telephones for personal calls-all in the name of maintaining a certain "personal sphere." It goes well beyond e-mails and the like, too, to cover a wide range of issues touching questions of workplace dignity. One striking French decision, for example, found it a violation of dignity rights when an employer in a retail store required that employees show a receipt for merchandise that they wished to take home. Treating workers with that sort of suspiciousness was regarded by the court as a violation of their expectation to be treated as honorable persons.

The contrast with American approaches to the workplace is telling. American privacy protections, at their metaphoric core, are the sorts of protections afforded by the walls of one's home. They have been extended beyond the literal home, of course, since the eighteenth century. Nevertheless, it remains the case that American protections become progressively weaker the further the affected person is from home. This is particularly true when courts apply the "reasonable expectation of privacy" test developed in the Fourth Amendment context.

The primary locus of one's "reasonable expectation of privacy" is of course in the home, and persons outside the home have correspondingly few privacy protections. This applies to workers as well, whose expectation of privacy in the workplace, according to the American cases, is sometimes close to nil. The same contrast holds in one of the most striking aspects of the comparative law of privacy: the treatment of criminal offenders, including accused persons and prison inmates. Continental privacy protections extend to these classes of persons as well.

Continental privacy law has been strongly concerned with the privacy rights of persons caught up in the toils of the justice system. In Germany, modern personality protection grows preeminently out of a 1976 case involving a homosexual prison inmate convicted of an act of terrorism. In that case, Lebach, the German Constitutional Court found that it would be a violation of the inmate's personality rights to broadcast a made-for-television movie about him. Lebach has been regarded since as the font of late-twentieth-century personality doctrine.

French law too has made strong efforts to guarantee the privacy of accused persons as a fundamental aspect of the presumption of innocence, and more broadly of the "honorability" of the accused. In line with this, both Germany and France make considerable efforts to guarantee that prison inmates will enjoy protections for their privacy, in ways that are unimaginable for Americans. All persons haled into the criminal justice system enjoy, at least in principle, protections that are not available to their American counterparts.

Differences in cultural tradition, in short, have made for palpable differences in law. The differences are most striking, and most categorical, where the values of free speech are involved. Here it is above all the classic problems of privacy law-sex and nudity-that provide the most revealing examples. They are my topic in this last Part discussing continental law.

With regard to France, some of the striking contrasts in the law were traced by Jeanne Hauch in a 1994 article with the wonderful title Protecting Private Facts in France: The Warren & Brandeis Tort Is Alive and Well and Flourishing in Paris. Hauch offers, among others, the example of Oliver Sipple. Sipple was the unfortunate man who thwarted the attempt of Sara Jane Moore to assassinate President Gerald Ford. He was homosexual-a fact that he very much wanted kept out of the press. This proved to be impossible under the American law of "public figures."

Of course, in any democracy the private doings of at least some public figures are a matter of legitimate public interest, and every democratic system recognizes that. Since the 1960s, though, the American "newsworthiness" exception has grown mightily, and peculiarly, in scope. Freedom of expression is a value of constitutional magnitude in the United States, whereas the protection of personal honor is not, which means that freedom of expression almost always wins out.

That is what doomed Oliver Sipple's effort to keep his homosexuality out of the papers. Although Sipple's entry into the public eye was the result only of his heroism in a moment of danger, the California Court of Appeal held that there was a legitimate public interest in his private life. In any case, the court held, "he did not make a secret" of his sexual orientation, at least in San Francisco. Sipple (whose family in the Midwest had known nothing of his California life) eventually committed suicide.

It is precisely cases like this that Europeans see differently. The right of free expression that protects the press is always balanced in continental Europe against an individual right to "dignity," "honor," or "personality," which implies a right to personal privacy-as was shown by a 1985 French case that Hauch uses as a foil to the Sipple decision. The case involved a man who attended a gay pride parade in Paris, dressed in a way that made it clear that he was himself gay. His image was captured in a news photo.

Continental law has long held that persons appearing in public may be photographed, but that no photograph may be published that focuses on them as individuals, unless they consent. Moreover, to the French way of thinking, the fact that one has revealed oneself to a restricted public-say, the gay community of Paris-does not imply that one has lost all protections before the larger public. These principles matter, and the French court accordingly acknowledged the plaintiff's right to oppose publication of his image.

The contrast between the treatment of Sipple and the treatment of this French victim of publicity is typical of a much deeper contrast in attitude, which one commentator on the supposed "failure" of American privacy law describes this way:

Privacy is not the only cherished American value. We also cherish information, and candour, and freedom of speech. We expect to be free to discover and discuss the secrets of our neighbours, celebrities, and public officials. We expect government to conduct its business publicly, even if that infringes the privacy of those caught up in the matter. Most of all, we expect the media to uncover the truth and report it-not merely the truth about government and public affairs, but the truth about people.

The law protects these expectations too and when they collide with expectations of privacy, privacy almost always loses. In Europe, by contrast, personal honor very often wins out. As one German author put it in 1959-a time when Germans began to reassert their own distinctive national traditions-there is simply an inevitable tension between the worldview of a Goethe, for whom the development of "personality" was "the greatest blessing of the children of the earth," and the worldview of a Jefferson, for whom press liberty was the indispensable foundation of a free society.

Europeans are by no means completely deaf to the pleas of Jefferson, but the attitude of Goethe always haunts their thinking too. That does not mean that Europeans are doctrinaire. They have their own doctrine of "public figures." But that doctrine cuts far less deeply, as numerous cases indicate. And even when the courts allow "intrusions" into the lives of "public figures," commentators grumble. Many more examples can be offered-most especially involving nudity, and most especially involving the Internet.

In German and French legal culture, we still find much the same attitude that we found in the 1877 decision regarding Ingres's nude sketch of Madame Moitessier: One ought to have control over one's nude image. This means, of course, that one can sell the rights to an image, just as one can in America-at least provisionally. Nevertheless, there are limits. In one 1974 case, for example, a French actress was permitted to suppress movie scenes in which she had willingly appeared naked: One's nude image is simply not definitively alienable under continental norms. In other cases, models have been able to suppress the republication of their nude photos in magazines other than the ones they posed for-a matter in which "French law," a commentator observes approvingly, "is totally opposed to American law."

The same sort of attitude has also affected both continental cyberlaw and the continental law of public nudity. The Internet has produced two recent leading cases in particular, one in Germany and one in France, in both of which courts imposed liability on Intemet service providers that housed nude images of celebrities. In the German decision, Steffi Graf, the former tennis star, successfully sued Microsoft for its refusal to guarantee that it would prevent dissemination of a "fake" a picture of her head superimposed on the nude body of another woman.

The leading French case involved the model Estelle Hallyday, who similarly sued a service provider this time a free service provider for housing her nude image. Hallyday's suit put the provider in question out of business. There have been a number of such French cases since. Indeed, there has been criminal liability: One young man who published nude photos of his ex-girlfriend on the Internet (with commentary) received a suspended sentence of eight months' imprisonment and a fine of 25,000 francs-a serious sentence in France. These cases do not establish an unconditional right. In particular, here again, European law does understand how to make exceptions for public figures. There is no absolute control over the dissemination of one's nude image in continental law. Nevertheless, there is no doubt that the continental courts are on the watch.

The situation is different in America. Theoretically, the same rights exist in some form in American law. Nevertheless, both culture and practice differ. Congress has passed legislation that aims to forbid imposing liability on Internet service providers as such. Perhaps more strikingly, unlike the European courts, American courts see little point in issuing injunctions once images have been irrevocably diffused over the Internet.

Such was the fate, for example, of Dr. Laura Schlessinger, a well-known conservative radio commentator, who posed for some cheesy nude photos for a man who was her boyfriend and mentor in the 1960s. In 1998, Dr. Schlessinger's (now ex-) boyfriend sold the photos to Internet Entertainment Group (IEG), an organization that specialized in putting exactly such nude photos of celebrities online. IEG promptly put the photos on display. Indeed, in a show of almost parodic contempt for norms of privacy, the IEG site was equipped with technology that allowed paying viewers to zoom in on any part of Dr. Schlessinger's anatomy.

There is little doubt that any continental court would have enjoined an outfit like this from distributing the photos. Even in America, Dr. Schlessinger did succeed in obtaining an injunction for a time. After a few weeks, though, the court lifted the injunction on the ground that the photos were already widely available on the Internet. From a certain point of view, of course, the real result of Dr. Schlessinger's suit was no different from the real result in the cases of Steffi Graf or Estelle Hallyday: The curious can still find the relevant nude pictures of all of these unfortunate celebrities online. (Indeed, critics of the Hallyday decision loudly complained that her nude images remained available on at least twenty sites.)

But European courts still feel obliged to forbid the circulation of those pictures, even when it is futile to do so, in order to express the importance of protecting "private life." Moreover, European courts feel obliged to penalize the persons responsible, be they Internet service providers or delinquent ex-boyfriends. American law is, our French commentator observes, "radically different."

This is not, let me emphasize, because Europeans are more squeamish about nudity than Americans. Quite the contrary. Germans in particular appear fully nude in places like public parks (in the summer) and public coed saunas (in the winter) with a sans-gene that Americans can hardly fathom; and French women go topless, not only on the beach, but also on the banks of the Seine. There are certainly limits: For example, one German court recently held that jogging in the raw went a bit too far. Nevertheless, as I began by observing, it is most assuredly the Americans who are most troubled, and even put off, by nudity.

The difference is not that Europeans refuse to be seen nude, but that they insist that they want to be the ones who should determine when and under what circumstances they will be seen nude. The difference is that the decision to appear nude, for Europeans, belongs to their control of their image. Indeed, even when they appear nude in public, individual Europeans have sometimes tried to claim a right not to be shown naked by the media. Scenes of naked bodies, whether on the beach or in the parks, are of course irresistibly tempting to journalists.

Photographs are inevitably published, and the persons portrayed sometimes sue. Such suits are indeed the ultimate test of the continental notion that people should have absolute control over the diffusion of their image. These suits have failed in France. But German courts are less categorical. Under the German law of the fight to one's image, the control of pictures of the naked body belongs "exclusively to the individual." This was the rule at stake in the case of a Munich man who filed suit after newspaper photos were published showing him naked in the Englischer Garten.

The court took his claim seriously enough to hold that he had in principle suffered harm to his "personality" rights, though it ruled against his claim for damages. Even in ruling against his claim for damages, though, the court emphasized that his genitals were not exposed in the photo. Had his genitals been exposed, the case might have come out differently. The German court thus found it important to state the principle that nude persons have a right to control their public face, just as clothed people do.

In this, the law only tracks German sensibilities more broadly, and in particular the German etiquette of public nudity. Indeed, any serious scholar's research into continental privacy norms should include a good stint on a German Liegewiese. As any German there will tell you, it is a matter of ordinary politeness that nude people have a right not to be stared at. Taking off all your clothes, even in a public park, does not constitute a surrender of your privacy.

Such is the sort of attitude that we must grasp if we want to understand continental law: We must understand that there could be such a thing as private public nudity. It is an attitude that American law simply does not comprehend, as we can see most strikingly from the Supreme Court's 1995 decision in Vernonia School District 47J v. Acton. This was a case that presented the question of whether high school athletes could be subjected to mandatory drug testing. In holding that they could, the Supreme Court offered, among others, an argument that took the following form: Athletes regularly shower together in the nude.

Since they voluntarily expose themselves through this "communal undress," they have a "reduced expectation of privacy" with regard to whether their urine will be tested for the presence of drugs: Once a person appears nude in public-even before a highly restricted public-he has, in the eyes of the Court, at least partly surrendered his claim to privacy. To the continental ear, this is a bizarre non sequitur.

The fact that students have willingly appeared naked in one circumstance says strictly nothing about whether they have broadly surrendered their right to control access to data about them, and certainly nothing about whether they have consented to a urine test. For Americans, by contrast, the right to privacy is, at its metaphoric core, a fight to hide behind the walls of one's own home. Those who have abandoned the protection of the home, and a fortiori the protection of clothing, have at best a diminished claim to privacy.

Indeed, continental ideas of privacy are just not much at home in American legal culture. To be sure, there is certainly American law on the books that sounds something like what we find on the books of Germany or France. American law has its famous four forms of the privacy tort, as analyzed by William Prosser in 1960: intrusion upon seclusion, appropriation of the name or likeness of another, public disclosure of private facts "not of legitimate concern to the public," and disclosure of private facts in such a way as to portray victims in a "false light."

There is considerable legislation too, like the Video Privacy Protection Act of 1987, passed in reaction to journalistic investigations of Robert Bork, and various other acts and bills, both state and federal. American legislatures do pass privacy protection statutes of various kinds especially, as Jeffrey Rosen has observed, in the wake of "heartstring-tugging" scandals. While many of these statutes treat the government as the principal threat to privacy, not all of them do. Though less than a third of the states have general laws on the protection of privacy, there certainly are state protections. There are even state constitutional protections for privacy.

There are decisions giving protection to one's image-notably cases involving the nude or sexually charged images of young women who did not intentionally pose in a provocative way, or who are the victims of sexual assaults, or who otherwise seem to be living "a life of rectitude." There are cases involving nongovernmental invasions of the "privacy of [the] home," and especially of the privacy of the bedroom: Where the walls of the home are breached Americans can be sensitive. There is a lot of American scholarship that vigorously defends the European point of view. And of course, there is the famous article of Warren and Brandeis.

Nevertheless, as our many and heated conflicts with Europe suggest, the American attitude remains different. It is not true that American law is absolutely different from European law. No generalization about any legal system is ever absolutely correct: Law is always something of a jumble, and there are always exceptions to any general description. The differences that we can see are always comparative differences, not absolute ones. Nevertheless, the American climate of values remains basically inhospitable to the European way of looking at things. We do find patches of more or less continental law in America, just as patches of snow sometimes survive in a hollow on an early spring day. But over time, most efforts to make American law look more continental tend to melt away.

This is indeed how we should understand the fate of "that most influential law review article of all," Warren and Brandeis's The Right to Privacy. Warren and Brandeis undertook the seminal, and still most cited, effort to introduce a continental-style right of privacy into American law. In theory, their right is still part of the law almost everywhere in America. Nevertheless, it is generally conceded that, after a century of legal history, it amounts to little in American practice today. The story of the relative failure of Warren and Brandeis is precisely a study in how poorly continental ideas do in the American climate.

In fact, it is best to think of the Warren and Brandeis tort not as a great American innovation, but as an unsuccessful continental transplant. For, though commentators have failed to recognize it, what the two authors set out to do was precisely to introduce the continental protection of privacy into America. It is hardly news that Warren and Brandeis worked in a world of Boston respectability closely akin to the high society of late-nineteenth-century Europe. Warren was a Boston Brahmin, a child of one of the socially dominant families of the city. Brandeis was the son of Bohemian-Jewish immigrants who had fled to America after 1848.

Their article was written in a fit of outrage over newspaper reports of a party given by the Warrens, and its main target was the gossip pages of the "yellow press," which Warren and Brandeis were convinced represented a new phenomenon. Like a number of authors of the period, they were upset by these press intrusions. "The press," the coauthors complained, "is overstepping in every direction the obvious bounds of propriety and of decency.... To occupy the indolent, column upon column is filled with idle gossip, which can only be procured by intrusion upon the domestic circle."

The only answer to the challenge, they argued, was to insist on a "right to privacy." This would protect individuals not only against the press, but also against intrusive photographers and the like. Nor would the new right be confined to high-status people like the Warrens:

> The design of the law must be to protect those persons with whose affairs the community has no legitimate concern, from being dragged into an undesirable and undesired publicity and to protect all persons, whatsoever their position or station, from having matters which they may properly prefer to keep private, made public against their will.

All of this was obviously much in the continental style, up to and including its desire to level up, to guarantee the tight of all citizens "whatsoever" to be safe from "undesirable and undesired publicity." The high-status tenor of the Warren and Brandeis article is indeed something any reader can see immediately, and critics of Warren and Brandeis have said so. But if we look closely at the article we can see something else: We can see that Warren and Brandeis took continental law as their starting point. In fact, it is not difficult to retrace the research steps that Warren and Brandeis took.

Like the authors of any law review article, they looked for authority for their position. The first and most natural place to look for their right to privacy, the two authors strikingly observed, lay in the protection of "honor" through the law of insult. And in the law of insult, they tightly noted, there were already lively traditions to draw upon in both France and Germany by the end of the nineteenth century.

As we have seen, by 1890, when Warren and Brandeis wrote, the right to privacy was a longstanding topic of study and discussion within the continental traditions of the law of insult. Indeed, continental discussions were reaching a fever point in the 1880s. Warren and Brandeis were perfectly familiar with this. They cited the French privacy legislation of 1868 at length, and admiringly. They also cited German scholarship on the law of insult-in particular Carl Salkowski's standard Institutes and History of Roman Private Law, a very German text, which interpreted ancient Roman law through the lens of German philosophy:

> Iniuria in the narrower sense is every intentional and illegal violation of honour, i.e., the whole personality of another.... This may be committed by insulting oral or written words or signs (so-called verbal and symbolic injuries), by deeds (so-called real injuries), by slander, and speeches and acts which cast suspicion upon, or are prejudicial to, the social or pecuniary position of any one, or other acts interfering with the right of personality.

From Salkowski, or from some other German source, Warren and Brandeis borrowed the term "personality," and they characterized their right to privacy, in orthodox German fashion, as one aspect of the protection of "personality" more broadly. Indeed, it is likely that Warren and Brandeis knew more about the continental tradition than they chose to cite. Brandeis, who had been brought up in a Germanophile Louisville household, had been sent to high school in Germany during the 1870s, and he remained a passionate admirer of German culture.

It seems wholly improbable that he did not know of the lively German literature on "personality" when he adopted the term for his article. (If he only cited Salkowski it may be because Salkowski's was the only German text that had been translated into English.) Moreover, at least some of the French cases on the right to one's image must have been known to educate Bostonians. The Dumas case in particular had been an international cause celebre. In any case, French privacy protections had been publicized by E.L. Godkin, an author often identified as an influence on Warren and Brandeis.

As Godkin had explained, "In France a man can legally prevent or punish the mere mention of his name in any disagreeable connection, if he be not in political, literary or artistic life"-law that Godkin insightfully credited to a French "sensitiveness to ridicule or insult which has probably never existed in any Anglo-Saxon country." Nevertheless, though Warren and Brandeis certainly knew the continental traditions, and cited them, they did not claim that it was possible to introduce continental practices directly into American law.

They understood the continental tradition too well for that. The continental approach, they observed, was not available within the common law tradition-for the simple and insurmountable reason that the law of insult, and the protection of "personal honor," did not exist in America. "[O]ur system, unlike the Roman law, does not afford a remedy ... for mental suffering which results from ... contumely and insult [involving] an intentional and unwarranted violation of the 'honor' of another." No matter how vigorous and appealing the ideas of Royer-Collard, Jhering, Gareis, Beaussire, and the rest might be, they could not be fitted into the common law precedents, which simply said nothing about personal honor, or at least nothing useful.

Warren and Brandeis's article thus started from the admission that the United States was doomed to be a nation without continental-style "privacy" protections, at least in their full form. But it continued by insisting that this was no cause for despair: Even in the absence of a law of insult, there were other resources to which one could turn. Indeed, Warren and Brandeis maintained, the protection of "honor" was not as promising a vehicle for the protection of "privacy" as continental writers imagined. The apparent analogy between honor and privacy was merely "superficial." Another road would have to be taken:

> It is not however necessary, in order to sustain the view that the common law recognizes and upholds a principle applicable to cases of invasion of privacy, to invoke the analogy, which is but superficial, to injuries sustained, either

by an attack upon reputation or by what the civilians called a violation of honor; for the legal doctrines relating to infractions of what is ordinarily termed the common-law right to intellectual and artistic property are, it is believed, but instances and applications of a general right to privacy, which properly understood afford a remedy for the evils under consideration.

There was no ultimate need for "honor" in order to protect privacy; artists' rights would do. But even here, of course, Warren and Brandeis were pursuing a continental tack, and most particularly a German one. The Germans, as we have seen, had created their law of personality by drawing both on the law of insult and on Urheberrecht, on intellectual and artistic property. This is exactly what Warren and Brandeis, like Gareis and Kohler before them, did as well.

The resulting article is, of course, a common law classic, a tour de force effort to capture the drift of a case law system in a state of productive flux. Yet let us note that, even in their account of common law evolution, Warren and Brandeis did not sound all that different from their continental, and especially German, predecessors. As we have seen, French and German writers held that privacy had emerged as a limitation on property, and an evolutionary outgrowth of the growing sensitivity to the needs of "personality." Warren and Brandeis echoed these ideas.

In a style unmistakably like that of Jhering, they tried to trace the evolving "spirit" of the law. Copyright, rights in "intellectual and artistic property," they observed, had always been understood as a property right. Yet primitive ideas of property were falling by the wayside as the common law evolved. It was a general evolutionary trend of the common law to get beyond the protection of mere material "property rights," offering new protections for the immaterial damage of emotional and moral harms.

This was true of privacy as well. Cases that had been interpreted as property cases, as cases in copyright, in fact revealed a growing judicial sense that it was necessary to "protect the privacy of the individual" from invasion-not just from the literal invasion of one's property, but from metaphorical invasions "either by the too enterprising press, the photographer, or the possessor of any other modern device for rewording or reproducing scenes or sounds." At the same time the common law of torts had gradually come to cognize the harm in various forms of mental suffering.

These two trends conduced to the same evolutionary end: Common law thinking was giving rise to the new "Warren and Brandeis tort," the tort of invasion of privacy. All of this made for an inspired contribution to the international literature on the protection of privacy-one that Europeans themselves still cite. But what Warren and Brandeis could not do was bring the European structure of values to the United States. Indeed, it was not just the continental law of insult that Warren and Brandeis were unable to introduce into America. It was much more broadly the constellation of ideas about personal honor that undergirded it.

Freedom of expression has been the most deadly enemy of continental-style privacy in America. To cite once again our German scholar of 1959, the conflict has always been one between the values of Jefferson and the values of Goethe. Of all American liberty values, freedom of the press is the most poisonous for continental-style privacy rights. Starting with the famous Sidis case of 1940, American law began, in an American way, to favour the interests of the press at the cost of almost any claim to privacy. Perhaps the most striking examples come from the Supreme Court, with its decisions in Cox Broadcasting Corp. v. Cohn and Florida Star v. B.J.F.

These were cases in which the media published the names of rape victims-in the latter case despite the fact that dissemination of the victim's name was a crime under state law. In both cases the Supreme Court found that the First Amendment protected media outlets against suit. Freedom of expression just about always wins in America-both in privacy cases and in cases involving infliction of emotional distress, like Hustler Magazine, Inc. v. Falwell, which denied recovery to preacher Jerry Falwell after Hustler published a particularly gross parody. This is the kind of question on which continental law, with its focus on personal honor, comes out differently.

That does not mean, of course, that American law never protects the control of one's image. But even where it does, it tends to do it in an American way. This is perhaps clearest in the doctrine of the "right of publicity." The "right of publicity" is a characteristic American doctrinal invention, which we owe to Melville Nimmer's work of the 1950s. In a sense, it is a doctrine of the protection of one's image. Nimmer argued that persons had an ownership right in their image, and that they could sue others who had misappropriated it. But it should be obvious that the notion of one's image as a piece of property, as a commercial commodity, is different in spirit from the continental protection of image.

And indeed, while continental lawyers endorse this American innovation, they are careful to distinguish it from their own distinctive traditions. (Indeed, Americans themselves are confused by the question of whether the right of publicity really belongs within the realm of privacy protections or not.) And unsurprisingly, the American doctrine produces different results from continental doctrine. As critics complain, the "right of publicity" has tended to lose all of its moorings in the Warren and Brandeis idea of privacy, becoming essentially a vehicle for protecting the enterprises of celebrities like Bette Midler and Vanna White.

Moreover, nothing in the doctrine of the "right of publicity" prevents Americans from alienating the rights in their image, no matter how humiliating their subsequent use may be. If your image is your property, you can sell it. In Europe, by contrast, as we have seen, sales of your nude image remain voidable-a very important doctrine, in particular, for protecting the interests of persons who, in moments of youthful folly, have allowed themselves to be photographed in embarrassing positions.

Finally, an American interest in one's "publicity" is an interest in one's property, not an interest in one's honor. This too sets the American tradition apart from the continental, and it affects the analysis in such famous matters as the "Here's Johnny!" case. In that case, the entertainer Johnny Carson sued a portable toilet maker who had adopted the well-known tagline "Here's Johnny!" for its product.

An appellate court held that Carson's publicity rights had been violated. But it was careful to insist that Carson's rights were commercial rights only, not privacy rights against humiliation or embarrassment. Here again, we can see a contrast with continental law, and with German law in particular. Even commercial enterprises can be "insulted" in Germany. German firms have "personality" rights, and they are indeed protected against embarrassing or humiliating uses of their slogans or logos, through what is called the doctrine of Markenverunglimpfung. Some cases litigated under the American "right of publicity" may come out the same way that they would in European "right to one's image" cases. But the underlying values are different, and courts feel obliged to say as much.

Indeed, even if some cases come out the same way, many come out differently. And there are many areas of the law, as we have seen, where Americans do not even perceive the sorts of privacy violations that seem to Europeans obviously present. The Europeans are right. At the end of the day, Americans do not really grasp the European idea of the protection of privacy.

But does this mean that Americans don't understand the moral imperative of privacy in the creation of "personhood"? Such is the conclusion that commentators repeatedly draw, both in Europe and in the United States. Yet I hope it is clear that the problem is more complex than that. If Europeans protect "privacy," it is not because they understand universal moral truths that Americans fail to understand. It is because they live in societies that have been shaped by certain kinds of cultural expectations and certain kinds of egalitarian ideals.

After many generations of experience, Europeans have come to value a certain kind of personhood: a kind of personhood founded in the commitment to a society in which every person, of every social station, has the right to put on a respectable public face; a society in which privacy rights are not just for royalty, but for everybody. This is a concept of personhood that has been formed by the peculiarities of continental culture and continental history, and it has produced a law of privacy that has been formed by the same culture and history. For persons who live in these continental cultures, there will always be some practices that seem, in an intuitively obvious way, to represent violations of privacy. Yet the same practices may not seem like violations at all to non-Europeans.

As for Americans: They have their own concepts of personhood, their own traditions, and their own values. And the consequence is that there will always be practices that intuitively seem to represent obvious violations to Americans. Most especially, state action will raise American hackles much more often than European ones.

This is indeed almost too obvious to need describing for American readers. Suspicion of the state has always stood at the foundation of American privacy thinking, and American scholarly writing and court doctrine continue to take it for granted that the state is the prime enemy of our privacy. To Americans, the starting point for the understanding of the right to privacy is of course to be sought in the late eighteenth century, and especially in the Bill of Rights, with its vigorous circumscription of state power.

In particular, "privacy" begins with the Fourth Amendment: At its origin, the right to privacy is the right against unlawful searches and seizures. It is thus a right that inheres in us as free and sovereign political actors, masters in our own houses, which the state is ordinarily forbidden to invade. Over time, to the American mind, the early republican commitment to "privacy" has matured into a much more far-reaching right against state intrusion into our lives.

The classic statement of this American view came in 1886, at the same time that European scholars were developing their own characteristic ideas of privacy protections. The case was Boyd v. United States. In forbidding the government to seize the documents of a merchant in a customs case, the Supreme Court, after discussing the eighteenth-century background at length, issued an aggressive declaration of the "sanctity" of an American home. The court focused on a cause celebre of the eighteenth century: the case of John Wilkes, the British political dissenter whose papers had been seized by government agents.

Bibliography

Anker, R. and C. Hein, 'Why Third World Urban Employers Usually Prefer Men', *International Labour Review*, Vol. 124, No. I, Geneva, 1985.

Beech, C., *Women and Women into Information Technology*, a report by the British Computer Society, 1990.

Byrne, E., *Women in Science and Technology: The Institutional Ecology Approach*, Interim Research Report, Department of Education, University of Queensland, 1988.

Chew. S.B. and R. Chew, 'Information Technology as a Strategy Human Resource Development', in E.C.Y. Kuo, C.M. Loh and K.S. Raman, *Information Technology in Singapore Society: Trends, Policies and Applications*, Singapore University Press, 1990.

Davidson, M.J. and C.L. Cooper (eds), *Women and Information Technology*, Psychology and Productivity at Work Series, London, John Wiley and Sons, 1987.

Deakin, R., *Women and Computing: The Golden Opportunity*, London, Macmillan Press, 1984.

Eriksson, I.V., B.A. Kitchenham and K.G. Tijdens (eds), *Women, Work and Computerization: Understanding and Overcoming Bias in Work and Education*, Amsterdam, North Holland, 1991.

Faruqui, A.M., M.H.A. Hassan and G. Sandri (eds), *The Role of Women in the Development of Science and Technology in the Third World*, proceedings of the conference organized by CIDA and the Third World Academy of Sciences, Trieste, Italy, October, 1988.

Harrison, P. (1983), *The Third World Tomorrow*, NY, Pilgrim Press and Harmondsworth, Penguin

Irvine, J., 'Women into Information Technology', *Information Technology and Public Policy*, Vol. 8, No. 3, Summer, 1990.

Kluzer, S., *Computer Diffusion in Black Africa: A Preliminary Assessment*, unpublished paper, SPRU, University of Sussex, Brighton, UK, 1988.

Lim, G.K., 'Women's Participation in the Computer Industry in Singapore', in Ken Tijdens *et al.* (eds), *Women, Work and Computing: Forming New Alliances*, Amsterdam, North Holland, 1989.

Lovegrove, G. and B. Segal (eds), *Women into Computing: Selected Papers*, 1988-1990, London, Springer, 1991.

Mitter, S., 'Computer Aided Manufacturing and Women's Employment: a Global Critique of Post Fordism', in I.V. Eriksson, B.A. Kitchenham and K.G. Tijdens (eds). *Women, Work and Computerisation: Understanding and Overcoming Bias in Work and Education*, Amsterdam, North Holland, 1991.

Mumford, E., *Where are Tomorrow's Top Women Executives?*, Manchester Business School Review, Vol. 4, No. 3, 1980.

Ng, C. (ed.), *Technology and Gender: Women's Work in Asia*, Women's Studies Unit, UPM and Malaysian Social Science Association, 1987.

Ng, C. and J. Othman, 'Information Technology, Gender and Employment in Malaysia', in S.C. Bhatnagar and M. Odedra (eds) *Social Implications of Computers in Developing Countries*, New Delhi, Tata-McGraw Hill, 1992.

Odedra, M., *Information Technology Transfer to Developing Countries: Case Studies from Kenya, Zambia and Zimbabwe*, unpublished Ph.D. thesis, London School of Economics, 1990a.

Odedra, M., 'Poor Management leads to Gross Under-utilization', *Computer in Africa*, Vol. 4, No. 5, July, 1990b.

Parikh, I., *Women in Management: an Annotated Bibliography with Emphasis on Commonwealth Sources*, London, Commonwealth Secretariat, 1987.

Stamp, P., *Technology, Gender and Power in Africa*, Ottawa, international Development Research Centre, 1989.

Subramaniam, P.R., *The Future for Women in Information Technology*, M. Sc. dissertation, London School of Economics, 1991.

Tijdens, K., M. Jennings, I. Wagner and M. Weggelaar (eds), *Women Work and Computing: Forming New Alliances*, Amsterdam, North Holland, 1989.

Virgo, P., 'The Case for Women into Information Technology Campaign', *Information Technology and Public Policy*, Vol. 6, No. 3, Summer, 1988.

World Bank, *Sub-Saharan Africa: From Crisis to Sustainable Growth*, Washington DC, World Bank, 1989.

Wright, B.D. (ed.), *Women, Work and Technology: Transformations*, Chicago, University of Michigan Press, 1987.

Index